9 95

THE COMPLETE HANDBOOK OF HOW TO START AND RUN A MONEY-MAKING BUSINESS IN YOUR HOME

THE COMPLETE HANDBOOK OF HOW TO START AND RUN A MONEY-MAKING BUSINESS IN YOUR HOME

Marian Behan Hammer

PARKER PUBLISHING COMPANY, INC.

WEST NYACK, NEW YORK

© 1975 *by*

Parker Publishing Company, Inc.

West Nyack, New York

Library of Congress Cataloging in Publication Data

Hammer, Marian Behan
   The complete handbook of how to start and run a
money-making business in your home.

   1. Self-employed. 2. Supplementary employment.
3. Small business. I. Title.
HD8036.H34   658'.022   75-8517
ISBN 0-13-161265-4

Printed in the United States of America

How This Book Can
Help You Make Money

Do you, like millions of others, find that getting by with your current income is becoming increasingly difficult? Would you prefer to spend your time making money at home every day rather than waste hours traveling back and forth to work through heavy traffic? Are you interested in being your own boss, or in making money through an enjoyable leisure-time pursuit? Does the idea of someday being really rich appeal to you?

If your answer to just one of these questions is "yes," this, then, is the book for you. Everything you need to know to start and build your own successful money-making business is right here in this complete and detailed handbook.

Most fortunes, as you know, are made by people who own their own businesses. But running a business and running a successful business in which you make money are two different things. I want to help you make money. If you have drive and incentive, this book provides workable methods and ideas you can profit from.

Perhaps you have a talent, a hobby, or an interest and have thought of starting a small business of your own, but don't know where to begin. This book tells you in clear, practical stages how you can set yourself up, with a minimum of effort and cost, and succeed in a profitable home business.

Perhaps you have a definite business in mind but have been afraid to venture forth by yourself, or reluctant to risk your savings because of unfamiliarity with marketing, distribution, and selling techniques. This book will guide you, simply and candidly, in all of these areas.

In what type of business can you make the most money? The first chapter will help you decide which business you are best suited for. It will show you how to choose a business for yourself in which you are sure to make money.

In succeeding chapters, you will learn about the many different kinds of businesses, what the starting requirements are, how much money is needed, where to get it, and what to expect from your initial investment. You will discover how and where to sell your product or service and how to keep customers coming back time and time again.

In all, this book presents over 150 business ideas for your consideration, all of them tested and successful. Some require only your time or energy to get started, while for others, financial backing is needed. You can start your home business on a small scale while still holding down your regular job, or you can start out full-time with a large or small investment. You will learn how to put your energy to work in your spare time to earn extra income. With most of the ideas presented in this book, you will find that the amount of time and commitment required is flexible and may be expanded or reduced to fit the needs and abilities of the individual.

However, this is not a mere book of small business ideas, but a truly helpful guide to making money in your special field. To succeed in any endeavor, you need a sound basic knowledge of what you are doing. Because this book offers business building ideas, it helps you to avoid most, if not all, of the common mistakes that lead to business failures, and helps you to conduct your affairs in a manner that will logically lead to making money.

Although the book concentrates on starting a business, the tested procedures that are presented throughout can make money for the seasoned businessman as well as the novice. Frequently, you will discover that the application of success principles which cause one type business to flourish are interchangable and can make money for you in your business as well.

Nor will you read this book once and put it aside. As the title claims, it is a handbook, one which you will find yourself reaching for again and again. It takes you from the point of starting a small business in your own home to the successful position of expanded sales and enlarged profits. Chapters on finance, promotion, advertising, and other specialized business activities help you keep pointed toward profit.

In addition, many examples, check-lists, trade publications, government helps, and reference materials are listed which help to put and keep you on the road to success and big money in the business of your choice.

But let's get on with the work at hand—making money for the best boss in the world—yourself.

Marian Behan Hammer

CONTENTS

THE COMPLETE HANDBOOK
OF HOW TO START AND RUN
A MONEY-MAKING BUSINESS
IN YOUR HOME

1

How to Select a Home Business for Profit

Thinking of starting your own business? It's a good idea provided you know what it takes and have what it takes. Not everyone has the right combination of talent, experience, and determination to make it in the business world.

Will you succeed and make a fortune in the business of your choice? The answer to this utopian question can be "yes"—if you use the right approach. This chapter will help you to take an objective look at yourself as a prospective business person.

FINDING THE RIGHT BUSINESS

The dream and opportunity of making big money in business, which challenged earlier generations, is still very much alive today. New products, ideas, and services are being discovered daily. Many reap fortunes for their promoters.

What is the *plus margin* which insures success for a new business venture? It includes the following:

1. Entering a field about which you know something.

2. Sufficient financial backing.

3. Determination to succeed.

The last factor is perhaps the most important, since determination will often make up for shortcomings in some other area. If you have a desire to start out in a business about which you know little

15

you can always learn more about it—through study, observation, and practice. A financial problem can be eased by borrowing or by starting out in a business enterprise that requires little or no capital. But without strong positive reasons for going into business, you will surely fail.

On the other hand, a determined person will work harder to overcome obstacles which might discourage others. If you have a willingness for self-discipline, long hours, and hard work, you will probably succeed.

We all know that rapidly growing markets and rapidly developing technology breed small firms. And although all of these do not survive, many of those that do are the beginnings of large enterprises. We have only to read the stories of the home bakery that developed into a large chain; the candy-maker who initiated a product that became known from coast-to-coast as "Cracker Jack"; the chemist who launched an intriguing line of cosmetics which eventually became a nationally-known firm.

Emerging technologies listed in a recent issue of *Industry Week* magazine include an account of ocean waves as an energy resource, and a new measuring technique for bacteria detection. Perhaps one of these will be your path to wealth and success. For you, too, can make it big. The opportunities for small business operation are so vast that it would take more than the pages of this book to list them all.

As an example, consider the birth of the following small businesses gleaned from the classified ad section of the New York Times.

> Renovating an old house? Experienced man will strip paint from wooden moldings and remove old wallpaper.
>
> Will videotape your next social affair. Weddings, birthday and anniversary parties, reunions, can be videotaped for instant replay. Can be seen again and again.
>
> On a budget? Picasso can't, but we can. Let us paint your walls with zingy supergraphics. Custom designed. Inexpensive.
>
> Food costs got you? Pick your own fruit and vegetables at our low farm prices.
>
> On a diet? I make clothes smaller for men and women. Suits $12; dresses $7; pants $4.

In starting a business, you might also keep in mind the story of *Ralston Purina*—a business that filled a need. "Get into a business that fills a need for lots of people, something they need all year around in good times and bad." This was the sage advice that in 1894 convinced young William H. Danforth to manufacture animal feed.

It was the time of horsepower economy, but only two kinds of horse and mule feed were known, corn and oats. Oats were costly, and every year thousands of horses died from colic caused by bad corn. "Cheaper than oats and safer than corn" became the slogan for a new blend of feed grain. Four years later, the company began to package a whole wheat cereal for people. Today the famous Ralston Purina checkerboard trademark can be found in almost every American home and Purina Chows for animals and poultry are known the world over.

But *finding the right business* doesn't always come easy. For Elliot Watson, pushing retirement in a forge shop, "it took a lot of looking." Elliot wanted a business that he could start while still holding down his job and one that would net him a fair income after he retired. "It had to be one that didn't cost much to set up, didn't take long to learn and produced a decent profit," he said.

Elliot spent several weekends visiting small industries until he found the right one—the ornamental concrete business. With a $2 bag of cement he can make a bird bath or statue that sells for $100.

His only investment is in molds. As the project thrived, he made sure that part of his profits went into buying more molds. Over three summers, he has built a wide line of castings, from lawn toads to religious wall plaques. He is also building a nice bank account.

MAKING PROVEN BUSINESS IDEAS
WORK FOR YOU

This book is not fundamentally one on how to run a going business, but rather, how to start and run one that is right for you, and how to make it pay off. In looking over established businesses which have attained a high degree of success, you will find that most business ideas fall into one of three categories: services, manufacturing, and selling.

A service is a job performed for an individual or an organization. For example, you can make big money by doing something for an individual which he cannot, or will not, do for himself. Wig-washing, tutoring, baby-sitting, and catering are all personal services which can be the start of a thriving home business.

Service to home-owners and families can also reap big profits for you. Rex Johnson, a dog-lover and retired factory worker living in Detroit, Michigan, adds to his income by grooming members of the canine community. Others bring in substantial extra money by offering such services as lawn maintenance, snow removal, tax consulting, and house painting.

Big money can also be made when you perform services for industry. Once you gain a reputation for work-well-done, your service is in constant demand. You might be interested in performing a clipping service, a telephone answering service, or like an interprising young high school graduate in Chicago, you could start a relamping service in which you replace burned out bulbs in large plants and department stores.

Another way to start on your way to big money is through manufacturing. This means making or producing something useful from raw material. Although most people don't have the space in their homes or garages for a large manufacturing operation, there are many small items that can be made in your home, garage, or an outside workshop. Most crafts fall into this category. How about candlemaking, leathercraft, shell products, doll clothes, plastic casting, electronic devices, or wood products?

Another proven way in which we see profits soar is from the land boom. Real estate has always been a popular investment, and today your land can make money for you. Whether you own many acres or merely the lawn in front of your house, there is income to be gained. Take notice of the many trailer camps, motels, archery ranges, boarding houses, swimming pools, and garden centers—all making money.

The businesses mentioned thus far are all areas that have proven successful for beginning business people. These and the thousands of other profitable enterprises are avenues through which you, too, can seek a business beginning. However, whatever product you decide to make, or service you plan to offer, *selling* will be an integral part of it. Whether you are pushing pine-scented candles or a unique pet-sitting service, it is your job of selling that will pull in those orders—and dollars.

Perhaps selling of itself is your forte, and you want to start a business in which you dispose of a product or service rendered by someone other than yourself. There are many good opportunities for a home business in the selling field. How about a mail order business, house-party and in-home selling, or door-to-door selling?

Services. Manufacturing. Selling. With such a vast selection to choose from, how do you know which home business is right for you? As you know, starting any new business can be risky. But your chances of making it go will be better if you understand the problems you'll meet and work out as many of them as you can before your start. That is why this book was written. To help you find your business. To start you out in a field that will net you big profits right from the beginning.

EVALUATING VITAL CLUES THAT POINT
THE WAY TO YOUR BUSINESS SUCCESS

The secret to making money from your own small home business lies primarily in knowing yourself and training yourself to cash in on what skills you have. My suggestion is that you try to write your qualifications down on paper. Think back to the achievements and experiences of your past life. What activities did you enjoy? Why did they bring you satisfaction? If you can write down your achievements and experiences, then analyze them honestly, you should be able to judge with a fair amount of accuracy the type of business in which you will best succeed.

For example, how do you rate people? If you like to be around people and find that your achievements involve competition, this indicates that you have some of the right qualities for a business that involves selling or service. You'll probably succeed in a business in which you associate with people and handle situations involving others.

If, on the other hand, you tend to keep to yourself and enjoy working alone, you might do well to investigate the manufacturing end of a business. Your success will be in a field where you are doing things yourself, where you aren't required to persuade or motivate people.

How good a worker are you? Do you have the qualities needed to operate a business on your own? If you are a self-starter, someone who has always been striving to achieve a goal, you will have no trouble operating a business of your own. Perhaps you have been elected to office in various social clubs or organizations. Did you enjoy the responsibility? If so, you will probably do well in the business world.

Which sports have you been active in? Have you been captain of a football or basketball team? Have you ever coached or managed a team? If your answer is "yes" it probably means that you enjoy organizing and motivating people and will, therefore, like work which involves these things.

How about your health? Are you in reasonably good physical shape? It takes vitality to live with a business 24 hours a day. Emotional health is also important. Any type of business is competitive. To be able to roll with the punches and have a certain amount of emotional toughness is helpful.

The following checklist will help you to evaluate your personal inclinations and characteristics. As you read the questions, it might be helpful to jot down your answers on a separate sheet of paper.

> Are you a self-starter? Can you get things done on your own or do you need a push to get you started?
>
> How do you feel about other people? Do you like to be around people or do you prefer working alone?
>
> Can you lead others?
>
> Can you take responsibility? Do you enjoy taking charge or would you rather let someone else do it?
>
> How good an organizer are you?
>
> How good a worker are you?
>
> Can you make decisions?
>
> Do you have stick-to-it-iveness? Once you make up your mind to do something, do you usually finish what you start?
>
> How good is your health?

Honest answers to the above questions will give you a fairly accurate indication as to whether or not you have what it takes to run a business. If you find that you are weak in certain areas, perhaps you could arrange to find a partner who is strong on the points you're weak on.

APPRAISING YOUR ASSETS

One of the keys to success in business is having the intelligence to solve the problems and make the decisions that come up from day to day. In business, as in everything we do, high general intelligence is an asset. Unfortunately we weren't all born with a genius IQ.

Therefore, the value of basic training and education cannot be over-emphasized. Some of the most intelligent people fail in business because of wrong attitudes, lack of motivation, or lack of basic knowledge of the product or service they provide.

John Addams graduated from college fifth highest in his class, but he was a failure in the business world because he wasn't willing to spend the time required to learn the basic concepts of management. On the other hand, Geraldine Bisonne, a high school graduate with only average ability, made an instant success of her children's party-planning business. Her experience with smaller brothers and sisters, plus baby-sitting experience, got her started. Her positive attitudes and strong drive, plus a high degree of maturity and willingness to work hard, zoomed the business to success.

In starting any type of business you would be wise to first measure your practical experience. Are you familiar with all of the things which you must do to make your business a success? Most people who start their own business have as a paramount thought the idea that they will "be their own boss." But many are either unwilling, or unaware of the necessity, to spend the time to learn all about their proposed operation, to start small and grow from a modest beginning.

Even though you may have a strong desire to start a business in your home and are well motivated, your business will be doomed to failure unless you know what you are about. "Experience," claims an old adage, "is the best teacher." It's true. We learn best by doing. Maybe you've had experience in your past life that will aid you in a business venture—a hobby that can be developed or experience working for someone else in the same field. Or perhaps a short course of study is all you need before you set up shop.

Many people branch out into business by making a special talent work for them. A doll, and his woodworking ability, helped William Sprague, of Elizabeth City, North Carolina, get his retirement business started. Woodworking has been a part of his life as long as he can remember, and his grand-daughter's doll is the model he uses to get the right measurements for the doll furniture he makes and sells locally and in distant parts of the country.

Sometimes it is necessary that you expand your talents to cover an ever increasing business need. Jenny LaToure, whose knitting needles brought her fame and fortune by way of the hand-knitted ski-cap she designed and sold, took on a knitting class. In this way she taught several women how to knit the cap and was soon paying them to help her meet the increased demand for her product.

A young man in Denver started stripping down furniture, removing old paint and varnish from antiques and the like. Once his business got rolling, however, he found that he had to learn upholstering in order to keep up with his competition.

Although special talents can be a big asset to you in starting a home business, you must also have the right attitude and temperament. Temperamentally, most successful small business people are competitive. They enjoy the day-to-day struggle to get things done. They are always aiming to improve their business, constantly pushing to achieve their goals. Even quiet, easy-going people who are successful in business have a competitive spirit. Underneath their calm exterior, they have positive attitudes. They believe in themselves and they're sure in their own minds that they have the ability and determination to achieve the business goals they set for themselves.

Another important attribute for the success of a business venture is good health. Obviously, you can't carry on the necessary work, or endure the long hours that setting up a new business requires if you're not in good mental and physical condition. Starting and running a money-making business is an active strenuous life style filled with tensions, reverses and discouragements, as well as fulfillment, joy, and profit.

Mental and emotional health is also vital. If you are an optimistic, positive, outgoing person you are more likely to succeed in business than if you are a cynical worrier, easily depressed. Such a person might easily worry himself into an ulcer or heart attack before his business ever got off the ground.

Just as knowledge, experience, temperament, and health, time is also important for your success in the business world. A person motivated by wanting to "make a bundle" in a hurry will probably be disappointed. It usually takes one or two years before a business catches on and begins bringing in big returns. It takes time for a product or service to gain a reputation and time for customers to know you. Most business people who have become successful were willing to sacrifice some comforts at first to accomplish their dream of success.

CONSIDERING YOUR FINANCIAL ASSETS

One of the most important steps in building a successful home business is a sound profit plan. What steps will you have to take to get started in the business of your choice and how much will each step cost you? For example, how much will it take to purchase the necessary materials and supplies to begin operation? What about the cost of insurance, telephone, license, and other items that will affect profit?

Once you have considered these things and made a list with estimated costs, you will have some idea of how much cash-on-hand you will need. Many thriving businesses were originally part time ventures utilizing cash from a regular income to get started. Others were started using resources and materials already on hand thereby requiring small cash investments of only $5 or $10. In many instances, money in a savings account will be enough to put you in business. Or perhaps you can fall back on stocks or bonds, or government savings bonds.

If, however, you have your sights set on a more expensive project, you may find it necessary to seek a loan. Therefore, it might be helpful for you to make a list of your equities. Do you own a house or a mortgage on some other property? If your house cost $12,000 and the balance of the mortgage on it is $7,000, you can reasonably claim an equity of $5,000 as a tangible asset. You can also list the value of your equity in any lots, recreational property, or other real estate where your title and rights are clear.

Are you the beneficiary of someone's will? This potential income can also be listed as an asset.

There are also other tangibles to be considered. What about your car? Do you plan to use it in your business? If so you can list its present value as an asset. Since you already own it you won't need to lay out cash for a required piece of equipment. Presently-owned machines, tools, furniture, and other items necessary to the conduct of your proposed business can also be considered assets.

How about personal property? Obviously, the contents of your home also constitute tangible assets. Furniture, TV's, stove, refrigerator, as well as rings, jewelry, watches, and the like. However, you take a risk listing them as assets. Should your business fail, they would be considered as tangible assets of the business and therefore subject to seizure.

EIGHT SURE-FIRE RULES FOR MAKING
MONEY FROM YOUR BUSINESS

Once you have decided on the type of business you wish to start, one of your chief aims is to make money. But some infant businesses not only fail to make money, they actually cause their owners to go bankrupt. This can't happen to you if you follow the rules set out below.

1. Select a business that you like. No one can commit himself totally to a job that he dislikes doing. On the other hand, if your business is something that calls for the kind of work you enjoy, you are going to work harder with the least amount of effort.

2. Start small. Many home businesses fail because their owners plunged in with every cent they owned. Remember, you can start your business while still holding down a full-time job, thereby making it possible to carry on as usual until your new business can stand on its own. This technique has been used by many people to build a fortune without risking their life savings.

3. Persistence pays off. A demand for your product or service won't surface overnight. It takes time to become established. Don't become discouraged.

4. Make your product or service "the best." No one is going to buy your product or service if he can get something better for the same price somewhere else. Giving your customers "a little more," even if it's only a friendly smile, will increase your chances for success.

5. Familiarize yourself with the business. If you don't know all of the in's and out's of your proposed business, you can easily find yourself on the road to failure. Learn all you can before you open for business.

6. Careful cost-figuring helps. Before you start your home business, carefully analyze all the costs involved, not only in getting started, but in maintaining the business from day to day. Many businesses have floundered because the owner failed to set aside enough working capital.

7. Operate in a business way. Because you are working out of your home is no reason to be sloppy about business procedures. Nor should a part-time business be handled as though it were a hobby. Hobbyists don't make money. Businessmen do.

8. Keep records. Probably the most important item for the new business entrepreneur is that he learn to keep complete records. These are not only valuable from a financial point, but they are also vital in establishing a customer list.

2

Where to Get Facts and Information You Need for a Money-Making Home Business

Finding the business project that is just right for you can mean the difference between your business success or failure, between financial loss or monetary gain. But what kind of information and facts do you need? Where and how do you find them?

ACQUIRING THE KNOW-HOW THAT MAKES MONEY

Acquiring the know-how that makes money is no secret. Helpful facts are everywhere and all sorts of information about every conceivable business is yours, in most instances, merely for the asking.

For instance, one of the easiest ways to learn about a business that is of interest to you is to observe how others in that field operate. Every business, large or small, had to have a beginning and reports on another's method of success—or failure—can be of great help.

People already operating a successful business are usually willing to help a beginner get started (but you should make it clear that you don't plan to compete in their area). Often, they regard your interest as a compliment and their friendly advice can frequently save you costly blunders. They can offer suggestions as to the best sources for materials and sometimes markets that they themselves are not interested in. Then too, each business has its own peculiarities and can best be learned from someone familiar with it.

Suppose operating a day nursery appeals to you. What is the first thing you do? Logically, your initial step is to visit one. See how it is equipped; ask questions about its operation; inquire about license regulations; check on advertising techniques. One word of caution, however. Seek help from a day nursery located in an area far removed from your intended place of business—on the opposite side of the city, or in a nearby town. In this way you don't pose a threat to the established business and will receive more explicit help from the owner.

Practical information can also be acquired from studying the business know-how of big organizations. Big businesses have found a successful formula for making money. Frequently they are willing to furnish the budding business opportunist with sound, proven, and tested business-development techniques and strategies. Checking their operation can sometimes help you to decide where to locate, how to advertise, where to market your products, or how to finance your operation.

No matter what the business or how large the company, don't be afraid to ask for help. The public relations departments of such firms are a good place to start. They are always co-operative and can give you a great amount of information on how the business got started. If they don't have facts on the particular phase of business know-how you seek, quite often they will put you in touch with others who can give you what you need.

If, in your business, you buy merchandise from a wholesaler, ask him for information you need. Because your success means more profit from him, he will do everything possible to help you sell your product. Likewise, the man who sells you the equipment necessary to carry out a service.

For example, suppose you're interested in making and selling small wooden candlestands. Information which will prove most helpful will be cheerfully given by these suppliers of carving tools:

Charles F. Bingler Sons, Inc. 498 Sixth Avenue New York, N.Y. 10009	Geo. S. Baker & Co. 578 Spring St., N.W. Atlanta, Georgia 30308

Other sources of information could be:

J. W. Danker Marquetry Co. 702 Evergreen St., S.E. Grand Rapids, Michigan 49507	Period Furniture Hardware Co., Inc. 123 Charles Street, Boston, Massachusetts 02154

If there is one rule for the beginner which is advocated by almost every business authority, it is this: *Proceed Cautiously.* Try out your ideas on a limited scale first. Then as your venture begins to show a profit, you can expand and build on it.

Here is an example of how one man felt his way to big business. Two years before his retirement, Loyal Jensen had saved a few hundred dollars and wanted to invest in a business that couldn't lose. Because he and his friends had to travel to an adjacent city for a massage, he felt confident that a massage studio in his hometown would be a success.

Since he had long been a paying customer, he had acquired a good deal of know-how in most aspects of the business and although he, himself, was not a licensed masseur, an ad placed in a help-wanted column was answered by a young man with suitable skill and a pleasing personality. The cost of basic equipment was negligible and he could operate from Jensen's home.

Loyal opened his studio while still holding down his regular job. As the town grew, so did the number of clients. By retirement time, the studio became a full-time business with added equipment and two masseurs in attendance.

TAPPING SOURCES OF INFORMATION
THROUGH YOUR LIBRARY

Probably the most accessible source of information the budding business person has is the library. On its shelves are literally thousands of books which can serve as guides for avenues of business endeavor or for almost any undertaking in which you think you might be interested.

Does furniture construction intrigue you? John Stewart, a successful cabinet maker I know, often begins work on a project by first going to the card file in his library and abstracting those cards having to do with wood, refinishing, or whatever phase of furniture information his current business demands. Frequently he goes home with an armful of books which include such titles as:

> *The Encyclopedia of Furniture Making,* by Ernest Joyce—Drake Publisher Limited, 1970.
>
> *Cabinetmaking and Millwork,* by John L. Fierer—Charles A. Bennett Co., Inc., 1967-1970.
>
> *Fine Furniture For the Amateur Cabinetmaker,* by A. W. Marlow—Bonanza Books, MCMLV.

Actually the card file is just the beginning, as a visit to your public library will prove.

Most libraries have many other basic reference sources. Anything that contains information arranged chronologically or alphabetically may be considered a reference source. Usually these materials cannot be taken out on loan, but they can be used in the library. Often they are kept on or very near the desk of a staff librarian who can save you time if you communicate your needs to her.

Among the most useful for the person seeking business information are newspaper and periodical indexes. These can provide you with timely information which you may need in your business and can get nowhere else. For example, you may need income tax information or business predictions which are too new to be found in hard-cover books. A check of your newspaper indexes will provide the answers.

Although most newspapers don't index their contents, a few major ones do. Frequently a particular fact—date, location, spelling of a name—can be learned from the index alone, without referring to the complete news story. Most libraries keep a microfilm record of complete hometown papers, as well as indexed items from major newspapers.

Indexes to newspapers include:

The New York Times Index carries more items than any other newspaper index. During the year these indexes appear at two-week intervals and are eventually consolidated into an annual index.

The London Times Index will be found in large city libraries. It indexes European news, business and general, and can be useful if you sell overseas.

Indexes to magazines and other periodicals are more numerous. They catalog articles and news published by almost every business magazine and trade journal. For example, the *Engineering Index* lists and describes material in over 1,000 engineering journals and includes abstracts of selected articles. Others of interest are:

Indexes to periodicals:

Reader's Guide to Periodical Literature indexes periodicals of broad general and popular interest.

Applied Science and Technology Index is a subject index to periodicals in fields of aerodynamics, automation, ceramics, chemistry, construction, electricity, food technology, and tele-communications.

Business Periodicals Index is a subject index to periodicals dealing with advertising, insurance, labor laws, marketing, and specific businesses, industries, and trades.

There are also many other indexes important for their subject matter specialization, such as *Accountants Index* and *Insurance Index.*

Directories too, are part of your library's basic reference materials and they frequently can provide you with the concise information to help you learn more about operating a money-making business.

Suppose, for instance, you make flowers and want to know who puts out the type of crepe paper you need. Or perhaps you want to find out who manufactures the electrical parts you need for your hand-crafted lamps. Look in the *Thomas Register of American Manufacturers,* or *McRae's Blue Book.*

Foreign directories can provide you with pertinent information on importing and exporting. Also useful as a directory is the library's collection of out of town telephone books. In the yellow pages you can find the answers to a surprising number of questions. For example, Vince Martin, of Delray Beach, Florida, was stumped when it came to naming his newly established dog grooming business. A look at the list of dog clipping businesses in the yellow pages of a Los Angeles directory provided him with a choice of several provocative names.

If you have questions that don't require extensive research, your library can give you the answers through a reference telephone service. With a simple phone call you can often save yourself a time consuming trip and obtain a single fact—as a firm's name, or an address from a business directory.

And don't overlook your librarian as a source of information. Confide in her. Frequently, by identifying yourself and your business, you can better help her to understand your problems. You'll be suprised what books, pamphlets, and other reference material she'll be able to find for you. Sometimes, if you live in a small town, she'll even send away, through inter-library loan, for books and reference materials that are available only in the big city libraries. In addition she can often steer you to business-oriented lectures at nearby colleges and high schools, or those sponsored by local groups and organizations.

In addition to the aids already mentioned, your library has many other services that will prove helpful to you as a beginning business person. Their referral and copying services, business bibliographies, and guides to government publications can prove invaluable.

USING YOUR CITY AND STATE AGENCIES

Now let's check some agencies in your own city and state for helpful facts and information. These can supply you with much useful material, and many successful business people I know use this source frequently.

Do you need to know something about consumers or credit? Most states have a consumer council that will give you information in this area. They also offer *free* counseling service should you find yourself in financial trouble.

Want to operate a beauty salon in your basement? Be sure to check the zoning laws in your community first. Licensing requirements are also something you should know about before you become too deeply involved or invest in expensive equipment. Each city has a list of these agencies in the phone book, or if they are not listed independently, information can be obtained at your city, town, or village hall. Explain your plans to the proper officials. Usually you will find them most helpful, often able to give needed advice and counsel.

Another valuable agency is your Better Business Bureau. Not long ago, a friend of mine needed information concerning a "business opportunity" advertised in the newspaper. Before he invested any considerable sum of money, he wanted to be sure that the venture was a sound, reputable one. His B.B.B. confirmed that it was.

The Bureau also has two pamphlets which they distribute to warn against misrepresented earning opportunities. Both *Tips On Work-At-Home Schemes,* and *Home-Work Schemes,* may be obtained *free* upon request.

Although a bank's main function is to loan out money at interest, your banker can be of great help to you in other ways. Remember, he wants to see your business succeed as much as you do.

At your neighborhood bank, officials will be well acquainted with what is going on in the area, and therefore will have a better understanding of the needs of your community. By inviting your banker's criticism, as well as his advice, in frank talks about your plans, you will receive the benefit of his judgment and experience.

Oftentimes your bank may distribute free pamphlets or other literature helpful to your particular business. For instance, leaflets entitled *What Customer Credit Can Do For You,* and *Farming For Profit,* can be picked up from the counter of a Mid-western bank.

Local insurance agencies can also be a source of help and information. Some insurance companies provide financing to small businesses, while others conduct seminars on such topics as: Managing the Small Business; Developing a Marketing Plan for a Small Business; Preparing to Seek Financing; etc.

MAKING MONEY WITH GOVERNMENT HELP

You'd be surprised how much help—free or for a few cents—you can get from the U.S.Government. There is a vast storehouse of information here just waiting for you, if you will only go to the trouble of asking for it.

One of the best sources of information from the government is the Superintendent of Documents, United States Government Printing Office, Washington, D.C. 20402.

You get a list of material being published each month by sending for the monthly catalog of United States Public Documents. At the same time, you can ask to be put on the list of Selected United States Government Publications—this is a *free* booklet and is mailed to you every month.

Glance through any list of government publications and you will find a wide variety of business-oriented subjects offered. Here are a few:

1. Commercial Strawberry Growing
2. Pruning Shade Trees and Repairing Their Injuries.
3. Better Lawns, Establishment, Maintenance.
4. Commercial Rabbit Raising.
5. Back To Work After Retirement.
6. Small Business and Labor.
7. Paint and Painting.

These are just a sampling from two bulletins. Each bulletin contains about 120 titles—all providing a wealth of material when those particular subjects relate to your business.

Another convenience to you is the growing number of Government Printing Office Bookstores outside of Washington, D.C., which have in stock approximately 1,000 of the most popular titles. Thus far these stores are located in the states listed below. Exact addresses can be found by looking in the white pages of your telephone book under *United States Government listings.*

Atlanta, Georgia	Kansas City, Missouri
Birmingham, Alabama	Los Angeles, California
Boston, Massachusetts	New York, N.Y.
Canton, Ohio	Pueblo, Colorado
Chicago, Illinois	San Francisco, California
Dallas, Texas	Detroit, Michigan
Denver, Colorado	

Another branch of the government which will welcome your inquiries and be glad to assist you is the Small Business Administration. This is a permanent, independent government agency created by Congress in 1953 to help small businesses grow and prosper. Through its network of field offices (listed below) in the principal cities of every state, as well as Guam and Puerto Rico, it offers small businesses financial assistance including lease guarantees, management assistance, and various types of loans.

From the SBA you can learn how to bid for government contracts, what goods and services are bought by the military and civilian government agencies, which purchasing office buys them, and much other related know-how.

If you need help to start a business or run one more successfully, you can obtain free counseling and guidance from the SBA. This agency also offers conferences, workshops, and clinics. Free pamphlets describing all these programs of assistance are available. Write to

Small Business Administration
Washington, D.C. 20416

or contact your nearest SBA field office.

Field Offices:

The Small Business Administration maintains field offices in the cities listed below. Field personnel will be glad to assist inquirers with their problems. Consult the local telephone book for street location and phone number or write the office in the city nearest you.

ALABAMA:	ARKANSAS:
Birmingham 35203	Little Rock 72201
ALASKA:	CALIFORNIA:
Anchorage 99501	Los Angeles 90013
ARIZONA:	San Diego 92104
Phoenix 85004	San Francisco 94105

COLORADO:
  Denver 80202
CONNECTICUT:
  Hartford 06103
DISTRICT OF COLUMBIA:
  Washington 20417
FLORIDA:
  Jacksonville 32202
  Miami 33131
GEORGIA:
  Atlanta 30303
GUAM:
  Agana 96910
HAWAII:
  Honolulu 96813
IDAHO:
  Boise 83702
ILLINOIS:
  Chicago 60604
INDIANA:
  Indianapolis 46204
IOWA:
  Des Moines 50309
KANSAS:
  Wichita 67202
KENTUCKY:
  Louisville 40202
LOUISIANA:
  New Orleans 70130
MAINE:
  Augusta 04330
MARYLAND:
  Baltimore 21201
MASSACHUSETTS:
  Boston 02210
MICHIGAN:
  Detroit 48226
  Marquette 49855
MINNESOTA:
  Minneapolis 55402
MISSISSIPPI:
  Jackson 39201
MISSOURI;
  Kansas City 64106
  St. Louis 63103

MONTANA:
  Helena 59601
NEBRASKA:
  Omaha 68102
NEVADA:
  Las Vegas 89104
NEW HAMPSHIRE:
  Concord 03301
NEW JERSEY:
  Newark 07102
NEW MEXICO:
  Albuquerque 87101
NEW YORK:
  Buffalo 14203
  New York 10004
  Syracuse 13202
NORTH CAROLINA:
  Charlotte 28202
NORTH DAKOTA:
  Fargo 58102
OHIO:
  Cincinnati 45202
  Cleveland 44113
  Columbus 43125
  Toledo 43602
OKLAHOMA:
  Oklahoma City 73102
OREGON:
  Portland 97205
PENNSYLVANIA:
  Philadelphia 19107
  Pittsburgh 15222
PUERTO RICO:
  Santurce 00908
RHODE ISLAND:
  Providence 02903
SOUTH CAROLINA:
  Columbia 29201
SOUTH DAKOTA:
  Sioux Falls 57102
TENNESSEE:
  Knoxville 37902
  Nashville 37219

TEXAS: WASHINGTON:
  Dallas 75202   Seattle 98104
  Houston 77002   Spokane 99201
  Lubbock 79401   WEST VIRGINIA:
  Marshall 75670   Charleston 25301
  San Antonio 78204   Clarksburg 26301
UTAH: WISCONSIN:
  Salt Lake City 84101   Madison 53703
VERMONT: Milwaukee 53203
  Montpelier 05601   WYOMING:
VIRGIN ISLANDS: Casper 82601
  St. Thomas 00802
VIRGINIA:
  Richmond 23226

In addition, the SBA issues countless other publications which will be valuable aids to you. Copies of these single pamphlets are available *free* from all SBA offices. Periodically, a series of pamphlets are compiled into "annuals." These are sold only through the Superintendent of Documents Office.

The four big categories of *free* pamphlets are: Management Aids; Marketers' Aids; Technical Aids; Bibliographies. Here's a sample of titles in each category.

Management aids:

  #52 Loan Sources in the Federal Government.

  #53 Small Business Profits from Unpatentable Ideas.

  #188 Developing A List of Prospects.

Technical aids:

  #50 Reduce Waste—Increase Profit.

  #77 Are You Using Your Space Effectively?

  #83 Judging Your Electric Power Needs.

Marketers' aids:

  #120 Building Good Customer Relations.

  #121 Measuring the Results of Advertising.

  #142 Steps In Meeting Your Tax Obligations.

Bibliographies:

  #1   Handicrafts and Home Businesses.

  #46 Woodworking S Shops.

  #54 Interior Decorating.

These are just a few sample titles of what is available. You can obtain a full list by requesting publication #*115A, "Free Booklets,"* from the Superintendent of Documents or your nearest SBA office.

Another publication, #*115B,* is also yours merely for the asking. This lists "For-Sale Booklets," which you can purchase, usually for less than one dollar each.

The two main categories of For-Sale Booklets are: *Small Business Management Series* and *Starting and Managing Series.*

Using SBA catalog #*1.12:6, Cutting Office Costs In Small Plants,* Frank Balle, a plastic toy-manufacturer, discovered that by re-organizing his filing system he could save about 18 hours each month, which figured out to a savings of approximately $86.

In the same way, Bill O'Connor, who operates a small machine shop, feels that reading SBA catalog #*1:15:1, Starting and Managing A Small Business Of Your Own,* helped him to avoid many of the pitfalls that can trap the person going into business for the first time. For example, within a six-month period he had saved himself more than $460 just by following the booklet's advice on equipment and materials necessary for his beginning business.

In addition to the Small Business Administration, there are several other government agencies which can be helpful to you in starting and operating a business. For example, suppose you want to start a bicycle repair shop. To test whether your community has enough business to support such a venture, you can use information from surveys and statistics.

The U.S.Dept. of Commerce is a major source of information on locating such data. Other aids from this department include marketing and sales programs for new products, as well as listings of available patents for new product development. Publications of the department are available by request.

If you are a veteran, or otherwise eligible, you may apply for a *veteran's business loan* from the Veteran's Administration, Washington, D.C. 20420. Your request can be for the purpose of buying, starting, or expanding a business. Or a loan can be made for the purchase of machinery, tools, and other business equipment, or improvement and repair of a business building. You can also put in a request for working capital.

Another source for loans is the Economic Development Administration, United States Department of Commerce, Washington, D.C. 20230.

Low-interest, long-term loans are granted to establish or to expand plants in designated redevelopment areas, if funds cannot be obtained through ordinary channels, such as banks. Individuals belonging to minority groups, or those whose background, experience, or skill in business management and techniques are lacking, can seek and find help through this branch of government.

Still another loan source is the Farmers' Home Administration. Loans up to $60,000 can be made for the development of farm land for recreational facilities, as camp grounds, riding stables, ski slopes, cycle trails, etc. Operational loans are also available. However, you must fulfill two conditions to be eligible for a loan. 1. You must have the know-how to start and operate a recreational enterprise. 2. You must be unable to obtain financing through ordinary channels.

Besides this service, the Farmers Home Administration distributes a large variety of popular publications which can be of great help in the operation of many business ventures. Send for *Popular Publications for the Farmer, Suburbanite, Homemaker, Consumer,* Farmers' Home Administration, U.S. Department of Agriculture, Washington, D.C. 20250.

The pamphlet you will receive includes such diversified subjects as:

	Order No.
Beekeeping for Beginners	158
Building A Pullet-Rearing House	M1142
Special Forest Products For Profit	AB278
Raising Guinea Pigs	L466
Saddle Horse Barn Plan	M1029
Simplified Clothing Construction	G59

There are over 6,000 subjects to choose from, and you may request single copies of up to 10 different publications *free.*

LETTING YOUR NEWSPAPERS GUIDE YOU

A most useful source for the person going into business is one you find in your own home everyday—the daily newspaper. Of particular interest, aside from your hometown paper, is the *Wall Street Journal,* or the Sunday edition of the *New York Times.* Many times, a check of the "Business Opportunities" columns can be rewarding.

For example, a note to those opportunities you think might appeal to you can sometimes result in ideas for your own business.

You can also find places to obtain aid on tax shelters or money sources for business growth. You would, of course, check these out thoroughly with your Better Business Bureau, before going ahead on your own.

Business and finance sections of your paper can be a constant current source of needed information. However, don't limit your reading to these portions alone. Frequently, in scanning through the remainder you will come across a news item that can prove beneficial to you.

For instance, glancing through the general news section of your paper, you see the following headline: *Crime Rise Fuels Security Services.* Reading further you find that most businesses, as well as individuals, are confronted with an upsurge in burglary, employee theft, shoplifting, industrial espionage, vandalism, and arson.

According to the article, anti-crime companies have a high profit margin on their investment. Does this give you an idea for a business of your own?

Ginny Platt started her home career after reading a newspaper article not unlike the one mentioned above. On an inside page of her town's small, weekly newspaper, she happened upon a piece titled, *Pest Control Rises Into Status Symbol.* The body of this article carried the message that the attitude toward pest control has changed drastically over the last few years. An authority gave the opinion that, whereas years ago, a company might even lose business if the words "exterminator" or "pest-control" were written on the side of the truck, today people become upset when the truck is unmarked. According to him, it has become a sort of status symbol to have regular pest control service and people demand service even when they don't need it.

Ginny wrote to the quoted authority for more information, which she received in abundance. She was delighted to learn that although pest control equipment could run into the thousands of dollars, she could start out with chemicals and a spray for about $110. After a short correspondence course in pest control from a large, state college, she was able to pass her state examination and obtain her license. Working full time that first year, her net income came to $1300.

Many times a business article can be of tremendous help to the established business person as well as a source of inspiration or a starting point for the beginner. Take, for example, the headline *Bicycle Sales Boom!* For the individual already in business, this article may give valuable advice on the techniques of selling. For the beginner, the statistical report of bicycle sales may readily suggest the need for bicycle repair shops.

Very often merely reading an article about another's business or hobby can inspire you. Or perhaps, on the social page of your newspaper, you will discover the announcement of a business celebrity who is scheduled to speak at a Knights of Columbus dinner or other organizational meeting in your town. Plan to attend. Asking questions of someone who has already solved some of the problems of a beginning business can be most helpful and encouraging.

Almost every newspaper has a section devoted to mail-order and franchising. In a typical business section of the Sunday *New York Times,* or the Wednesday *Wall Street Journal,* you will find many offers of already established businesses, as well as available locations and opportunities to begin on your own. Your mail-order and franchise pages present you with the very latest information in this field, and by answering the ads, you will receive the kind of information you will need to have about individual companies.

DISCOVERING INCOME OPPORTUNITIES
FROM MAGAZINES

The more you know about a business which interests you, the easier it will be for you to make a success of starting and operating it. There are several monthly magazines, available on most newsstands, that can give you an insight into earning big money.

Waiting for an appointment in her dentist's office, Mrs. Margaret Dutton picked up an issue of *Industry Week* Magazine. In it was an account of how one large printing company cashed in on its delivery service.

Since Mrs. Dutton owned and operated a small printing business herself, this information was vitally important. Applying the principles set forth in the article she was able to offer her customers "free delivery." She could do this by extending the use of facilities already available—her station wagon. This service brought her many new customers and thereby increased her monthly income by 10 percent.

Another issue of the same magazine related the story of a man who buys California mountain tops at an extremely low price and makes a profit from owning them. Loren R. McQueen is president of

Communication and Control Inc., and leases radio antenna sites for handling long-range, two-way communications.

A friend of mine, after reading this account, didn't rush out to buy the tops of mountains, but she did buy land on a mountainside at $200 per acre. Bit by bit she has converted her land into a well-paying ski resort near Denver, which, in season, brings her an income of more than $100 a day.

Industry Week, like most other business magazines, also offers regular features on business outlooks, technology, marketing, and research, plus special reports on current business issues.

Trade journals too, can be very helpful and although they are not for sale at newsstands, many are available through your library business periodical department. A trade magazine is devoted to a specific business or industry or trade. It can give you not only the news of its field, but many helpful ideas for carrying on.

A hardware trade journal, for example, may have a story on how a merchant in Michigan increased spring sales by offering free packages of flower seeds to customers making purchases in his store. In another part of the country, other hardware dealers read about his successful selling plan, and may try the same idea. Trade journals also supply you with the names and addresses of manufacturers, wholesalers, or other suppliers in a particular field.

Although trade magazines are not available on your newsstand, there are many general consumer magazines that are. These, too, can often give you an insight into earning extra income. For example, recently an article written by seven young millionaires, on "How To Make A Million Dollars," appeared in *Coronet.*

An article in *Reader's Digest* gave an account of how the founder of McDonald's (a high school dropout, no less) got started with hamburgers, and how he parlayed his beginning business into a leading franchise.

Home and garden magazines are full of ideas devoted to homes, gardens, and workshop items. One publication ran an article about a man who makes family coats-of-arms as a profession. Another article explained how a local store owner catered to the growing interest in wines and wine-making in his neighborhood by developing and selling do-it-yourself kits.

For articles on current events look to your national and world affairs magazines such as *Newsweek, Time,* and the *National Review.* Knowing what's going on in the world can be vital to your business success.

Antique and hobby magazines offer a vast amount of material, often with step-by-step directions for business projects. In one such publication, Glenda and Bob Harper, ran across plans for making miniature furniture. With Bob retired, the $150 additional income each month from their tiny furniture factory is most welcome.

Another couple, newly married and living on the shores of Lake Huron, in Michigan, got the idea for giving lessons when they read an article, "Sailing For The Fun of It," in a hobby magazine. In the summer months, they average about $40 a day, and since there is little overhead save the wear and tear on their sailboat, it's clear profit.

Magazines such as *Popular Science, Popular Mechanics,* and *Mechanix Illustrated* present new and interesting developments in many fields, and are virtually exploding with helpful "how-to" advice. Here are some titles chosen at random from recent issues.

Darkroom Basics

The Six Strongest Glues for Woodworkers

Build A Pelican Class Sailboat

Guide To Pencil Engravers

Build A Doorbeep

Now Anyone Can Lay Parquet Flooring

Three Table-Saw Tips

Build A Low-Cost Speaker

Stained-Glass Candle Lamps

New Ideas From the Inventors

Custom Furniture You Can Build

Car-Care: 13 No-Nos For Your Car

Shop Tips

Build A Sled for Your Snowmobile

Men's magazines, too, can frequently be of use to you in your business. *Argosy, True,* and others of this type feature articles on camping, hunting, fishing, travel, automobiles—all subjects that can provide ideas or inspire you toward a business venture.

The same holds true for those magazines oriented toward a female readership. Most offer "how-to" pieces on a variety of subjects including the arts of cooking and sewing, workshop projects, and crafts.

In an issue of *Woman's Day,* for instance, the editors offered you directions for making jewelry designs, as well as information on how to make a "touch-up beauty box," in its workshop column. *Redbook* devotes space each month to a section called the *Handicrafter.* One issue gave specific directions on how to make the following items.

Quick-point animal pillows.	Place mats and napkins.
A child's bulletin board.	A tray and coaster set.
A kitchen bulletin board.	A blanket with macramé-fringed ends.
Totes for toys.	A vinyl carryall.

Some women's magazines even feature an article each month which tells the story of a successful business woman and how she got started. "Careers At Home," a feature in *Family Circle,* by Mary Gibson, became so popular over the years that the author recently published a book of the same title. Copies of this 296-page book ($5.95) are available from

Family Circle Books, Dept. 434,
P.O. Box 450, Teaneck, N.J. 07666

Ladies' Home Journal edits a column called, "How To Make Money in Your Spare Time," while a regular feature of *McCall's* is titled, "Launching Your Own Business."

There is probably nothing more stimulating than reading the "income opportunity" magazines. These are devoted exclusively to helping the small-business person. *Income Opportunities* appears on the newsstands monthly with regular departments devoted to selling, real estate reports, mail-order know-how, and latest franchise developments, plus accounts of how successful businesses got their start.

Another magazine I found on the newsstand, which can help to put cash in your pocket, is *Guide To Earning Extra Income.* Published once or twice during the year by Ziff-Davis Publishing Company, it offers help on the development of many home business ideas, as well as mail-order, franchising, and business know-how. It's "Reader Service" features a "pass-along" page. In the event you wish to respond to an ad in the magazine, you merely clip and mail these coupons for free information.

A Taylor Rental Coupon, for instance, will bring you information in the return mail about the advantages of operating one of these $10,000 to $14,000 rental franchises. A coupon of the North American School of Accounting will bring you information on their training program plus a free booklet, *Your Future In Accounting.*

And a Univeral School's coupon will bring to your door a free book on earnings and opportunities in Accident Investigation.

Mailing in these coupons usually obligates you in no way, and helps you to analyze the thousands of business opportunities which are offered.

Salesman's Opportunity is a monthly concerned chiefly with selling techniques, but it also offers advice in other areas. For instance, the following article titles were listed in one issue:

New Opportunities for Women   News of Money-Makers

How I Became A Winner   A Profitable Service Business

PROFITING FROM OTHER
MISCELLANEOUS MATERIAL

In many communities educational courses are offered for those who wish to learn the "tricks of the trade" in the business world. Usually a fee is charged. You might start by consulting the Continuing Education Department, or the Business School, of your local colleges and universities.

A telephone call, for instance, or a brief letter of inquiry to the director will alert you to time, place, and other particulars. Some colleges offer an extensive curriculum of evening classes for both the beginning and advanced business person. Since these courses are usually no-credit, the entire program may cost no more than $15.

Other colleges and universities are affiliated with business management groups, organizations which conduct business seminars on campus. For many participants, the course is free, since they are sponsored by various trade and/or professional organizations.

Besides offering courses and seminars, the Extension Services of your State College will be glad to supply you with information and printed instructions on many subjects—agriculture, household repairs, animal husbandry, furniture refinishing—to name but a few. Colleges also engage many speakers during the school year. Some of these talks could be of interest to you in your business. Ask for a brochure listing speakers and events for each semester.

You might also consult your local Board of Education for information about high-school evening courses. Check the programs of the Young Men's and Young Women's Christian Associations in your city. Often Community Centers and Art Institutes offer classes in various crafts, arts, and sciences. Sometimes, hobby shops give instruction in metalworking, leathercrafts, decoupage, antiquing, macramé, and the like. In short, ideas are everywhere. It's up to you to find the right one and make it your own.

3

How to Make Instant Money with Time Your Only Investment

In this age of the machine and the computer, consumers are eager for a personalized service or a handmade product and they are prepared to pay for it. Perhaps you can create foods others enjoy, oil paintings that people will pay for, carved wooden objects that bring a good price, or perhaps like Annabel Morrison, you have a talent for making people look beautiful.

Annabel, a young housewife and mother, who before her marriage worked in a posh New York beauty salon, started her home business from scratch with a *two-chair beauty parlor* in her basement. Her laundry tubs served as shampoo sinks and she did all the work herself. Friends were her first customers, but as word of mouth spread the news of her new business, she found it necessary gradually to expand. Today, she employs five operators in her complete "house of beauty" on the first floor of a lovely old, renovated Victorian mansion in downtown Detroit.

At the onset, Annabel serviced five customers daily during the week, eight on weekends. She charged $3 per head for a shampoo and set, $10-$15 for a permanent, and grossed a minimum of $500 a month. Five years later, with two operators helping her, she grossed $1250 per month. Then, as now, she kept abreast of hair fashion trends by constantly reading and attending beauty seminars whenever possible.

Whatever your skills and abilities, *taking an objective view* of their money-making potential will reap higher rewards for you. Don't downgrade your talents simply because their performance seems simple to you. Don't discard their use as money-makers because they have languished unused for a time. Take them out of mothballs, polish them up, and look at them objectively, in the light of money-making assets.

Perhaps, right now, you possess all the knowledge you need to successfully handle a home business based on your special talent. On the other hand, if you feel a bit rusty, you may wish to take advantage of some additional training or a "brush-up" course to enable you to qualify for a successful business venture. Many such instructional courses may be completed at home by mail and are not prohibitive in cost. Others, also for a small fee, can be learned at various centers in your town or city. Such centers include the YMCA/YWCA and church affiliated organizations, or continuing-education courses at your local high school or college.

When you feel that you are ready to take the plunge into the business arena, there are two basic approaches to be considered.

1. You can use your skill to fulfill a need for your customers—that is perform a service such as baby-sitting or antique-finding.
2. You can share your skill through instruction—by teaching others what you know.

PROFITING FROM YOUR TALENTS

Do you have a good command of a foreign language? Do you know how to knit or crochet? Can you speak in front of an audience? Now is the time to put this special skill to work for you, and turn it into extra income.

Take tutoring for example. Language tutors are always in demand. They are especially sought-after today with the big boom in foreign travel. Time spent abroad is very popular with high school and college students who tour the continents during summer vacations. Others take part in student exchange programs during the school term.

Another market for your tutoring service are businessmen. Many have jobs that occasionally take them overseas, and being able to speak the language of business associates in a foreign country is a distinct advantage.

You might also consider aliens who come to live in our country.

They must learn English. Then too, don't forget the children in our schools who may need coaching. If you are good at figures, you might wish to teach math. High school students need help with algebra and geometry, and "new-math" tutors are in demand for grade school pupils.

Tutoring can be done in the evening or on a weekend, in the quiet of your own home or in the home of the person to be tutored. A French woman, living near a university, tutors for $10 per hour and handles about 16 pupils in a week. You can set your own fee and the number of hours you wish to work.

Often, you can advertise free in school bulletins and club news letters. Sometimes your own children serve as your best advertising media.

Books from the library which will prove helpful are similar to the two listed below.

> *Teacher and Child,* by Haim G. Ginott, Macmillan, 1972—a guide for teachers and parents.

> *Teaching English As A Second Language,* by Mary Finocchiaro, Harper and Row, New York, 1969.

If tutoring is not for you, perhaps, like Elinor Gibbons, a young homemaker, your way to making money is as a decorating consultant. Possessed of an innate aesthetic sense which allows her to bring a room to life with very little money, and empathy for the middle-income housewife, who can't afford costly decorating fees, Elinor set up shop in her home, advertising herself as a "consultant in home decoration." In this role she would enter a customer's home and discuss the redoing of a room or rooms with the owner. Then, using her client's money, she would set forth to buy draperies, paint, wall paper, curtains, furniture or whatever else was needed to complete the room—often with her client in tow. She would also contract for painters, plasterers, and other workmen.

The reasonable fee she charged for the loan of her aesthetic talent was sometimes by the hour, sometimes by the job. For instance, if a customer wished to consult Elinor about a window hanging, or the color coordination of a room, the fee would be $10 per hour. If, on the other hand, she contracted to do the entire job, her fee would be in accordance with the amount of time it required.

For a **Small** Business Bibliography—*Interior Decorating #54,* send a request to the Small Business Administration, Washington, D.C 20416.

For publications and services which will assist you in your decorating endeavors, write to:

American Institute of Decorators　　Decorative Fabrics Institute
41 East 57th Street　　　　　　　　500 Fifth Ave.
New York, N.Y. 10022　　　　　　　New York, N.Y. 10018

American Institute of Interior Designers
673 Fifth Ave.
New York, N.Y. 10022

Books from the library which will provide help are:

Interior Decoration As A Profession, by Victoria Kloss, Ed. Books Div. of Universal Pub., and Distributing Corp., 1963.

Decorating Small Apartments, by Olga Stier, Morrow, 1969.

Better Homes and Gardens Decorating Ideas Under $100, Meredith Corp., 1971.

There are also a number of popular magazines which contain a wealth of home decorating information. Included among them are:

The American Home, Curtis Publishing Co., 300 Park Ave., New York, N.Y. 10022.

Better Homes and Gardens, Meredith Publishing Co., 1716 Locust St., Des Moines, Iowa 50309.

House and Garden, Conde Nast Publications, Inc., 420 Lexington Ave., New York, N.Y. 10017.

If you are particularly well versed in a subject, have an unusual collection or hobby, or achieved an accomplishment of some kind, lectures can be lucrative. People are anxious for knowledge and know-how, and organizations of all types are always on the lookout for an interesting speaker.

Don't cross this opportunity for income off your list because you think you have to be a great orator or a brilliant speechmaker to succeed. On the contrary, it isn't at all difficult to talk to groups about something you're really keen on. Sincerity and knowledge of your subject are your greatest assets.

John Smith, an authority in the coin-collecting field, has been booked by groups all over the country. He sometimes gives as many as five lectures a week. At $150 per evening, he does quite well financially.

Another man, an old hand at using a metal-detector, started giving lectures in his home town at $25 per talk. He was "guest speaker"—at Boy Scout meetings, Knights of Columbus banquets, even women's clubs.

To get started, you might send a letter to clubs and church groups in your community explaining the subject matter of your talk and giving your qualifications for presenting it. You set your own fee which will be paid by the organization or group who sponsors you. They will also usually arrange the program as to place, time, and length of your talk and take care of news releases and other publicity. Usually you will be expected to talk for about 45 minutes. If your subject warrants it, you can allow some time for questions.

Another slant on the lecture market is the promotion of lectures by others with you acting as an agent. In this instance, your job involves providing the speaker, the place, and the advertising. Your profit is split equally with the speaker, and is usually about $200 per lecture, since most of your speakers will be well known, crowd-pulling attractions.

The following books, available at your library, will prove helpful.

> *How To Make Money Speaking in Public,* by Eskelin, Parker Publishing Company.
>
> *Humor In Public Speaking,* by Day, Parker Publishing Company.
>
> *Eloquence in Public Speaking,* by McFarland, Prentice-Hall, Inc.

If the thought of addressing more than one person leaves you tongue-tied, how about writing for profit? Perhaps you are another Margaret Mitchell, whose exciting success with her first novel, "Gone With The Wind," has become a legend.

Although most of us can't hope to write a best seller, there are other avenues open for profit. How about short fillers or personal experiences for magazines and newspapers? Trade magazines and business "newsletters" are always on the lookout for items of interest to those in the trade. Or perhaps you could become a salesman with a typewriter—an advertising copywriter.

There are techniques that must be mastered to succeed in the craft of writing, but if you can furnish the time and talent, technique can be learned. Check with the schools in your area for classes in the art of writing.

Another ability that can make money for you is a knowledge of antiques. Frequently, an individual will be on a quest for a special antique item. Sometimes a dealer will be on the lookout for something unique for a customer. If you can locate the piece in question, you can earn a picker's fee. Or, as one who is able to identify antiques, you might wish to become a curator and be handsomely paid for your efforts by auctioneers and dealers who liquidate estates.

John Kolurski, who worked with fine furnishings all his life, retired a short time ago and used his knowledge of antiques to further yet another business. He is a picker and curator for one of the best known auction houses in New York.

As a picker, his fee is 30 percent to 50 percent over and above the actual cost he pays for an item. For example, if he buys an antique rocking chair for $100, he will sell it at $150, thus making a profit of $50. His fee as curator for an auction is 4 percent-5 percent of the total amount of sales. Therefore, if bids add up to $10,000, his profit is $500.

No license is required to judge the antiquity of an item, but a "picker" is, in a sense, a dealer and in most cases must obtain a $1 vendor's license from the state.

To put yourself in business, advise the auctioneers and antique dealers in your area of your ability and place yourself at their service. You might start by going through the listings in the yellow pages of your telephone book..

The following library books should be helpful to you.

Know Your Heirlooms, by Thomas H. Ormsbee, The McBride Co., Inc.

How To Sell Your Antiques at A Profit, by Ann Kilborn Cole, David McKay Co., Inc., New York 1969.

The Complete Antiques Price List, by Kovel, Crown Publishers ($5).

SELLING YOUR PERSONAL SERVICES

Today personal services are becoming a rare commodity. But in the machine age of today, they are needed more than ever. So much in demand are they, that in many communities, just making your service known gets you off to a profitable start.

For instance, if you have a pleasant speaking voice, you can turn a telephone service into dollars by offering to note incoming calls for absent businessmen as well as plumbers, carpenters, roofers, painters, masons, insurance agents, and antique dealers. You might also solicit patronage from doctors, lawyers, nurses, dentists, and funeral directors.

You can begin with a message-relay-service using your own

phone, later graduating to an answering service utilizing special telephone equipment. Contact your telephone company for more information on this, as area requirements vary.

There are also other services with which you can make use of your telephone in a profitable way. Many small firms and organizations rely on telephone sales solicitation to advertise or promote their product. Or you might try to sell an appointment for a salesman. If you are a tactful individual, you could qualify as a collection-service-caller. With credit buying on the rise, many retailers find themselves with unpaid accounts and customers are frequently contacted by telephone.

Although large organizations make these calls from their offices, Eileen Tuttle, a victim of arthritis, made them from her home. Her clients were small businessmen, doctors, storekeepers, advertising firms, and the like. For her service, she charged a fee of one-third of the amount collected.

Another telephone service is one which reminds customers of birthdays, anniversaries, and holidays such as Valentine's, Mother's, Father's, Sweetest, Memorial, and St. Patrick's days. Aside from individuals, many gift shops, florists, and department stores could use this service.

When he was small, Dick Alleer's forgetful father paid the boy ten cents to remind him to buy his wife a gift on her birthday. Applying this same principle, Dick, now grown, operates a thriving telephone reminder service in his midwest home town. Stores use his service to contact potential new buyers as well as to remind old customers of a special date. His service fee is $15 per month for 100 calls.

Books on telephone service include:

> *Telephone Answering Service.* Counseling Note #8, *free* from your nearest SBA office, or from SBA, Washington, D.C. 20416.

> *Phonemanship,* by William A. Garrett, Farrar, Straus & Giroux, 19 Union Sq. West, New York, N.Y. 10003.

If your handwriting is legible, it can be worth money to you in starting a personalized addressing service. Each year many business-men, professional people, and small firms send out hundreds of Christmas cards and other material to clients, employees, and friends and will pay well to have them and the accompanying envelope hand-written. This is also true of organizations and politicians who mail invitations for various functions to a select group of people.

There are many busy people in your community who want that personal touch and could use this service. Call on them, or better still, write a letter explaining your service. You might also place an ad in the personal column of the classified section of your local newspaper. This is what Patrick Keatirg, did. Now he and his wife Ann, supplement his school teacher's income with their earnings.

Library research is yet another way to make money at home. As more and more businesses become aware of the value of public relations, the need for reliable research material increases. Many firms publish small booklets or newsletters that go out to clients and employees. Writers, politicians, corporations, civic groups, charities, and small shops are in need of special information relating to their business, or in the preparation of literature.

Your service may be operated on a local or national basis. You can start out with material gathered at your public library, but as your business grows, you might wish to subscribe to various technical journals and trade papers as well as magazines and newspapers, clipping those items on all current ideas of interest to your clients.

Further information can be obtained from *Clipping Service,* Counseling Note #33, a two-page, *free* booklet available from Small Business Administration, Washington, D.C. 20416.

If you are skilled at shorthand, typing, using a dictaphone or mimeograph machine, you could become a *free-lance secretary.* Availability on short notice is a must in this field since you will often be called upon to fill in for a regular employee who is absent due to illness or some other reason, or off on a holiday. If you are reliable and constant you can build up a repeat business which can net you a good profit.

Marcia Gibbons got started by mailing a personal letter outlining her capabilities to doctors, lawyers, dentists, and small businessmen in her home town. At first, she charged $2 per hour and worked for as little as one or two hours at a time. However, as her reputation spread, business boomed. She now commands a fee of $3 per hour, does not accept jobs of less than 3 hours duration, and works a full five-day week.

You might start out using Marcia's method of contacting customers, by inserting an ad in your local paper, or by calling in person on business and professional people in an industrial complex or shopping area near your home. Your fee can be charged by the hour, day, or week.

You could also offer other typing services which could be done in your home, such as typing term papers and theses for students, or typing manuscripts for writers. For student clients, place an ad in the campus newspaper; for writer clients, advertise in one of the writer magazines. Such an ad should read:

> John Doe
> 121 First St., S. W., Grand Rapids, Michigan
> Phone: 313-347-7769
> Includes: Minor corrections, extra carbon copy,
> Smith Corona Electric-pica type

Helpful secretarial books from your library include:

> *The New World Secretarial Handbook,* by A. E. Klein, World Publishers—a fact-filled reference to the latest procedures and techniques.
>
> *Secretary's Complete Model Letter Handbook,* by Claire N. Eddings, Prentice-Hall, Inc.
>
> *Modern Secretary's Complete Guide,*by Twyla Kramer Schwieger, Prentice-Hall, Inc., 1971.

Another big business today is baby-sitting. Working mothers are demanding adequate day-care facilities for their children; vacationing parents are in need of someone to supervise offspring in their absence; mothers and fathers on a "night-out" need a baby sitter.

Maintaining a baby-sitting business is a responsible job and great care must be taken in the selection of sitters. Advertise in local and church papers for trustworthy people, and follow up with a request for references from each applicant along with a personal interview. High school students are fine for short periods, but when parents leave on an extended vacation or an overnight stay, they much prefer that an older, more mature person be left in charge of the household.

To advertise your service, place an ad in the classified section of your local newspaper under childcare. You might also, as did Alice Simmons, a mother of teenagers who started in business 18 months ago, contact pediatricians' offices in your community and try for a bit of free advertising there.

Alice guarantees her sitters at least 2 hours fee per job, which breaks down to $1 per hour. Of this she keeps 35¢ and pays the sitter 65¢. If the customer needs them for less time, they still must pay for two hours. With her girls sitting for an average of about 50 hours each day, Alice makes a gross profit of $22.10 per day.

Since baby-sitting fees vary widely from one area to another, check the going rate in your community. In one town it may be 50¢ an hour, in another $1.50. Many baby-sitting services bill customers on a monthly basis, but Alice finds that better results are obtained when the sitter collects the money as she leaves the job.

There are many good publications with regard to baby-sitting available.

> *How To Start A Baby-Sitting Service* is offered *free* to residents of Massachusetts who write to the Department of Commerce, Women's Division, 150 Causeway Street, Boston, Mass. 02114.

> *Baby Sitting Registry,* Counseling Note #13, can be obtained *free* from your SBA field office or SBA, Washington, D.C. 20416.

Library books include:

> *When Teenagers Take Care of Children,* by Ivor Kraft, Macrae Smith, 1965—the official guide for baby sitters.

> *A Manual for Baby Sitters,* by Marion S. Lowndes, Little Brown, 1961.

Everyone likes a clean house, but today's homemaker has a difficult time finding adequate domestic help. *Cleanliness can mean cash in your pocket* if you launch your own cleaning business.

Perhaps you might wish to start out by doing much of the work yourself, using your own tools. But as your business catches on, you can gradually invest in automatic cleaning equipment and employ assistants. You won't scrub floors, run vacuum cleaners, dust furniture, or wash windows yourself, but employ people skilled in these jobs and operate your business much the same way as the above baby-sitter service is carried out.

Two enterprising young college students started out by lugging their mother's vacuum cleaner, floor mop, and various other cleaning devices to a client's home, where they rolled up their sleeves and went to work. As time went on, they bought their own cleaning equipment—most of it "used," at bargain prices. Today, these two career-minded girls employ eight to ten other students, and own almost $1000 worth of cleaning equipment.

For general house-cleaning, the girls charge at the rate of $3 per hour, $2.00 of which is paid to the worker. This nets the business about $50 per day. The fee for walls, woodwork, and windows is $4 per hour.

Office cleaning and apartment refurbishing can also reap big profits for you. Today, with apartment living on the rise and a high tenant turnover rate, vacated apartments must be washed and cleaned before each new tenant moves in. There is a growing need for such a service. If you don't want to invest money in your own machines, you can lease them and other supplies from most industrial supply companies. $25 per month will lease $500 worth of equipment and free you from maintenance worries.

As in baby-sitting, your workers must be trustworthy, since their performance will reflect on you. Customers can be serviced on a weekly, bi-weekly, or monthly basis, and a fee quoted beforehand depending on the work to be done.

Customers will be easy to find. An ad in the local newspaper will probably result in more calls than you can handle.

If you are adept at spotting misprints in a written piece, your way to prosperity may lie in proofreading for profit. Check with the publishers and printers in your locality. Often small shops are pressed for time during seasonal rushes, and there are various other organizations that use a lot of printed matter in the course of business on a yearly basis. All of this must be proofread. Free-lance writers also require the service of a proofreader.

To attract customers you might advertise in writer's publications and business magazines. A fee for your service can be charged on an hourly basis, or at an agreed-upon-price per typewritten page.

Helpful books include:

> *A Manual For Writers of Term Papers, Theses, and Dissertations,* by Kate L. Turabian, The University of Chicago Press, 1970.

> *The Elements of Style,* by William Strunk, Jr., The Macmillan Co.

Envelope stuffing is an occupation we frequently see listed as a home business money-maker. The truth is, you'll never become a millionaire by stuffing envelopes. It can net you a reliable source of income, however, particularly if you also address the envelopes for bulk mailings. Today, direct mail advertising is being used by a wide range of businesses throughout the country and many direct mail firms use home typists to address the envelopes.

Fees for typing addresses range from $15 to $20 per thousand—more if you also stuff the envelope. It is left to you to determine the number of hours you wish to work and the amount of work you wish to do.

A pet-sitting service mushroomed into big business for Ted Stalder, a young man in Miami Shores, Florida. It all began when neighbors, preparing to go on a week-end holiday, asked him to stop by each day and feed their pet ocelot, with food which they had provided. For the time spent, the job netted Ted a good profit and soon he was sitting for other neighborhood pets of a more common variety—dogs, cats, fish, gerbils and hamsters, and various types of birds.

His service has grown to include not only feeding, but providing each canine or feline charge with one or two exercise outings each day, as well as the administering of medication that is prescribed. When clients are gone for longer than a week-end, dogs and cats are brushed every third day.

In the beginning, Ted charged $2 per day for his service, adding another $1 if the pets required exercise or medication. A bath and grooming session cost the customer $5 extra. Business was best during the summer months when Ted sometimes took in well over $100 per week.

As word of his service spread, Ted learned that many people prefer this type of treatment for their pets rather than having them confined to the pens in a kennel. Although his rates today are somewhat higher than those of a kennel, his customers don't seem to object when their pets can remain in a home environment and receive individual care.

News of Ted's service passed quickly by word of mouth, but to get started you might place an ad in your local paper or a placard on view in the pet stores in your area.

Helpful information can be obtained from:

> The National Association of the Pet Industry
> 431 Chauncey Street
> Brooklyn, N.Y. 11233
>
> Florida Tropical Fish Industries, Inc.
> 1713 Cortez St.
> Coral Gables, Fla. 33532

Books from your library:

> *Cats and All About Them,* by Lewis H. Fairchild, Howell Book House Inc., N.Y.
>
> *Dog Care and Keeping,* by Will Judy, Judy Publishing Co.
>
> *Hamster Guide,* by G. E. Folk, Jr., TFH Publications, Inc.
>
> *Monkey Manual,* by A.O. Janze, Universe Books, Inc.

TURNING TEACHING INTO PROFIT

If you have a special skill or art, you might try teaching it to others. In addition to home instructions, many people also earn income from teaching their favorite subject in centers such as the Y.M.C.A., in high school night sessions, and in college continuing education classes. The list of subjects being taught in this manner is staggering: crafts of all kinds; music and voice; all manner of self-defense skills such as karate, fencing, wrestling; various culinary arts; and sports skills of all kinds, including golf, tennis, skiing, surfing, skin-diving, and swimming. Acquaint yourself with books like those listed below if you would qualify as a teacher in the sports field.

> *Honor Blackman's Book of Self Defense,* by Honor Blackman, The Macmillan Co., 1965
>
> *Teaching An Infant to Swim,* by Virginia Hunt Newman, Harcourt, Brace and World, Inc., 1967
>
> *The Complete Book of Sky Diving,* by Arthur Liebers, Coward-McCann Inc., New York 1968

In our mechanized world, more and more people are anxious to learn how to create something with their hands. Whether your forte is knitting, woodworking, ceramics, or art, you can maximize your profits from your craft by teaching others how to do it.

Using your own workshop as a classroom and requiring that students bring their own materials, will get you off to a good start. You can, perhaps, begin with an evening program, graduating to day class schedules as your pupils multiply in number. Also, as attendance increases, perhaps you will want to sell necessary craft materials to your students.

If you are already teaching a craft class outside your home, obtaining pupils for a home class will not be difficult. Should you not have this advantage, a poster in your area craft shops and an ad placed in your local newspaper should put you in business.

If you have viewed *Yoga* as merely stuff on the counter-culture, look again. Businessmen find relief from headaches in it; young people acclaim it a source of deep inner peace; housewives attribute weight loss and relaxation to its postures. If you have studied this Hindu Philosophy and have considerable knowledge of it, or interest in it, you may undertake to teach it to others.

Classes in Yoga can be set up in a recreation room, a garage, even a living room—any place which provides enough space for about eight to ten pupils to stretch out and move about with freedom. You may wish to start out with one class daily, although many instructors find a need for both day-time and evening classes, especially if they wish to provide time for working men and women. A $2 fee is usually charged, per student, per session.

You can't get rich giving music lessons, but there are income opportunities in the music field. All you need, to do quite well financially, is a musical talent and the ability to teach others.

Guitar and drum lessons are still sought by the teenage set, and piano lessons remain as popular as ever, but many youngsters are branching out into other avenues of musical endeavor. The flute, the organ, and various types of brass instruments are gaining in popularity, as are solo and group singing lessons.

The price of lessons can vary anywhere upwards of $3 per hour, depending on whether the pupil comes to your home or you go to his. By teaching in your home, you have no overhead or investment other than your advertising, since the student supplies his own instrument.

To get started, place an ad in the musical instrument column of the classified section of your local newspaper. You might also make yourself known to the musical instrument dealers in your area, who could refer students to you.

Library books which can be of help to you include:

Piano Teachers Professional Handbook, by Gordon B. Terwilliger, Prentice-Hall Inc., 1965.

Youth Choirs, by Paul Jerome Miller, Harold Flammer, Inc. New York—explains how to organize and rehearse and maintain a group.

How To Build A Church Choir, by Charles H. Heaton, The Bethany Press.

Are you a good driver? If so, perhaps like George Field you can make driving lessons pay off. Today, several agencies and most high schools offer students a driver's education program. This consists of classroom instruction as well as behind-the-wheel driving. After an initial test, the student is issued a permit which allows him to drive a car *if* he is accompanied by a licensed driver. This is his *practice period* and your time to make money.

When a neighbor boy's father offered to pay George to ride with the boy during his practice trips, George, having more than an average amount of patience and steady nerve, accepted. He soon discovered that, like his neighbor, many parents are too nervous or too busy to accompany these fledgling drivers, and his new business boomed. Now, when he is not driving about with a "new" driver, he is engaged as a driving instructor in a high school program.

The following books are available at your library:

> How To Drive Better and Avoid Accidents, by Paul W. Kearney, Thomas Y. Crowell Co., New York 1964.
>
> The Book of Expert Driving, by E.D. Fales, Jr., Hawthorn Books, Inc., New York, 1970.

Everyone is aware of weight reducing salons, an idea that took shape by exchanging pounds for dollars. Today, a trim figure is not merely a matter of pride, but of health, and more and more women and men are looking for some type of exercise that will not only insure a good figure, but good health as well. Most people can't seem to get down to exercising on their own. Group participation takes their mind off what they're doing and makes it painless.

However, all salons are not the plush, machine-operated, beauty spas one reads about in slick magazines. Many are unpretentious recreation rooms in the basement of someone's home where exercise programs are directed for neighborhood groups.

All you need to get your business rolling is an accurate scale, a full length mirror, and plenty of exercising space. A word to your neighbors or an ad in your local paper, plus a couple of posters in strategic places should bring you your first customers.

In much this same way, Gloria Belden initiated a charm school in her home. Beginning with housewives in her own neighborhood, this former model outfitted a spare bedroom with mirrors, make-up tables, weighing scales, and boxes of facial tissue.

Her course consisted of weighing in and recommended exercise to be done at home, plus classes in diet, posture, skin care, make-up, hair styling, manicuring, and clothese coordination.

Although her first clients were housewives, she has extended her program to include a class for teenagers and one for pre-teens. She also conducts an evening class for men with emphasis on colors and the coordination of clothing. Fee for each course is $25, or $5 per session, bringing in a gross income of $10,000 per year.

CASHING IN ON YOUR CREATIVITY

Many people are gifted with an innate creative ability which manifests itself in their homes, their work, their dress, their handling of a situation. This gift allows them to turn the common and ordinary into something beautiful or unusual.

Often these people can sell their *ideas for big money.* It isn't always that they come up with something entirely new, but that they have the vision to see another use for some product already in use, at a time when the consumer is ready for it.

In Detroit, a Catholic potato chip manufacturer, looking for an unusual service project, came up with *Kosher Potato Chips,* prepared with pure oil, according to Jewish law, for use during Jewish holidays. In Baltimore, a 29-year-old medical student has invented a new snap-on, interchangeable button system for general apparel and uniforms. Thanks to a Tulsa housewife, a bedpillow in the shape of a doll, with printed face and dress, becomes a little child's cuddly companion during the day, yet is a strong, well-made pillow that retains its usual function for sleep times.

The first step to take with your new-born idea is to seek the services of a patent attorney, or some other knowledgeable person, to determine whether or not your invention is patentable. A patent or copyright can protect your work from being used and sold by anyone else for a period of three and a half to 28 years.

A Roster of Attorneys and Agents Registered to Practice before the U.S. Patent Office can be obtained for $1 by sending a request to the U.S. Patent Office, Washington, D.C. Two other pamphlets which can be obtained from the Superintendent of Documents, Washington, D.C. are: *General Information Concerning Patents* and *Patents and Inventions, an Information Aid for Inventors.* Copyrights are registered by the United States Copyright Office, Library of Congress, Washington, D.C.

Library books which will be helpful are:

A Technique for Producing Ideas, by James Webb Young, Advertising Publications—gives a formula for producing ideas.

Successful Inventor's Guide, by K.O. Kessler and N. Carlisle, Prentice-Hall, Inc.

Profits from hand printing were the start of a thriving reproduction service in Denver. Because he had a knack with pen and ink, Charles Anthony was often asked by friends and acquaintances to make posters announcing this or that activity, and to print place cards or fashion covers for small booklets and brochures.

When he decided to charge for his services, it wasn't long before he had accumulated $100 which he used to buy a second-hand mimeograph machine. As business and bankroll increased, he added more machines, including a new photocopier. He also handles photo offset work, but sends it out to a printer. Last year, his income was over $10,000, including that from handprinted services, which Charles admits are still his first love.

Books on printing at your library are:

Dictionary of the Art of Printing, by William Savage, B. Franklin Pub.

Printing and the Allied Trades, by Robert R. Karch, Pitman Pub. Co.

Also available at most libraries is the directory, *Printing Trades Blue Book* which gives information on dealers, trade associations, and unions in the printing industry.

You can also obtain a free copy of *The Printing Business* from Bank of America, Small Business Advisory Service, San Francisco, California 94120.

You can earn money from gift-shopping if you are thrifty and clever and able to spot a bargain. Today, many people are too busy to take the time necessary to shop for gifts and are willing to pay to have someone else do it for them. You might begin, as one enterprising young woman did, by soliciting customers from among those who are employed in a large industrial office complex. You will probably find, as she did, that many businessmen are glad to have you choose a gift for wife or girl friend for Christmas, Valentine's Day, birthdays, wedding anniversaries, and other such occasions.

Today, this woman keeps a file system, listing each customer and the dates for gift-giving on his calendar. A week or so before due date, she telephones the client, checks with him as to the type of gift he wishes bought and the amount he wishes to spend. She delivers the gift to him, wrapped and ready for presentation. At this time, she collects the purchase price of the gift plus her $5 fee.

Another excellent field where you can really capitalize on your creative ability and put money in your pocket is party planning for others. The range for celebrations and party giving is wide—showers, engagements, birthdays, holidays, welcoming new neighbors, parties of farewell, anniversaries, retirement parties, graduations—the list goes on and on. People give parties at home, in backyards, on the terrace, on boats, at country clubs, and in private halls.

If you are a creative person, each party you undertake will be a new and interesting challenge. Your job is to create the party, to do the organizing, planning, and execution within the budget allowed and in the best possible taste. Perhaps you might wish to confine your abilities to one type of party. You could specialize in weddings or children's parties.

Until you have built up a following, your best advertising medium is the special services column of your local newspaper. Later, you can place a small ad in the yellow pages of your telephone directory, or with a local radio station.

Your library has many helpful books on all kinds of party planning. Here are a few.

> *The Gesell Institute Party Book,* Harper and Bros., New York—a practical handbook of party planning for children from ages 3-15.
>
> *The Complete Shower Party Book,* by Margaret Gleeson, Doubleday, 1971.
>
> *Party Fun for Holidays and Special Occasions,* by Margaret Elizabeth Mulac, Harper, New York, 1960.
>
> *The Party Planner,* by Lois M. Freeman, Golden Press, 1964.
>
> *Parties for Children,* by Lois M. Freeman, Golden Press, 1964.
>
> *The World Book of Children's Games* (ages 4-12) by Arnold Arnold, World Publishers, 1972.
>
> *The Omnibus of Fun,* by Helen and Larry Eisenberg, Association Press, N.Y.—a library of advice and information on planning and running parties and celebrations of many kinds for all ages.

Many people have gained income opportunities from artistic endeavors. Painters, as you know, often sell oil and watercolor pieces for large sums of money. Designers are paid handsomely for their ideas. The work of sculptors is in demand at high prices. But there are other artistic abilities that have also proved themselves profitable.

In Cleveland, Margaret Nelson, a perky 83-year-old woman, not only sells her hand-trimmed bejeweled Easter eggs for $5 to $14 apiece to a waiting line of customers, but during the year she also teaches a class of 70 in her home and at the Senior Citizen Center.

A young couple in upper Michigan, Joel and Mary Lou Peterson, spend the entire year putting together frames and gathering cones and pods that go into their beautiful Christmas wreaths, swags, and centerpieces. When they aren't raking in the money from the sale of these items, which sell between $10-$55, they are giving demonstration-lectures at area clubs and organizations, for a fee of $50 to $100 per appearance.

In all of these endeavors, however, as I mentioned earlier in this chapter, *timing is of the essence.* The most fantastic new idea or the cleverest innovation will come to naught if your timing is not right. I suppose the many inventions of Leonardo da Vinci are our most striking examples of misplaced timing. Marvelous though they were, at the time they were invented there was no demand for them.

On the other hand, need was the motive that got Rob Dubbs started in his Rent-A-Helper business. Today, more and more busy people need someone to help with a chore they don't have time to do themselves. Basically, Rent-A-Helper is an agency which brings together a client who wants a job done and a helper who is able and willing to do the job.

Rob and his helpers are not professionals in any one line of work, but they can perform almost any task competently. Jobs for which a helper is available include: yard work, $4 per hour; personal services like ironing $2.50; shopping, $3; or a trip to the laundramat, $2.50; light housework, $3; silver polishing, $2; window and wall washing, $4; cooking a meal, $4; maid for a night, $5; painting, $3.50; dog walking, $1; and horse exercising, $2.

Upon completion of a job, the client pays his helper, who in turn pays Rent-A-Helper 10 percent of the fee. Helpers have earned as much as $130 per week, and Rent-A-Helper grossed well over $15,000 last year.

Rob first advertised his business through a short series of classified ads in his local newspaper. As the word of his service spread, he discontinued this practice and now most new clients are referred by old ones. Usually he has more requests than he and a staff of helpers can handle.

4

Turn Your Pastime into Profit

Almost everybody has a hobby, something that he enjoys doing "just for fun," in his spare time. Your pastime can mean big money and can be developed into a business that may mushroom and make you a small fortune.

George Eastman built what began as little more than a hobby into a multi-million dollar photography business. A nationally-known department store is in existence today because its founder enjoyed sewing. Even one of our large automobile industries took shape because a man enjoyed "tinkering," in his spare time.

DEVELOPING YOUR HOBBY INTO A
MONEY-MAKING HOME BUSINESS

Many people regard a hobby as a nearly effortless venture, with no more work involved than gluing stamps or postcards into an album, or collecting old bottles on a shelf. This is simply not true. A hobby usually requires considerable work, time, and knowledge on the part of the hobbyist. He is usually quite well skilled in his craft before he is able to derive an income from it.

However, if you don't already have a hobby, you can still get started on something and even make money while you are learning. Today, in almost every hobby, there are simple, inexpensive ways to begin. With a kit from a hobbycraft shop, it's easy to try out one or several crafts that appeal to you. This way you find out whether the one you select is really as interesting as it appears before you commit your time and your pocketbook to any great extent.

In this chapter, you will find listed all of the arts, crafts, and skills which can be termed *hobbies,* but which can easily become small business enterprises. There are many ways to develop these into big money-makers. Sometimes the move is the result of an accident; sometimes it is deliberate.

Take Jerry Wenner, for example. Although blacksmiths greatly outnumbered other metal craftsmen in early America, there are few such men upon the scene today. Therefore, the Wenners and their neighbors, horse owners for years, had been having difficulty getting their horses properly shod. That's when Jerry, whose great-grandfather was a village blacksmith, started doing it himself.

Later, when a pay cut was added to a long winter's drive between home and office, Jerry's hobby came to his rescue and he did what many of us would like to do. He quit his job and made his hobby his business—and now finds himself far better off financially.

Today, with more and more people investing in pleasure horses, business is booming. Unlike his grandfather, who worked with the traditional bellows and forge, Jerry travels about the countryside in a small truck especially equipped for his work and uses a modern gas torch.

Soon he will also be able to practice horse dentistry. This is not considered animal medicine, but it is a time-consuming craft which he is learning from a veterinarian. Acquiring this added skill should not only tend to enlarge his business further, but it will be a distinct advantage since the Wenners are already into the business of breeding quality, halter class Appaloosa horses.

Another example of hobby turned business is the story of *Antique Monthly,* the publication on antiques that has become a giant in the industry and winds up in over 100,000 homes each month.

Mrs. Gray D. Boone, its editor, developed her interest in antiques at an early age. As a young girl she spent many summers with a relative who lived in a big old house and had a love for history. Her interest grew with time, until eventually this love of antiques, coupled with a flair for writing, led to the birth of a successful business.

Sitting at her kitchen table, Mrs Boone typed up the pages that would become the first small newspaper publication on antique know-how. With the help of her newspaper-publisher husband, that first edition caught on, and as the operation grew, it moved from the kitchen to a spare bedroom. With a staff of six full-time and six part-time employees, the bedroom was shortly abandoned for a modern new building. It now has its own press and circulation center. Its offices are carpeted, paneled, and furnished with antiques.

USING HANDICRAFT HOBBIES
AS BUSINESS STARTERS

Many hobbies can open the door to income potentialities for you. For instance, a handcrafted product, manufactured in your home, is but one easy way for you to enter business for yourself. The list is practically endless and new techniques and materials offer vast opportunities.

In upper Michigan, leathercraft has paid off big for Don Phillips. He had worked with leather as a hobby for many years, having learned the craft from his father, an avid deer-hunter. Recently, after visiting New York and viewing several Broadway productions which featured leather clothes, Don turned to creating his own leather clothing. He tans and dyes deer and other animal hides to make beautiful, soft, supple garments—coats, jackets, slacks, hats, purses, belts, and some footwear. He designs the items, cuts them according to his customers' measurements and stitches them by hand or machine. His prices range between $20-$300. In the first year, his gross income was well over the $8,000 mark.

But it isn't necessary to hunt your own deer to make money with leather. Hides are sold in tanneries, leather shops, and handicraft supply stores. Tools, too, are available from hardware, craft and leather stores, and shoemaker suppliers. They may also be ordered from the catalogs listed below.

Leather is easy to work with and there are innumerable articles you can make that are much in demand today. Aside from the articles of clothing being worn by teenager and adult alike, leather has become one of the newest mediums of sculpture. It is also used to make wine-bottle holders and other contemporary items, plus the old stand-bys—billfolds, belts, and wallets.

If you have never worked with leather, start out with a beginner's set of tools, inexpensive materials, and a good instruction book. When you buy leather, bring a paper pattern of the pieces you'll need. Then you won't get caught short on material or buy more than you'll need. Books from your library that can be of help to you include:

Contemporary Leather, by Dona Meilach, Regnery, 1972–a complete
how-to-book on modern ways with leather.

Working With Leather, by Xenia Ley Parker, Charles Scribner's Sons,
1972.

Leather supply catalogs can be obtained from the following
companies:

Tandy Leather Co.
1001 Foch St.
Fort Worth, Texas 76107
has stores in almost every
state. For the one nearest
you, write to the parent
store at the above address.

Ziegel Eisman Co.
50 Paris,
Newark, N.J.
(kangaroo leather only)

Tilton Tanning Corp.
Tilton, N.H.

Advance Glove Mfg. Co.
972 W. Lafayette Blvd.
Detroit, Mich.

Berlin Tanning Co.
Berlin, Wis.

Hoffman Stafford Tanning Co.
1001 W. Division
Chicago, Ill.

Garden State Tanning Inc.
Fleetwood, Tenn. 19522

Byron W. D. & Sons, Inc.
Williamsport, Md.
(fancy leather)

L. H. Hamel Leather Co.
Haverhill, Mass.

Irving Tanning Co.
134 Beach
Boston, Mass.

American Wm. Co.
215 Willow
Philadelphia, Pa.

Ashtabula Leathercraft Mfg. Co.
Ashtabula, Ohio

Poetsch & Peterson
325 S. Maple Ave.
S. San Francisco, Calif.

These are just a few of the leather supply sources. For one closer to
your home, check the *1972 Thomas Register* at your library.

Woodcraftmanship is another hobby that can bring in big profits.
Today, when people are being swept along in a back-to-nature
experience, articles made of wood are quickly sold.

In his small basement workshop in eastern Ohio, a retired
mechanic pieces together guitars, mandolins, banjos, and lutes which
he sells for $45-$60 each. He designs his own patterns from which he
makes new instruments as well as doing repair work on old ones. This
hobby, which he started five years ago, now supplements his income.

On the other side of the state, James Rogers also profits from a part-time hobby he started by carving objects from wood. Today, this man is one of only five independent master pipe makers in the country. His originally-designed and hand-carved pipes are in great demand. Men buy them for their personal use and wives find that they make great gifts. Less expensive pipes sell for $40. Others, depending upon the type of wood used and the amount of carving done, bring much higher prices.

The avenues open to the worker in woodcraft are numerous. Toys, furniture, novelties, household articles, models—all can be made of wood. Whatever your forte, whittling miniatures, wood-carving statues, or chip-carving animals, fame and fortune can come to you.

Two demure lady hobbyists living in Cleveland faithfully dupli-cate the construction details and quality standards of craftmanship of 18th-century antique furniture in their basement workshop. Their income averages more than $1,000 a month, and in this age of an-tique revival, they are always behind with their orders.

In Arizona, Bill Baxter, a tough ex-football player carves, paints and dresses authentic Hopi Kachina dolls, and is considered one of the finest doll-makers in the West. He whittles the little figures out of cottonwood roots and has sold them for $100 to $150 each.

So you see, there is no end to what you can make from wood. Starting with a modest kit of tools, which you probably have on hand right now, you can make all sorts of useful and ornamental items. These products can be sold through mail-order, direct selling methods, or placed in retail stores and boutiques.

Some publications on wood products which will be helpful to you can be obtained from Forest Products Laboratory, Forest Service, U.S. Department of Agriculture, Madison, Wis. 53705.

> *Identification of Furniture Woods,* U.S.DA Misc. Cir. 66—free.
>
> *Books and Pamphlets on Finishing of Wood and Furniture,* SWP-63-050, free.
>
> List of Publications for Furniture Manufacturers, Wood-workers, and Teachers of Wood Shop Practice, free.

Among the many helpful books that can be found on your library shelf are:

> *Practical Wood-carving Projects,* by Enid Bell, World Publishing Company—written by a well-known teacher of woodcarving, this book is a complete manual on the tools and craft, with many illustrations.

Wood Carving With Power Tools, by Ralph Byers, Chilton Books—gives information about carving animals and other objects.

Checkering and Carving of Gunstocks, by Monty Kennedy, Stackpole Books—gives patterns and instructions in gun ornamentation from many experts.

Some people earn their way to business success simply by tying knots. Knot making probably developed first in the time of the ancient mariner. Seafaring men knotted rope to while away their time on long sea voyages. Two examples of sailors work can be seen today at the Seasmen's Church Institute of New York City. These are large picture frames made with heavy seine twine, a traditional material used by sailors.

Today a revival of this old art form of knot tying is known as *Macramé.* A master knotter can make anything from fine needle lace to a tennis net, a fine cord belt or a hammock. Items made by this technique are remarkably strong as well as beautiful.

Macramé can be practiced wherever you are. You don't need any special instruments, only your own two hands. You control the tightness of the knots and the design. Materials include a multitude of cords or strings—cotton, nylon, plastic, linen—anything found at your grocery, hardware, knitting shops, or at an upholstery supply store will do. The list of projects to be made goes on and on: handbags, neckties, tassels and cords, belts, rugs, standing sculptures of heavy rope, hanging space sculptures with varied colored macramé knots.

Books available at your library are:

The Art of Knot Tying, by Paulette and Allen A. Macfarlan, N.Y. Assoc. Press, 1967.

Macramé, by Imelda Manalo Pesch, Sterling Publishing, 1971.

Macramé, by Mary Walker Phillips, Golden Press, N.Y. 1970—a complete step-by-step introduction to the craft of creative knotting.

The following supply sources carry a wide selection of cords and yarn.

Ace Hardware
local outlets

Briggs & Little Woolen Mills
York Mills, Harvey Station,
N.B., Canada

Countryside Handweavers
West Elkhorn Ave. Box 1743
Estes Park, Col. 80517

Creative Handweavers
P.O. Box 26480
Los Angeles, Calif. 90026

Esther Fear's
1807 Central Street
Evanston, Ill. 66201

Frederick J. Fawcett
129 South Street
Boston, Mass. 02111

P. C. Herwig
264 Clinton Street
Brooklyn, N.Y. 11201

House of Yarns and Fabrics
Box 98
Hampton, N. H. 03842

International Handcraft & Supply
103 Lyndon Street
Hermosa Beach, Calif. 90254

Lily Mills Co.
Department HWH
Shelby, N.C. 28150

The Mannings
R.D.2
East Berlin, Pa. 17316

Northwest Handcraft House
110 West Esplanade
N. Vancouver, B.C.C Canada

Pacific Fibre & Rope Co., Inc.
903 Flint Ave.
Wilmington, Calif. 90744

Marie Walling
4409 Bakman Ave.
N. Hollywood, Calif. 91602

Warp, Woof & Potpourri
1503 North Lake Ave.
Pasadena, Calif. 91104

The Weaver's Loft
320 Blue Bell Road
Williamstown, N.J. 08094

Weaving Workshop
3324 N. Halsted Street
Chicago, Ill. 60608

Wellington Puritan Mills, Inc.
P. O. Box 22185
Louisville, Ky. 40222 (local
    outlets; school order over
    $50 through the Mills)

The Yarn Depot
545 Sutter Street
San Francisco, Calif. 94102

The Yarn Merchant
8533 Beverly Blvd.
Los Angeles, Calif. 90048

Another hobby that can earn big profits for you is papercraft. A profitable business in this field can encompass anything from bookbinding to creating realistic-looking flowers, to making papier-mâché doll heads for puppets and marionettes. If you enjoy working with paper, there is a tremendous demand for your talent, and your product.

Even with a houseful of babies, two young women living next door to each other in Los Angeles, are splitting a $2,900 yearly profit from making paper flowers at home. Each flower costs about ten cents to make and sells for $1 wholesale or $2 retail, although some special flowers sell for as much as $6 wholesale.

The hobbyist who has succeeded in mastering the art of papercraft has a wide outlet for his talents. Crepe paper, construction paper, newsprint, grocery bags, waxed paper, metallic paper, from featherweight tissue paper to heavy corrugated cardboard—you name it—there's a use for it.

Paper is used extensively for decorations, holiday ornaments, greeting cards, costumes, flowers, kites, lampshades, jewelry, mobiles, collages, mosaics, masks, and abstract sculpture. Your way to fame and fortune in this field could lie in developing your own talents and your own ideas.

Many greeting card companies are in the market for new product ideas and will welcome yours. For information on the types of papercraft submissions of interest to them, you should query the following:

American Greetings Corp.   Russ Berrie and Co., Inc.
10300 American Rd.   20 Bushes Lane
Cleveland, Ohio 44144   E. Paterson, N.J. 07601

Peck, Inc.   Vagabond Creations
516 Lafayette Road   2560 Lance Drive
St. Paul, Minn. 55101   Dayton, Ohio 45409

Books available from your library include:

> *Make It With Paper,* by Louise and Orvelo Wood, David McKay Company, Inc., New York, 1970—a how-to book in which hundreds of paper objects are presented with basic patterns and techniques for making them.

> *The Art of Papier Mache,* by Carla and John B. Kenny, Chilton Book Company, 1968.

> *Creative Paper Crafts,* by Chester Jay Alkema, Sterling Pub., Co., Inc., New York—offers inspiring ideas from simple projects to those for the experienced craftsman.

> *Making Paper and Fabric Flowers,* by Carolyn Wilder, Hearthside Press, Inc., New York, 1969.

Making money from pottery and ceramics is an easy transition for the hobbyist. It is a field of endless opportunity in which many beginning potters make their first sale to a neighborhood craftshop. This can result in reorders as well as new orders by other giftshop buyers. As business builds, you can take samples on the road, or have an agent who will promote sales for you in other localities. A good average order would be about 3 or 4 dozen of each sample.

One master potter living in California creates an average of 2,000 original sculptured pots a year, which are sold for as little as $5 and as much as $500. During the summer months, she also teaches her art to gifted students for a fee.

Most potters work in home studios using three types of clay to make their various ceramic pieces—earthenware, stoneware, and porcelain. A potter's wheel is used for pots, bowls, cups, jugs, and pitchers—anything that will be hollow inside. A piece that involves a figure or a head is modeled by hand or shaped over a mold. You can also create items on a flat surface using a slab, or by coiling. (This is the method the Indians used in building up their pots.) A professional potter will use them all.

Equipment can run into thousands of dollars. The best wheel will cost around $480. A firing kiln can run to $2,000. But the beginner can start out less expensively by buying a used wheel. and firing can be done in an outside kiln, usually for a small fee. And, as you know, molded pieces or those created on a slab are less expensive to produce.

Books on ceramics at your library are numerous, and professional training is available at many colleges and art centers throughout the country. There are also several good monthly magazines published on ceramics. Check your library periodical room for these.

The following is a list of some of the major ceramic suppliers in the United States. You can write to them for supplies and information.

A.D. Alpine
11837 Teale,
Culver City, California
90230

Advanced Kiln Co.
2543 Whittier Blvd.
Los Angeles, Calif.
90023

Western Ceramic Supply Co.
1601 Howard Street
San Francisco, Calif.
94103

Western Stoneware Co.
Monmouth, Illinois 61462

American Art Clay Co.
4717 West 16th Street
Indianapolis, Indiana 46222

Newton Pottery Supply Co.
Newton, Massachusetts

Denver Fire Clay Co.
3033 Black Street,
Denver, Colo.

Van Howe Company
1185 South Cherokee Ave.,
Denver, Colo. 83223

U.S. Stoneware Co.
Akron, Ohio

Harrop Ceramic Service
347 East 5th Avenue
Columbus, Ohio 43201

Kentucky-Tennessee Clay Co.
Mayfield, Ohio

Cedar Heights Clay Co.
50 Portsmouth Road
Oak Hill, Ohio 45656

W. H. Fairchild
712 Centre Street
Freeland, Pennsylvania 18224

Jack D. Wolfe Co., Inc.
724-734 Meeker Ave.
Brooklyn, New York 11222

O. Hommel Co.
209 Fourth Avenue
Pittsburgh, Pennsylvania 15215

Norman Ceramics Co., Inc.
225 Mamaroneck Avenue
Mamaroneck, New York 10543

Stewart Clay Co., Inc.
133 Mulberry Street
New York, New York 10013

Craftools, Inc.
401 Broadway
New York, New York 10013

DEVELOPING A BUSINESS FROM
YOUR "FUN PROJECTS"

Do you enjoy baking bread, making jam, or putting together a batch of Christmas hard candy? Perhaps, then, your business future is already taking shape, for kitchen fun can frequently lead to big profits.

For example, several years ago a housewife in Ohio began baking a nut cake, an old family recipe, to give as Christmas gifts to her friends. So great was the response that the following year found her in business, selling to friends and friends of friends, earning $60 in one week. Then, suddenly, the business was too big to be run from her kitchen and the work too much for one individual. She now employs almost 20 women, full time, during the holiday seasons, and operates from a large rented kitchen with several ovens.

A thriving Lebanese bakery in Cleveland started with an old family bread recipe, a determined young couple, and a 4 x 6-foot oven in a rented flat. Today, the bread is sold, not only locally, but it is trucked to foreign food groceries all over the United States, including Chicago, Pittsburgh, Indianapolis, Washington, D.C., Louisville, Ky., and Raleigh, N.C. It is also shipped individually all over the country to bread lovers who have standing orders.

Most business people with whom I have talked have one general rule for the beginner who would capitalize on culinary art. That is to limit your production to one or two specialties, something that is not readily available from local merchants. In the beginning, it is also wise to be generous with samples, for until you have established a clientele, the food itself is your best advertisement. Pass it out to friends at every opportunity, donate it to clubs and organizations.

In Florida, an elderly widow sold her first batch of "Grandma's Ginger Cookies" to the local country club lunchroom. Soon members were asking to buy cookies to take home and the business was off to a good start.

To get started you need only one stove, the equipment you already have in your home, and the ability to make something that is different, has taste appeal, or that will save time and labor for the buyer. Many men and women have turned out large quantities of food and reaped big profits right in their own kitchens.

Most people want to "WOW" when they entertain. That's why catering is big business. As a caterer you would prepare food either at your customer's home or in your own kitchen. If the host or hostess has not already decided on a menu, it is up to you to suggest one. Your service can range from exotic party foods and buffets for private parties to tasty, but low-cost, meals for club meetings, church groups, and other local functions.

Or perhaps, like the petite, 35-year-old operator of a gourmet service in Detroit, you will want to serve only internationally accented foods. In this instance, a wide variety of foods is offered, including complete dinners as well as individual dishes, tea sandwiches, hors d'oeuvres, and desserts. The caterer prepares these at a basic rate of $2 an hour and requires a week's notice for orders. An order for a hundred hors d'oeuvres, in addition to her regular hourly charge, will cost a client $15.

There is no fixed system for establishing catering prices, but many small caterers find that the rule of thumb procedure, simply multiplying all costs by two, is a helpful way to set prices.

Word of mouth referrals, plus telephone contacts to likely prospects listed in the newspaper society pages keep the business operating on a full-time, highly profitable scale.

Books helpful to the caterer are many. Check your library and don't overlook the cookbooks you have in your own home. Recommended reading:

Manual of Catering, by W.H. Emery, Williams and Wilkins Co.

Cooking For A Crowd, by Annette L. Ross and Jean A. Disney, Doubleday and Co., Inc. 1968.

Come for Cocktails Stay for Supper, by Marian Burros and Lois Levine,
The Macmillan Co., 1970–a guide to planning successful cocktail
parties and cocktail buffets.

Two government booklets are available *free* from the Small Business
Administration, Washington, D.C. 20416, or from your nearest SBA
office.

Restaurants and Catering, SBB No. 17.

Catering Service, Counseling Note No. 15.

Although you must have a manufacturer's license to sell wine for
profit, and must meet government brewery regulations, winemaking
in your home can put money in your pocket.

Recently, millions of Americans have discovered wine as a new
aspect of gracious living and wine supply stores are blossoming all
over the country. However, keeping wine on the table can get quite
expensive, so many who have developed a taste for it are making
their own.

Wines are frequently made from fresh grapes, bananas, cherries,
and dandelions, or today, often with concentrates. The first step for
the amateur wine maker is to register with the Internal Revenue
Service. Once registered, the head of a family can produce up to 200
gallons of wine a year for family consumption. All that's needed to
turn out a tasty vintage wine is a gallon jug, an airlock, a hose, a
bottle of wine concentrate and jars of various powders. Oh yes, and
some knee-slapping, wine-making know-how.

Put these items together in a neat package and you have a
wine-making kit that you can sell to eager customers for $7.50. Or, if
you are an old hand at the wine-making art, you might want to start
a wine-making school.

For regulations in your state, check with your State Liquor
Control Department, listed in the yellow pages of your telephone
book.

Tape recording as a money-maker is another pastime fun project
that can pay big dividends, using only the equipment you have
already acquired in pursuit of your hobby. The first requisite being,
of course, that you own a dependable tape recorder and are well
versed in the operation of it.

Taped recordings of various life ceremonies and notable personal
happenings are gaining in popularity today. For example, it is a
frequent occurrence that the bride and groom have not only a
photographic story of their wedding day, but a recording of the

words "I do" as well. Tapes of children's parties are also high on the list, as are anniversaries and family reunions.

Bert Golde, an auto mechanic by trade, began taping weddings at $7.50 an hour, and his weekly income is now $100 higher because of week-end taping sessions.

In this business, a small advertisement in your hometown newspaper or church or school bulletin will get you started. Or, if like Bert, you want to keep your work to a minimum, word of mouth may be enough to keep you as busy as you may wish.

Information on tape recording and equipment can be obtained from the various tape-recording magazines on the market.

How about sewing for profit? Here again, the field is wide open and you can begin operations without any big money outlay. If you are handy with a needle or adept with your sewing machine you can parlay these abilities into a highly profitable home business.

Working alone, Elsie Parker, a woman in my hometown, grosses more than $800 per month making custom wedding apparel and accessories. Her first clients were obtained by sending letters to prospective brides whose engagements were announced in the newspaper and church bulletins. David Glass, a dress designer, also got his start by sewing custom fashions in his home. Now he makes more than $30,000 a year.

Opportunities for money-making sewing projects are numerous. Draperies and slip covers are always in demand. Likewise curtains and bedspreads. Or you might try infants' wear and children's clothing. Custom-made shirts for men bring a good price, as do handmade ties. Perhaps you want to specialize or cater to a specific market. How about teen lingerie? Or long dresses for young girls?

The wife of a doll's-furniture manufacturer is busy all year providing custom-made doll's clothes. Her active imagination, plus odd scraps of material and bits of fur and leather, provide unique wardrobes for a whole family of popular dolls and puts money in her pocket. Christmas is her busiest season, at which time she employs two other women to help her fill her orders.

There are always things to sew. Use your imagination. How about floor-pillows for the Yoga crowd?

Picture-taking is always fun, and it can be most profitable. Magazines and newspaper supplements pay $10 for black and white photographs, more for color. Wedding pictures sell for $25 to $250 per album. Ditto for graduation pictures. A good portrait photographer can easily net $150 or better each week.

No wonder, then, that Dick Bixler, a full-time, free-lance photographer decided to develop a business from this interesting hobby. Starting as a young boy with an inexpensive camera, Dick soon learned that good pictures earn good money. Part-time work in a photographic shop whetted his interest still further. His ability, supplemented both by practical experience and photographic studies, soon earned him the reputation of a sought-after photographer, and a well-paid one. Today, his camera equipment is valued in the thousand-dollar bracket and his jobs include newspaper and magazine work, industrial and business photography, as well as occasional portrait and studio work.

Aside from these areas, there are many other photographic endeavors from which you can net substantial profits. Perhaps you might wish to specialize—weddings, birthday parties, real estate, fashions, or commercial photography of some sort

Greater profits can be realized if your knowledge of photographic equipment, and skill in using and maintaining it, includes the ability to develop and enlarge your own pictures. Aside from a darkroom, you will need a work-storage area. A telephone is a must for the free lance; a small studio room for the portrait artist.

The following books will help you.

> *Successful Wedding Photography,* by Michael K. Arin, Chilton Book Co., 1967.
>
> *Practical Portrait Photography,* by Edwin A. Falk and Charles Abel, Chilton Book Co., 1967.
>
> *Feninger's Complete Photography,* by Andreas Feninger, Prentice-Hall, Inc., 1965.
>
> *Commercial Photography,* by Kenneth M. McCombs, American Technical Society.

Eastman Kodak Company, 343 State St., Rochester, N.Y. 14650 has more than 750 publications that provide authoritative, up-to-date information for camera users.

Also, a *free* catalog, *Directory of Photographic Books,* may be obtained on request from U.S. Camera Publishing Corp., 9 East 40th St., New York, N.Y. 10016.

From the Small Business Administration, Washington, D.C. 20416, a free bibliography is available which lists many additional references. Ask for *Photographic Dealers and Studios, SBB 64.*

MAKING YOUR COLLECTIONS PAY OFF

Ever since the time he was a small child and picked up his first Potawatomi arrow head, while on a summer tour of upper Michigan, Judd O'Hearn has been an avid collector. Over the years, as he pursued this fascinating hobby, he has acquired arrow heads from almost every American Indian tribe, and become somewhat of an authority on Indian lore.

Just recently, Judd discovered that collecting things can be more than fun—it can be profitable. People will pay to see an exhibit of his wide collection and hear his knowledgeable talks. His engagements take him all over his own and neighboring states and include bookings at clubs, schools, art centers, and local groups, with fees ranging from $40 to $150 per lecture.

Another man, who made his own cases in which to display his collection of coins, found that many people were more interested in the cases than the coins. He is now making big money through the manufacture and distribution of his *collector's display cases.*

Making money from dolls you have collected is another way to enter the business world. Here, again, you can exhibit your dolls for profit, particularly if they are representative of past generations. Your collection can be the basis of a lecture on antique dolls, or for many other ideas for doll lovers, including those who collect, manufacture, costume, repair, or offer any other service connected with dolls.

You might wish to create new dolls yourself, since one of the newer things are kits to make replicas of expensive old dolls. A woman who makes dolls in her Sidney, Montana, home sold 38 of her ten models in less than a year. Each doll carried a price tag of $45. Repair of antique dolls is also a booming business. Although many modern dolls, with their mechanical organs sealed in their plastic bodies, are almot unrepairable, there is an increasing need for someone who can artfully repair old dolls.

The making of wardrobes for old dolls can also provide a profitable income. Collectors want their antique dolls dressed in authentic gowns of the era. Or how about clothes design and pattern-making in this area?

If this interests you, Sylvia Bryant, a regional director for the

National Federation of Dolls, has published a reprint of the *Demorest Catalog, Fall and Winter Fashions, 1873-74* (about $2). She also publishes the *Peak Doll Directory,* an annual booklet listing persons throughout the country who offer doll repair, doll parts, and doll clothing, and *Advertised Prices Of Dolls,* which lists about 3,200 prices with description arranged alphabetically by types of doll. Send your request to Sylvia Bryant, 1208 Meade Ave., Colorado Springs, Colo. 80909.

Don't overlook the doll directories in your library.

Other helpful books include:

> *Doll's Dressmaking,* by Winifred Butler, Van Nostrand Co.
>
> *The Doll Book,* by Estelle Ansley Worrell, D. Van Nostrand Company, Inc.—offers step by step directions for making 5 basic dolls, with dozens of variations and directions for creating authentic hair styles and clothing for various periods.
>
> *Make Your Own Dolls,* by Ilse Stroble-Wohlschlager, Watson-Guptill Pub., New York, 1966—rag dolls and hand puppets.

Sometimes people acquire valuable collections without any effort on their part. Two sisters, Jan and Lillian Kelly, spinster school teachers, had collected a store of antiques. Living in the family home, they had inherited all the old junk left behind by departing brothers, sisters, parents, grandparents, aunts, and uncles—items like old furniture, china, radios, curling irons, sleigh bells, and candles molds. When they were forced to move into new quarters to allow throughway for state road expansion, they chose a smaller house in the city. But they brought their many possessions with them and now operate a thriving antique business from their home.

If you have no antiques or collectables of your own to start with, check your newspaper for auctions or garage sales. You will probably be able to pick up odd lots of china, furniture, and other interesting items, which you can then resell at a profit. A bit of paint or a touch of glue can mean the difference between a few cents output and several dollars intake. The more you know of antiques and their value on today's market, the better your chance for success.

Books from your library which would be helpful are:

> *Antiques: How to Identify, Buy, Sell, Refinish and Care for Them,* by Ann K. Cole, Collier Books.
>
> *How To Sell Your Antiques At A Profit,* by Ann Kilborn Cole, David McKay Company, New York, 1969.
>
> *Fortune in the Junk Pile,* Dorothy Jenkins.

From the Small Business Administration, Washington, D.C. 20416 you can receive free *Furniture Retailing, SBB 48*. This booklet contains references to many additional sources of information on antique furniture, including directories, trade associations, and journals.

Some of the best current sources for antiques information are the following magazines and newspapers. Check your library for back issues.

The Antique Dealer, 101 Springfield Ave., Summit, N.J. 07901.

Antiques, 55 Fifth Ave., New York 10017, $12 a year, $1.50 a copy.

The Western Collector, San Francisco, Calif. 94129, $5 a year.

Spinning Wheel, Hanover, Pennsylvania 17331, $4.50 a year.

Hobbies, 1006 South Michigan Ave., Chicago, Ill. 60605 $4 a year.

Collector's News, Grundy Center, Iowa 50638 $3 a year.

The Antique Trader, Kewanee, Ill. 61443 $3 a year.

Richard Smith has a boxful of whales' teeth rivaling those of captains of the old whaling vessels. Recently he offered this unusual collection for sale to a New York *scrimshaw* artist, who etches miniature drawings into the ivory of each tooth.

Actually the seller had acquired his first whale tooth as a curiosity many years ago. He bought it from a merchant to see if he could make jewelry from it. So pleased was he with the results that he began importing teeth for himself and for other hobbyists from a small whaling town in Europe. In short order, he had imported about a half-ton of teeth, which he sold for $10 a pound.

But that was before the Endangered Species Act cut off his source of supply. However, Mr. Smith still has over 700 teeth in his basement, a collection of ivory weighing over 400 pounds. At current prices, this assortment of teeth should pay off big.

Although collecting whales' teeth is a bit unusual, rock collecting is something that most of us do sometime during our life. A few souvenirs from the mountains, the beach, or a cavern and you're off to a good start. Soon minerals and gems are covering cabinets and filling shelves and you find yourself carding and identifying treasures from mineral sites and mine shafts. Your time is spent grinding and polishing to turn rough stones into lovely gems.

But rocks can become much more than a collection. When you become an expert or an authority in your field, they can put money in your pocket. Many collectors show their gems in area schools and for local organizations. Some teach lapidary work in colleges, while others guest-lecture.

You can also make money by cutting, polishing and mounting gems for sale. Some rock collectors who don't have the time or the equipment are willing to pay $1-$3 per stone for this service. Or you can sell these pieces through a museum, a club showroom, or the direct selling method. Items such as pins and tie tacks cost about 50¢ to make and retail to the public for $1 to $5.

Perhaps part or all of your present collection could be sold to other collectors. For instance, a recent sale of rare minerals brought the seller $5,000.

The following list of publications can be of great help to the rock collector enthusiast.

> *The Lapidary Journal,* 3564 Kettner, Blvd., San Diego, California—an annual, it lists the Gem and Mineral Clubs in North America and foreign countries. Each area has its own club or society.
>
> *Gems and Minerals,* a hobby magazine, Box 678, Mentone, Calif., 92359.
>
> *Rocks and Minerals,* a hobby magazine, Box 29, Peekskill, N.Y. 10566.
>
> *Rocks and Minerals,* a field guide by Herbert S. Zim, Golden Press, N.Y.
>
> *The Facetier,* Arrow Profile Company.

More information, supplies and equipment can be obtained from:

Arrow Profile Company
P.O. Box 38
St. Clair Shores, Michigan

Adams Lapidary and Gem Shop
8391 Market St.
Youngstown, Ohio 44512

Highland Park Mfg. Co.
12600 Chadron Ave.
Hawthorne, Calif. 90250

York River Mining Company
9612 Parkman Road
Windham, Ohio 44288

MAKING MONEY FROM LEISURE

Frequently, the things we do in our leisure time can lead us to the start of a profitable home business. The old idea that leisure is do-nothing-time is fast fading, and people today are engaged in all sorts of enjoyable activities—many of them, money producing.

Bob Sargent, a school teacher, started tying flies when he was a boy of 13. Now, at the age of 36, this skill nets him about $30,000 a year over his teaching salary. While a student at Northwestern University, he began tying flies and selling them to fellow students in order to finance his fishing trips. Then, for a few years afterward he tied flies and sold them wholesale, netting about $5.00 a dozen. He now has his own fishing-tackle shop in North Carolina, and ties no more than three dozen flies an hour, for which he earns about 75 ¢ each.

Tying flies is an art that requires good eyesight, and the ability to imitate natural fish food with a tiny hook and bits of feather, fur, thread, or tinsel. The body of a fly is usually made from fur—mink, muskrat, silver monkey, racoon, fox, polar bear, badger, otter, hare, beaver, or bobcat. Bob buys many of his pelts from trappers, but also uses the pelts of animals hit on the road, if they are in good shape. The part of the fly known as the hackle he makes from various bird neck feathers.

Booklets on fishing skills such as *Fly Fishing,* by Lefty Kreh, *code 8917,* and *Artificial Lures,* by Mark Sosin, *code 8904* are available from your library, your dealer, or directly from The Garcia Corporation Fishing Library, 329 Afred Ave., Teaneck, N.J. 07666.

Weaving can be profitable with income possibilities limited only by the skill and the ambition of the weaver. Simple articles such as table mats, afghans, scarves, and belts can be produced with small inexpensive table looms, while the experienced weaver may prefer to set up his own loom.

The quality of yarn is equally as important as your choice of a loom and it would be wise to seek professional help before investing in expensive materials. You will find a vast store of helpful information in the many books on your library shelf, plus correspondence with the suppliers listed below.

From the library:

> *Weaving Without A Loom,* by Sarita R. Rainey, Davis Publications, 1971—an easy and natural approach to weaving.
>
> *Step by Step Weaving,* by Nell Znamierowski, Golden Press.

Looms and equipment:

Gilmore Looms
1032 North Broadway Ave.
Stockton, California 95205

Kessenich Looms and Yarns
7463 Harwood Ave.
Wauwatosa, Wisconsin 53213

Purrington Looms
East Dennis, Massachusetts 02641

Structo Division
King-Seeley Thermos Co.
Freeport, Illinois 61032

The Norwood Loom Co.
Box 272
Baldwin, Michigan 49304

L. W. Macomber
166 Essex Street
Saugus, Massachusetts 01906

Nilus Leclerc
L'Isletville 6,
Quebec, Canada

Dyes:

W. Cushing & Co.
"Perfection" Dyes
North St.
Kennebunkport, Maine 04046

Tintex and Rit dyes obtainable
at five and dime stores.

General suppliers:

School Products Co.
312 East 23rd Street
New York, New York 10010

The Silver Shuttle
1301 35th Street N.W.
Washington, D.C. 20007

Handlooms:

Bailey Manufacturing Co.
118 Lee Street
Lodi, Ohio 44254

L. W. Macomber
166 Essex Street
Saugus, Massachusetts 01906

Dorset Looms
Woodin Road R.D. #1
Waterford, New York 12188

Morgan Inkle Loom Factory
Railroad Engine House
Guilford, Connecticut 06437

Gilmore Looms
North Broadway Avenue
Stockton, California 55205

Newcomb Loom Co.
Davenport, Iowa 52808

Northwest Looms
Rt. #4, Box 4872
Bainbridge Island, Washington 98110

The Handcrafters
521 W. Brown Street
Waupum, Wisconsin 53963

The Norwood Loom Company
Box 272
Baldwin, Michigan 49304

Kessenich Looms
7463 Harwood Avenue
Wauwatasa, Wisconsin 53213

The Pendleton Shop
Sedona, Arizona 86336

Kircher Looms
R.T. 3, Box 461
Loveland, Colorado 0537

Turnbull Looms
P.O. Box 4295
Mobile Alabama 36604

Leclerc Corp.
P.O. Box 491
Plattsburg, New York 12901

Leclerc West
P.O. Box 7012 Landscape Station
Berkeley, California 94707

Making money with hooked rugs comes closer to the ideal of making something out of nothing than most other crafts. Equipment needed is a simple rug hook (50¢), some rug binding (7¢ a yard), and a piece of good quality burlap ($1 a yard), and all the old material you can scrounge from your friends and acquaintances. You can use wool or cotton clothing, old blankets, and linens. The remnant pile of a yard-goods department will also yield interesting additions.

Your own creative ability in the field of color and design can be expressed in your work, such as dyeing your own material to get just the right color or hue you desire. Or you can make rugs to order, using your customers ideas.

Check your library for the following books:

Persian Patterns in Hooked Rugs, by Pearl McGown, Harper and Row Publishers, New York.

Rug Hooking Made Easy, by Charlotte K. Stratton, Harper and Row Publishers, New York.

Ideas For Canvas Work, by Mary Rhodes, Chas. T. Branford Co., 1970—includes information on appropriate mordants and dyes.

Basket weaving is a centuries-old craft which has recently made a big comeback, and if you're creative, it can net you big profits. Baskets of every shape and size are "hot" items which can be found in almost every home.

Russell Connors of Denver, Colorado, taking advantage of the wine craze, designed a unique wine-holder basket. He was able to display it in a local beer and wine carry-out store, and soon orders began pouring in. In three months, he had filled 39 orders and added $320 to his regular income. Later, he began to sell through mail-order and was on his way to big business.

Many handicraft shops sell basket-making supplies. This is fine for testing the craft, but when you decide to go into business with an item, you might better purchase your materials from a wholesale supply house. You will find a good selection listed in the directories at your library.

Today, because handwork of any type is beginning to regain the value it once held, both in the artistic and practical sense, many people are cashing in on needlework. Knitting, crocheting, needlepoint, crewel work, embroidery—all can lead you at a gallop into big business.

Mary Glenn, a young wife and mother in Pittsburgh, began

knitting and crocheting afghans to sell as Christmas gifts. Each one carried a price tag of $35, and the season's sales netted her a profit of $145. So successful were these first efforts, she now employs five other women, working year round to fill orders. Another woman teaches knitting in her home, and as a sideline offers knitting supplies for sale to her students.

Aside from the numerous books on needlework available at your library, you will find help and information from the following:

The Unicorn,
Box 645C
Rockville, Md. 20851
offers a 25¢ catalog
listing hundreds of needlework books and pamphlets,
many with graphed designs.

Amateur Needlework of Today, Inc.
111 East 59th St.
New York, New York 10022
for those who work in needlepoint or
crewel.

The Embroiderer's Guild of America, Inc.
120 East 56th Street
New York, N.Y. 10022

Every magazine stand, handicraft shop, and library displays numerous publications on the arts, crafts, and skills which make up the hobbies of millions of people. Those mentioned in this chapter represent only a few which have proved popular as big money makers. Most likely, your hobby can make money for you too. If you haven't thought about it before, the time to start is *now*.

5

Starting Your Home Business with Limited Resources

Every year thousands of men and women go into business for themselves, operating out of a basement, garage, or spare room in their home. Many of these businesses, which eventually develop into full-scale operations are started "on a shoestring."

GETTING STARTED ON A SHOESTRING

Today, the Hertz Corporation is a diversified equipment rental company operating world-wide with a fleet of over 160,000 corporation-owned and licensed vehicles, and generating well over $500 million in annual revenues. However, a half century ago when the business started, you could find the yellow and black emblem in only one back-street garage, in only one city, Chicago.

But it was an idea whose time had come and the business grew. First on the scene, Hertz remains the undisputed leader of one of the nation's vanguard service industries, an example of what innovating and planning can do.

On a lesser scale, Sandi Prentice, a young man I know, developed his candle-making business from scratch. Starting with one mold, an 11-lb. cake of wax, and a candle dye, he has built his business to the point where he sells through gift shops and department stores, has hired a salesman to help him, and is beginning to sell through the mail.

Because many people today are willing to pay more for handcrafted products that are decorative and different from machine-made look-alikes, he sells some of his more elaborate candles for $20 and $30 dollars apiece. Filling orders for Christmas and holiday candles alone keeps him constantly busy.

Although Sandi started on his own, learning as he went along, there are many places offering classes and guidance in the art of candle-making. Check with your local "Y" and art institute or local highschool for available classes.

Spearheading the profits thousands are finding in candlecraft, is the Custom Candlecrafter's Club of America, 1600 Cabrillo Avenue, Torrance, California 90501. For a small fee ($10) the institute starts you on a complete home study course which covers candle-making techniques and business methods, plus nine unique candle molds and the assurance that you can earn big profits even as you learn (example: your cost for a candle to retail at $3.95 is only 35¢).

Candle supply houses can also be of great help to the candle-maker. Most have candle-making kits, waxes, dyes, wicks, molds, materials for decorative effects, and for the advanced candle maker who wants to compound his own waxes and formulas. Free catalogs are available from:

Barker Enterprises
4208 S.W. 100th St.
Seattle, Wash. 98146

Lumi-lit Candle Company
Main Street
Norwalk, Ohio

Paurette Manufactures
in California

Another source of information is *The Journal of the American Candlemaker,* P. O. Box 1203, Santa Cruz, California 95060. And don't forget the many good candle making booklets in your local hobby store or handicraft shop, plus the selection of books on your library shelf. One of the best is:

> *The Candle Book by Carli Laklan,* M. Barrous & Co., Inc., New York, 1962—a complete book about candlecraft and candles for those who seek an exciting money-making venture. Every step from start to finish is described in detail as well as kinds of wax available, the size wicks to use, molds that are most successful, etc. It answers all questions on how to make candles, how to decorate them and how to turn this easy, entertaining craft into a profitable home business.

STARTING A BUSINESS WITH $50 OR LESS

In Detroit, a couple took a night school course in furniture remodeling, re-upholstery and slipcovering techniques. Starting with their own and their neighbors' old furniture, they set to work. Since customers supplied their own fabric, paint, or varnish, the couple's original investment consisted primarily of paint remover, paint brushes, antiquing materials, and upholstery tacks. From this modest beginning, they now operate a thriving furniture renovation business in their basement.

Another couple makes big money from unpainted furniture. They started in business several years ago by buying from a wholesaler a few pieces of unpainted furniture, which they painted and decorated with Pennsylvania Dutch designs and sold at a good profit. Today, they too have a thriving business and operate from a suburban shop where they employ several people.

You will find your library shelves filled with books on furniture. These listed will be especially helpful.

> *Refinishing Furniture,* by W. H. Kuhn, Arco Publishing Co., Inc., 1964.
>
> *Restoring and Maintaining Finishes—Spot Finishing,* by George A. Soderberg and Paul W. Karcher, Bruce Publishing Co.—explains the technique of repairing damaged areas of furniture and extensive information on methods of restoring and maintaining furniture finishes.
>
> *Upholstering and Re-upholstering,* by Clyde A. Griswell, Frederick J. Drake and Co.—incorporates the newest materials and latest methods of procedure.
>
> *Découpage,* by D. Harrower, Bonanza Books.
>
> *Decorative Painting—Folk Art Style,* by Hundley and Cole, Doubleday, 1971—steps to creating unique furniture.
>
> *The Furniture Doctor by George Grotz,* Doubleday, 1962—with tricks of the trade and easy-to-follow directions.

Beading is a centuries-old craft which has never lost its appeal. Materials are inexpensive and finished pieces bring good prices. A small tube of 900 Indian type beads sells for 20¢ ; a large tube of over 1800 for 40¢ .

Many small accessories and articles of wearing apparel such as headbands, belts, and moccasins, colorfully decorated with woven beadwork, are popular items with the teenage set. Beaded work on burlap shoulder-strap bags can be done in a short time. And many of today's homes are decorated with beaded door hangings and room dividers.

The list of books below will help you in making money with beads.

Beading; Basic and Boutique, by Barbara L. Farlie, Meredith Corp.,
1971.

Real Crafts by Catherine Roberts, Garden City Books, Chapter II; Indian
Moccasins and Beadwork, p. 45.

Bouquets From Beads, by Virginia Osterland. Charles Scribner's Sons,
N.Y.–explains principles and techniques of beaded flowers and foliage.

Bead Embroidery, by Joan Edwards,–Taplinger Publishing Co., 1966–an
expert text together with 230 clear drawings and diagrams.

New Patterns For Bead Flowers and Decorations by Virginia Nathanson,
Hearthside Press, Inc., New York, 1969–step by step fundamentals of
a host of beaded projects–lavishly illustrated.

Another way to make easy money is to customize for profit.
Everyone likes the personalized item, the one that is different or
made to order. For example it is said that in the Arab sheikdom of
Kuwait, a wealthy sheik bought a new Lincoln Continental and a
new Cadillac and gave orders to have them cut in half. He then had
the four pieces fitted together with the result that his new
"customized" cars had the front of a Lincoln and the back of a
Cadillac (and vice versa).

More believable is the man from Hatteras, North Carolina, who
buys plastic serving trays from his wholesaler, hand-decorates them
with shells he has picked up on the beach in front of his home, and
sells them to his customers for more than double what he paid for
them.

You can customize just about anything, but the one sure way to
make money is to buy at a low price and sell at a high price. One
woman buys huge quantities of plain drinking glasses, uses a stencil
to etch monograms on them, and sells them at a profit. Mosaic tiles
are used by a young businessman to enhance the tops of small coffee
tables–as well as his bank account.

For ideas on customizing for profit which might appeal to you,
the following books are recommended.

A Handbook of Crafts, by Elsie V. Hanauer, A.S. Barnes and Co., Inc.,
1966.

Metalwork and Its Decoration by Etching, by Oscar Almeida, Taplinger
Publishing Co., 1964.

Glass Craft: Designing, Forming and Decorating, by Kay Kinney, Chilton
Book Company, Phil., Pa.

The Art of Making Mosaics, by Louisa Jenkins and Barbara Mills, D. Van
Nostrand Co., Inc.–shows how to make unusual mosaic pieces.

The Art of Crewel Embroidery by Mildred J. Davis, Crown Publishers, Inc., 1962—shows how to make a variety of stitches, how to trace and enlarge patterns.

This year the halls of 15-million U.S. households will be decked, not with holly, but with *plastic*. Not only does this 20th century bonanza include plastic trees, flowers, and ornaments for the holiday season, but everyday giftwares such as candle holders, picture frames, night lights, bookends—even room dividers and decorative screens—and toys.

A friend of mine who fooled around with plastic as a hobby found that he could make big money manufacturing model kits. Working with his brother he turns out highway miniatures, Ho gauge, model railroad scale trucks and cars that sell for $1.95 apiece.

If manufacturing a product doesn't interest you, you might improve products made by others. An investment of $15 will buy a plastic laminating machine. With this you can seal in plastic such items as photographs, identification cards, social security cards, and most other items to be found in a wallet, plus wedding or birth announcements and newspaper clippings. Warner Electric Company, Inc., 1512 Jarvis Avenue, Chicago, Ill. 60626 will send you all the details.

Plastic is a material with endless possibilities. It can be melted, embedded, formed, and cemented. The books mentioned below, available in your library, offer a wide selection of ideas for its use.

Plastics—Projects and Techniques, by Alvin R. Lappin, McKnight and McKnight Publishing Co., 1965—basic information on cutting, heating, forming, and finishing plastics, plus suggestions for unusual ways of working plastic.

Plastics For Fun, by Alexander F. Bick, The Bruce Publishing Co.

Cope's Plastic Book, by Dwight Cope, The Goodheart-Willcox Co., Inc., 1960—plastic projects are illustrated, ranging from elementary to advanced. A description of various types of plastic and how they are made. It also describes methods of working with plastic, storing, sawing, machining, polishing, heating, cementing, dyeing, and commercial fabrication methods.

Adventures With Plastics, by Louis V. Newkirk, D.C. Heath and Co.—for the person who is just beginning to work with plastics. How to order plastics and supplies is included.

Fiber Glass: Projects and Procedures, by Gerald L. Steele, McKnight and McKnight Publishing Co., 1962—specializes in fiber-glass projects and their construction in the home. Includes characteristics of materials

and the equipment and processes used in working with fiber glass. Also
includes lists of manufacturers of fiber glass and supply sources.

Block printing is easy and yet it offers unlimited opportunity to
earn hard cash. A recent newspaper account told of a housewife who,
because she couldn't find wrapping paper with a Christian motif,
decided to design her own. Having accomplished this, she offered it
to one of the big greeting card companies. She is now getting top
dollar not only for her gift wrappings, but also for party tablecloths,
cocktail napkins, and paperware. Of late, she also prints cards and
has recently designed several wallpapers.

You can also block print on a roll of fabric or on garments that
are ready-made or on anything that will take the print. Hand-blocked
prints launder beautifully and are practical for many purposes—
couch covers, slip covers, bed spreads, table linens, curtains for a
kitchen, draperies for a period drawing room, skirts, neckties,
scarves—the list is endless.

In our affluent society, the consumer daily grows more dis-
criminating and is ever ready to buy materials which show originality
of design and attention to detail. To help you get a start in this
interesting and lucrative business, I suggest the following reading list:

> *Printed Textile Design,* by Terence Conran, Studio Publication, New
> York—shows all the aspects of printed textile design. Explains natural
> and synthetic fibers, gives a brief history of textile design and discusses
> the approach to manufacturers on whose patronage future prosperity
> must depend.

> *Block Printing On Textiles,* by Janet Erickson, Watson-Guptill Publica-
> tions, 1967—a complete guidebook. Beginning with linoleum cutting,
> the author analyzes all the basic materials and tools and their uses. She
> also treats block printing methods for the beginner, working with scrap
> rubber and other familiar, inexpensive materials. Valuable charts list
> fibers and fabrics, their qualities and typical uses.

> *Fabric Printing,* by Lotti Lauterburg, The Reinhold Publishing Co.,
> 1959—describes some of the simpler techniques of printing and dyeing,
> with a large number of illustrations.

> *Introducing Dyeing and Printing,* by Beryl Ash and Anthony Dyson,
> Watson-Guptill Publications, New York,—useful framework on which
> the ideas and improvisations of readers may be built.

Because bones can be profitable, a family I know has an
"English" roast of beef on the dinner table at least twice a week.
When the meat is gone, the marrow bone is boiled in alum and
limewater (one teaspoon of alum to each quart of water), rinsed in

several changes of water, and then bleached for several days in the sun. Then the bone is used to make napkin rings which are sold through a local gift shop.

Cattle bone is the principal material used for making bone articles today, although sheep bones are very hard and are excellent for jewelry and buttons. One woman even makes jewelry of chicken bones. Materials made of bone bring a high price today and are becoming ever more popular. Fine old wooden cabinets and boxes are enhanced by bone keyhole plates; stainless steelware is enriched by adding bone handles; jewelry pendants made of bone and hung on leather thongs sell well.

Tools for working in bone are few and if you don't want the bother of boiling and drying the bone, prepared bone in various sizes can be bought from a wholesaler and is also sold in hobby shops.

Working in Plastic, Bone, Amber, and Horn, by Erland Borglund and Jacob Flauensgaard, Reinhold Book Corp., 1968, gives explicit directions on working with bone and should serve to stimulate your own design talent.

There are *big* profits to be made from *art* today. Not only in owning and selling paintings, but in preserving and restoring them. However, this is not a job to be tackled without training. Alas for the bold do-it-yourselfer who removed the face of his ancestor from a prized family portrait with one soapy stroke.

But with so many people acquiring old paintings, there are many things that a knowledgeable restorer can safely do in his home workshop. Paintings need to be cleaned, lined, inpainted (retouching that is confined to areas where paint is missing) and finally protected with a new coat of varnish. If you have confidence in your skills you can try relining a painting whose canvas has deteriorated or touching up a canvas where the paint has chipped.

Perhaps your local art galleries and artist supply shops will display an advertising sign for you.

Publications for conservators include:

A Handbook on the Care of Paintings, by Caroline K. Keck, Watson-Guptill Publications, $6.95—tells how to care successfully for paintings and prevent deterioration. Recommended for conservators especially.

The American Artist Magazine, $1 per month or $11 per year. Subscription dept: American Artist, 2160 Patterson St., Cincinnati, Ohio 45214.

The Painter's Pocket Book, by Hilaire Hiler, Watson-Guptill Publications, $4.95—a book of methods and materials.

Notes On the Technique of Painting, by Hilaire Hiler, Watson-Guptill Publications, $6.95—a classic on materials and methods of painting," particularly famous for its compilation of the formulas, techniques and palettes of the masters—old and new.

GETTING INTO BUSINESS WITH $100 TO $500

If you have $100 or more to invest in your home business, you might consider the various ways of making money with a typewriter.

Armed with a second-hand portable, a new ribbon, and already-learned typing skills, Ann Markley offered a public stenographer service in the business-oriented area of Cleveland in which she lived. Convenience to clients, accuracy, and reliability help her to build a repeat business which keeps her on a full schedule every day.

If you live in a college town your typing services could include theses or term papers—or typing lessons. Excellent exposure can be provided by advertising in the school newspaper or other school publications.

Or if, along with fast and accurate typing skills, you have a flair for spelling, punctuation, and syntax, you have the basics needed for successful operation of a home typing service for authors and other writers. Free-lance writers are found in every town and city in the U.S. and the average writer doesn't type very well. Advertising in either of the two "writer's magazine" should get you started.

The Writer, Inc., 8 Arlington St., Boston, Mass. 02116.

Writer's Digest, 22 E. 12th St., Cinn., Ohio 45210.

By typing addresses on envelopes for bulk mailings you can earn $15 to $20 per thousand evelopes. With a high typing speed, this can be a most profitable occupation. Firms that handle this kind of work are listed in the yellow pages under "Direct Mail Advertising" and "Mailing Lists." Also, local printing firms are a good source of information.

Among the many books on typing to be found on your library shelves, read "How You Can Earn $10,000 Typing at Home," by Lenore E. Felgen, Felgen and Associates Publishers.

Because the field of original art is growing and because each painting must have its own "display case," picture framing has become a growth business, and custom framing can be a valuable source of high profit income. Some custom framers make their own frames, others buy from a wholesaler, and still others redo old or antique frames. Training in custom framing can be learned from professionals or acquired through self study.

Your local artist supply or hobby equipment shop might agree to post a "picture framing" sign for you, or suggest your service to their customers.

Library books which will prove useful are:

> *Better Frames For Your Pictures,* by Frederic Taubes, Viking Press, New York, 1970—explains how to make and finish your own frames.
>
> *Right Frame,* by Henry Heydenryk, James H. Heineman, Inc., 1964.
>
> *How To Make Your Own Picture Frames,* by Ed Reinhardt and Hal Rogers—a step-by-step study with photos, showing every phase of frame making as well as the tools you need.

Statistics tell us that more and more people today are acquiring dogs, some for protection, some for pets, but regardless of the reason, there is big money to be made by *pampering poodles.*

A Cleveland businessman, retired and a dog fancier, took a dog-grooming course from a local Poodle Parlor for a cost of $350. While taking the course, he clipped his own dog and several neighborhood canines, and so was able to earn even as he learned. He now operates a full scale dog-grooming service in his heated garage.

Dogs who come in for the full treatment get their toenails clipped and their ears cleaned. They get brushed, washed, and clipped, and afterwards are sprayed with perfume. The entire job takes about three hours and costs can range anywhere from $8 for a puppy clip to $25 for the entire treatment.

You may be able to advertise your service through pet supply stores, veterinaries, and boarding kennels in your area.

The following books from your library will help you.

> *The Poodle Handbook,* by Ernest H. Hart, T.F.H. Publications, Inc., 1966—includes how to clip your poodle, plus diseases and first aid.
>
> *Clipping Your Poodle,* by Sheldon and Lockwood, Arco Pet Library, 1972-$1.95—for the novice who wishes to make an efficient job of clipping and grooming. Lists equipment (basic) needed to start in business; also the various types of clips.
>
> *First Aid For Pets,* by Leon F. Whitney D.V.M., Vanguard Press—includes problems of hygiene and coat care.
>
> *Your Dog's Skin Problems,* by Dr. Frank Miller—helps on keeping a dog's coat in the best condition.

The Complete Dog Book—the official Publication of the American Kennel Club—the best and most up-to-date information available on care of pure-bred dogs.

If you are handy with automobiles, there is quick money waiting for you in an auto junk yard.

Starting with parts from a "junked" Volkswagen, Jerry Nuchler built his Auto Parts and VW Repair Shop to a full-scale, every-day backyard business. His main source of used parts is still the auto graveyard, where he can sometimes buy almost new parts for next to nothing. Now that business is flourishing, he carries some new parts in stock and has expanded his service to include other small foreign cars.

Books on auto repair, obtainable from your library, include:

The Principles of Autobody Repairing and Repainting, by Tait-DeRoche-Hildebrand, Prentice-Hall, Inc., 1971—complete step-by-step details for mastery of every skill needed in all phases of auto repair with more than 700 up-to-date illustrations that cover the whole range of skills you will require as an expert craftsman.

Car Repairs You Can Make, by Hartford and Daffron, Arco Book Publishers—an ideal book for the beginning repairman since no major tools are required for most of the repairs and yet it enables you to do a better job than many so-called pros.

Car Maintenance and Repair, by Arthur W. Judge, Robert Bentley Inc., 1967—intended for the use of the mechanically minded.

Automotive Engines, by Wm. H. Crouse, McGraw-Hill Book Co., Inc.—a basic guide to the construction, operation, servicing, and repair of American auto engines.

Another much needed service, which can net you fat dividends today, is *bicycle repair.* From cross-country racing to urban commuting, from short "escape" trips around the neighborhood to long tours through the open countryside, the cycling experience is catching on. One-speed, five-speed, ten-speed—they all have one thing in common—at sometime or other they will all need to be repaired or serviced.

A young man I know, in conjunction with his repair shop, buys up old or discarded bicycles, sometimes for as little as $3, polishes and repairs them and sells them at a tremendous profit. Another, who lives near a college campus, rents them for a modest fee, per hour, day, or week. Books about bicycling which you should read include:

The Complete Book of Bicycling, by Eugene A. Sloane, Trident Press, 1970—the most comprehensive guide to all aspects of bicycles, and bicycling, including history, repair, and maintenance, design and theory, touring and camping. $9.95.

Anybody's Bike Book, by Tom Cuthbertson, $3—a complete manual of bicycle repairs. Illustrated and written so that *anybody* can fix a bike.

If you cannot find these books in your library, they can be ordered from American Youth Hostels, Inc., Metropolitan New York Council, 535 West End Ave., New York, N.Y. 10024.

Money may not grow on trees, but for some people, trees are a main source of income. Jim Battler owns and operates a tree-trimming and pruning business that grew out of a neighborhood hedge-cutting job.

Starting out with an electric hedge-cutter and a few pruning tools he gradually expanded his business and his equipment to include a used pick-up truck, two chain saws, ropes, hooks, and other necessary items. During the recent epidemic of Dutch Elm Disease in Ohio, he became professional in cutting down thousands of dead elm trees throughout his part of the state.

For an extra fee he would cut and stack the logs for firewood, leaving a customer's yard free of all debris. Learning as he went along, he now has become a specialist in disease and insect control, has several employees, and offers a complete tree service to his customers.

When starting in business, referrals by greenhouse operators and nurserymen can be helpful. Library books on this subject are many, but you might begin with *The Pruning Manual,* by Everett P. Christopher, The Macmillan Co., 1966—sections are devoted to forestry, grafting, root pruning, wound treatment, and tools.

Lawn maintenance, too, can be a big money maker for you. In Denver, Jim Reynolds started out as a young boy cutting lawns in his own neighborhood. Using the family power mower and a pair of hand clippers, one job lead to another, and from his profits Jim was soon able to buy his own equipment, including a small, used riding mower. Each year, part of his profits went into more and better equipment.

Today, Jim's business is a full-time summer operation, employing three helpers full-time and two part-time. During the past two winters Jim has turned to snow removal for his customers, but will probably be forced to give up that portion of his business when he enters college in the fall.

Several years ago, a $100 used truck put Guy Rice in the driver's seat of a thriving business which today employs 40 people and maintains 60 trucks. Specialization was the key.

Guy got his start by focusing on city department stores that opened branches in outlying suburban areas. His first job—the transfer of dress goods between two store locations—caused him to outfit that first truck, which he drove himself, with racks and hardware to accommodate hundreds of hangered articles. Gradually he signed up more accounts and acquired more trucks to service them, until his network included a dozen states.

Guy's company is a contract carrier, which means that it handles merchandise for a limited number of clients, to and from specific locations. But there are several types of carriers and it is safe to say that almost all got their start from one-man, one-truck businesses.

If trucking appeals to you, you can begin by operating the business in your spare time. In a large city, you may be able to make a good living right from the start, and as you add more trucks your income can only go up.

The following list of books provides information on trucking and cartage services.

> *Commercial Motor Transportation,* by Charles A. Taff, Richard D. Irwin, Inc., 1961—a general text on trucking principles.
>
> *Motor Truck Facts,* Automobile Manufacturers Assoc., Inc., 320 New Center Bldg., Detroit, Michigan 48202—free—statistics on trucks and their uses.
>
> *National Directory of Motor Contract Carriers in Interstate Commerce,* Contract Carriers, Inc., 1616 P St., N.W., Washington, D.C. 20036—helps in clarifying the background and requirements of carriers.

PROFITS FROM YOUR $$ INVESTMENTS

Some people think that unless they have a large amount of money to invest in a business, they haven't a chance of succeeding. They couldn't be more wrong. Everyday we hear of someone who is making it big in a business he started on a shoestring.

Most of the large contracting companies started out as small, one-man operations. Concrete, tile, patio foundations, wall painting, bricklaying, plastering, paperhanging—in the yellow pages of every telephone directory the list goes on and on.

It takes only a small investment to start on any of these enterprises and although you need not be a genius to lay a brick or cement a sidewalk, it does require some knowledge. However, most dealers and wholesalers can give you practical advice if you but ask. You can also find interesting and practical information in magazines devoted to homes and gardens. To get you started the following books may prove helpful.

> *The Art of Bricklaying,* by J. Edgar Ray, Charles A. Bennett Company, 1971.

> *Concrete and Masonry,* by Richard Day, Arco Publishing Co.—presents valuable information on every aspect of masonry.

That a small beginning investment can result in the making of a fortune is evidenced by the story of the Revlon Company. Forty years ago, two Boston-born brothers named Joseph and Charles Revson and a chemist friend, Charles Lachman, started manufacturing nail enamel in a room on Manhattan's West Side. They had $300 in capital and a formula for a new nail polish that wouldn't streak.

Revlon, as the Depression-born corporate infant was christened (taking its L from Lachman) produced a variety of shades with catchy names such as "Windsor" and "Rosy Future," matched them to lipsticks and merchandised them with fashion promotions, store tie-ins, and lavish advertising. In the nineteen-fifties, sales volume soared to over $100-million. To this day, Revlon remains one of the giants in the field of cosmetics.

There is money to be made from hundreds of skills not everybody has. One of them is *Magic.* From the beginning of time, people have been obsessed with a desire to know what the future has in store for them. Today, we are seeing a resurgence of spiritualism and mysticism. We are in a mystic time.

If you can read palms, analyze handwriting, read card fortunes, or foretell the future through extra-sensory perception, or astrology, you can earn a lot of money. Working "for fun" at parties and bazaars or in the more serious science of parapsychology will net you a good income. For the use of cards or palm reading, whether taken seriously or merely as light entertainment, can be big business.

In the suburb of Chicago, Illinois, Betty Falk has taken advantage of the current interest in occult and prophetic matters to launch her newly-formed home business. Dealing particularly in prophesy, she not only reads palms and interprets handwriting, but conducts a class in these subjects for students once a week. Fortune telling with cards, plus these other abilities, have made her a much sought-after entertainer at many local fund raising parties. On occasion, she has earned as much as $100 an evening for two hours work.

Much knowledge of magic may be obtained through books for there are a great many on the subject.

> *Parapsychology: ESP-Seers and Psychics,* by Christopher Milbourne, Thomas Y. Crowell Company 1970—explains what the occult really is—covers every type of unexplained phenomenon.

> *ESP: A Scientific Evaluation,* by C.E.M. Hansel, Charles Scribner's Sons, New York 1966—a dispassionate and comprehensive study of psychical research from its origins to the present day, including telepathy, clairvoyance, prerecognition, and psychokinesis.

> *How To Tell Fortunes With Cards,* by Wenzell Brown, Sterling Publishing Co., 1968—a book written completely logically and realistically about revelation of personality from ordinary playing cards.

> *The Sibil Leek Book of Fortune Telling,* by Sibil Leek, the Macmillan Co., 1969—a knowing guide to the wisdom of Tarot cards and I Ching, palmistry and crystal-gazing, tea leaves and candle imagery, cards and dominos.

Although the work you do is invisible, the rewards you reap from reweaving aren't. Just as in regular weaving, invisible reweaving can be learned by anyone who has good eyesight and common needle-and-thread ability. It can be mastered through self teaching or through a correspondence course. One such course costs about $75. For this sum you get complete instruction in the best methods of repair of burns, moth holes, and tears, plus marketing guidance, referrals to local outlets, display posters and business cards.

In today's market, income-producing possibilities with weaving are limited only by the skill, imagination, and ambition of the weaver. For example, in Cleveland, a former sailor, who learned his craft while sailing many times around the world, makes and sells unusual picture frames. Using as many as six different colors of string, he uses his craft of string weaving to deftly work the pattern into a type of frame suitable for holding small photographs.

Ambitious weavers will find inspiration and a vast store of information in the many books on your library's shelves.

> *Weaving Is For Anyone,* by Jean Wilson, Reinhold Publishing Corp., 1967—a book for all weavers interested in different techniques— beginner or professional.

Contemporary Handweaving, by Ruth Overman and Lula Smith, Iowa State University Press, Ames, Iowa 50012—presents a simplified approach to handweaving with an introduction to the tools and techniques of weaving.

Weaving and Design, by Jack L. Larson and Azalea S. Thorpe, Chilton Co., 1961—a well illustrated book showing ways and means of creating design.

Handweaver and Craftsman Magazine, Waurterly, $5 per year—contains articles on textile design and techniques, tools and equipment for handweavers, markets, opportunities for exhibit. 246 Fifth Ave., New York, N.Y. 10001.

Homeowners are a constant source of ideas for profitable, proven businesses. Trying to cut expenses is a goal that every homeowner aims for, be he rich or poor, and if you can come up with a service that he needs at a price he can afford to pay, you have a potential customer.

One enterprising young man got his start in making custom signs by offering to the homeowner, for a small fee, the street-number painted on the curb in front of his residence. Another took advantage of a burglary scare in his town to manufacture, sell, and install a unique yard light. The renovation of a block of old townhouses in New York City was all the inspiration Nettie Albers needed to initiate her "authentic early American, home decorating service."

Take up your telephone book and thumb through the "yellow pages." Look at all of the services aimed at the homeowner. Improve on one of these, come up with something new, or offer a new twist—and you're ready for business.

"Make big money helping people avoid housebreaking," the ad read. So Gene Dunne sent away for the free details that showed him how to start as a burglar alarm specialist. After a short mail-order study course dealing with the many types and characteristics of alarm devices, he found a ready market right in his own apartment building. Since then his business has grown to include two private clubs, a candy factory, and several retail stores. He has also built up a good trade for locksmithing and keymaking.

Many of his customers lost their keys or wanted duplicate keys made. Others wanted locks replaced as they moved into and out of apartments and houses. For Gene, it all added up to a profitable full time business.

For further information about burglar alarms contact: Nasco, 11071 Massachusetts Ave., Dept. F2612, Los Angeles, Ca. 90025.

There is a new trend blooming in our land—the old fashioned art of door-to-door selling. Knock on any door these days and you can come away a little richer. Especially if you are selling a well known, name-brand product. Is there anyone who is not familiar with the Fuller Brush man, the Amway boy, or the Avon Lady?

Most of these companies operate in the same way. You, the salesman purchase a small amount of sample products (which in the case of Fuller costs not more than $10). The company supplies you with an order catalog and a specified territory. Since you receive a commission on what you sell, your profit depends entirely on how good a salesman you are.

You can obtain more information about the companies in your area by contacting the main office.

Amway Corporation
Home Care Distributor Department
7375 E. Fulton Drive
Ada, Michigan 49301

Avon Cosmetics
Home Distributor Department
Springdale, Ohio

The Fuller Brush Company
East Hartford, Conn.

Bestline Products, Inc.
Distributor Department
2350 Trimble Road
San Jose, California 95132

Most of the big businesses you see around you today were small ones a few years ago. Many began as "home businesses," and most were started by one individual using a small amount of capital. Remember, the little business venture that you start today can become one of the giants of tomorrow.

STARTING YOUR BUSINESS WITH $500 OR MORE

When you have $500 or more to invest in the business of your choice, there are three avenues open to you. You can start and run your own business; you can go into franchising; you can invest in mail-order. Since franchising is discussed in Chapter 6, and mail-order in Chapter 7, we will concentrate here on the business you start on your own.

A number of years ago, quite by accident, Nick Bosse found

himself in the tool rental business. Since his neighbors were always borrowing from his well-stocked tool room, he decided to turn an annoyance into a profitable business. Drawing on equipment already in his tool room he gradually added floor polisher, rug shampooers, and other electrical machines. Being able to repair his tools and keep them in good working condition was an asset and, for an added charge, he would even pick up and deliver. Today, a cost estimate of his "tools for rent" would total well over $35,000 and he is thinking of branching out to include camping and health equipment.

According to Nick, a good rule of thumb is that annual receipts should be $1.33 to $1.35 for every $1.00 invested in equipment. A full-time rental business usually requires at least $10,000 for equipment, but if you start on a small scale, as Nick did, and if you already own some tools, you can start with much less and cash in big on this fast growing service industry.

Or you might want to start out renting camping equipment or exercise machines or party supplies. Catalogs of large mail order firms such as Sears or Wards will give you other ideas and suggest other possibilities.

Sears Roebuck	Montgomery Ward
Chicago, Illinois	Chicago, Illinois

Aside from the service-oriented businesses, one of the areas furnishing the greatest opportunities for new small business is in manufacturing. Small manufacturing establishments complement the large industrial producers. They produce items for local consumer markets; for local business markets; for local construction markets. But whether you make machine parts or picture frames, they are usually contracted for (sold on order) before the first step toward a finished product is taken. When your product is already sold, manufacturing it can only mean money in your pocket.

Even so, some people go at it the hard way. An example is D.J. Williams, who four years ago, built his first cab-over camper by hand and sold it at a modest profit. He immediately ploughed his money back into more materials and built camper #2, then camper #3. But his patience, plodding, and enthusiasm paid off big and today his recreation-vehicles company sales are zooming past a $20,000,000 annual level. He has factories in Texas, Georgia, California, and Mississippi which turn out recreational vehicles to suit virtually every consumer need and budget.

Machine shops in the home, unless you live in a castle, are usually limited as to size and quantity of machinery. Most are one-man operations which specialize in custom items or job-type machining of small tools and dies.

Good used machine tools are available at substantially lower prices than new ones, but the machine shop operator will also need workbenches, material handling equipment, shop cupboards, work-bench lights, and in most cases an air compressor.

In our highly mechanized society, jobs performed by machine shops offer increasing profit opportunities. But before you decide on a shop of your own, count your sources of metals, the number of job shops already in your area, and your potential customers. A thorough survey may uncover a need in your community for the service you intend to supply, where a versatile machinist with a head for business can start his own machine shop with good prospects for a useful and profitable career.

Books from your library which can be useful are:

> *Machinists Library,* by P.O. Black, Theodore Audel and Co. 1970—basic machine shop information with a generous use of illustrations and how-to-do-it machine shop questions.
>
> *Machine Shop-Theory and Practice,* by F.H. Hallett, The Macmillan Company, 1961.
>
> *The New American Machinist's Handbook,* by Rupert LeGrand, McGraw Hill Book Company—an invaluable shop aid for machinists.
>
> *Complete Metal Working Manual,* by R.H. Cooley, Arco Publishing Company Inc., 1967—discusses techniques, machines and equipment.
>
> *Workshop Equipment,* by Arthur Wakeling, The Home Craftsman Publishing Corp.,—tells how to build your own workshop equipment.

If manufacturing is not for you, perhaps operating a job-shop which sells a product will pique your interest. Plumbing and heating is a good example of this type business. Air conditioning is another. As a retailer selling to the public, you still must merchandise your product and you also have the responsibility of installing and servicing the product you sell.

While all states and many local governments have codes and laws governing the installation of plumbing, heating, and air-conditioning equipment, these trades are easy to learn. This is best done by working for a professional for a few years. By the time you have studied under a master plumber or journeyman, you have acquired most of your needed tools and the cost of setting up shop is relatively small.

Because this type of service takes in such a wide range of specialties, particularly in the heating area, one of the best ways to get inside information is to consult someone who is operating a like business in a neighboring town. He can tell you all the tricks of the trade and the probable amount of your initial cash outlay.

Other sources of information would be current articles on plumbing and heating. These can be found in *The Engineering Index* and *The Applied Science and Technology Index,* available at your library.

Library books would include:

Heating and Air Conditioning, by Allen, Walker and Jamees, McGraw Hill Book Company, Inc.,—intended as a textbook for the individual who is studying the subject by himself.

ABCs of Air Conditioning, by Ernest Tricomi, Bobbs-Merrill Company, Inc.—complete down-to-earth explanation of the theory of air conditioning and practical applications.

National Plumbing Code, Illustrated, by Vincent T. Manas, Manas Publications, 1968—minimum requirements for plumbing.

Plumbing Repairs Simplified, by Donald R. Brann, Easi-bild Pattern Co., Inc. 1967.

Plumbing, by John G. Miller, D. Van Nostrand Co., Inc.,—a handbook of tools, materials, methods, and directions.

6

The Franchise Business You
Operate from Your Home

Many of us have had our homes cleaned by ServiceMaster, or our lawns cared for by Lawn King. And who among us hasn't munched a delicious hamburger under McDonald's "golden arches"? We readily recognize the familiar trademarks of these businesses, and we are vaguely aware that the "franchise" owners make big profits from them. But although the franchising industry is one of the nation's fastest growing areas of business, it remains a rather obscure concept for most of us. Perhaps this chapter will help to clarify this uniquely American marketing technique.

FRANCHISING—THE DO-IT-YOURSELF
SUCCESS KIT

Franchising represents the best of two worlds. 1. It offers you the chance to build a small business on your own in which you are the boss. 2. It supplies you with the knowledge, know-how and expertise of a large national company. You are provided with all the necessary tools except human aspiration.

Basically *what it is* and *how it operates* can be explained this way. A businessman perfects a product or service. When his business has become an outstanding success, he shows others how to succeed in the same way. For this, he charges a "franchise fee."

The business is operated as though it were part of a large chain, complete with trademarks, uniform symbols, design, equipment, and standardized services or products, but each franchise is *independently* owned. It is this personal and financial independence, created when a person invests his hard-earned savings, that is one of the greatest contributing forces in franchise success.

Franchising began before the turn of the century, with Rexall being given credit as the #1 pioneer. Louis K. Liggett began offering druggists the right to use the Rexall name in a joint marketing effort. That it is still in operation today speaks eloquently for its success.

However, it wasn't until after World War II that franchising really took off at a gallop. Opportunities were given to small investors to operate franchised roadside businesses. Today, these drive-in food stands are spread from coast to coast over the American landscape. And business people have discovered that franchising can be used for almost any type of business.

Where do you find franchise businesses? Anywhere and everywhere. Look about you. You'll see them in small towns, big cities, vacation playgrounds, and in secret hideaways. You know the names of scores of them—Kentucky Fried Chicken, Fish and Chips, Baskin-Robbins, Mr. Doughnut, Holiday Inn, Howard Johnson Restaurants, Evelyn Wood Reading Dynamics, Arnold Palmer Driving Ranges, Mister Softee, "One Hour Martinizing," Midas Muffler, Aero-Mayflower, A to Z Rentals, Culligan Soft-Water Service, United General Mini-Theatre, Hertz Rent-a-Car,—the list goes on and on. You name a business, there's a franchise for it.

You can make money by piggybacking the giants of the franchising industry. This system is one of the most powerful marketing devices on the economic scene. Franchising is a 100-billion-dollar-a-year business, and growing by leaps and bounds. There are approximately 350,000 franchise holders today, and the market is constantly expanding.

Because these businesses are successful enterprises with established formats, buying a franchise enables you to realize all the benefits of the free enterprise system and, at the same time, minimize your risk of failure. It helps you to avoid the pitfalls, headaches, and mistakes that so often accompany the start of a new business.

One reason for the phenominal success of those who own a franchise business is that *you operate under a nationally known name.* Most franchises got where they are in today's business economy by offering a consistently good service or product. The names of these companies are familiar to millions of people throughout the country and their product or service is accepted as being the best. When you are a franchisee of one of these nationally known and respected companies, you start out with a name that's a household word. This alone will probably get you into the black much sooner than if you started out with an unknown name.

What other advantages does a franchise offer you? There are many, but basically it is superior know-how. A franchisor like ServiceMaster's has found a successful formula for making money. The public accepts its services, its prices, its image, and the company has vast experience based on research and development. Very few ServiceMaster franchisees fail to make good. If you are willing to work at it, you are almost guaranteed a successful business. You begin operating with a national and regional reputation already built, whereas if you go out on your own, you'll have to start from scratch.

Another advantage you will get is continuing professional guidance and advice from your parent firm. Through experience they can tell you how much gross you should do to make a reasonable profit. They will advise you on equipment operation, sales aids, record keeping, buying tips, and all other aspects of the business. There is no need for costly trial-and-error methods. You needn't ponder over which piece of equipment would be best to buy or which would do a job most effectively. Nor need you worry about service on equipment, or what prices to charge. Usually all of this is taken care of for you with your franchise.

Thus far, I've painted a rather rosy picture of the franchise business, but it is only fair that we also examine the disadvantages involved. Probably the one that stands tall above the others is money—or the lack of it. For it does cost money to open a franchise business, and we will discuss this in detail a little further on.

Another point to consider is that although you are your boss—you aren't exactly. You must follow centrally dictated policies and procedures set down by the franchisor. You will be told what kind of uniform to wear, how long your hair can be, and what hours to work. If you don't follow all the rules, your contract can be terminated.

CHECKING INTO THE COST OF FRANCHISE

One of the most frequent obstacles to owning any kind of business is lack of money. This, of course, also applies to the business you operate through a franchise. In fact, the amount of money needed will usually be more than the cash outlay you could get by with in starting your own business on a small scale. There are several things you will be required to pay for, including a franchise fee.

How much will a franchise fee cost? The answer depends on several conditions. In what type of business are you interested? Where do you wish to locate? Will you operate alone or with a partner?

The cash requirements of franchising vary as widely as the variety of businesses available. You can invest anywhere from a few hundred dollars to over $300,000. A look at the following franchise fees will give you an idea of the wide choice the beginning business person has.

FRANCHISE	FEE
Bix-It, process furniture stripping	$5,000
Kinney Rent-A-Car	$15,000
Lawn-A-Mat, automated lawn treatment	$16,500
Domesticare, home cleaning	$1,500

When you have made this initial investment, what does your franchise fee buy for you? As with every business, there is no single formula which can be applied to every situation. The terms "cash required," "investment," "initial cash requirement," can mean different things in different companies. Sometimes "total investment" includes training and start-up aids and promotions; sometimes not.

Basically you are buying a trade-marked name and qualified help in getting started. Practically all successful franchising programs contain these basic benefits:

1. A legal contract—in which the relationship between you and the parent company is spelled out in detail.

2. Advertising and promotion—which the parent company conducts, including displays, commercials, direct mail material, ads, and other publicity and sales aids.

3. Continuing assistance—from the parent company such as information on new products and merchandising techniques, periodic financial reviews, and advice on special problems.

4. Territory, site and space—are often selected by the parent company in a promising marketing area.

Franchise fees alone, however, don't tell the entire story, and you can't judge the cost of a franchise program without first examining other financial obligations. With some companies, for instance, there will be added costs of equipment and supplies, either purchased or rented. The Better Business Bureau warns against franchisors who "milk" their franchisees by requiring that they buy exclusively from the parent company at inflated prices. Then, too, the company you choose may charge for tax and accounting services, or you may be expected to pay a percentage of your gross for a national advertising campaign.

In determining total costs, check every aspect of the deal and don't forget about *additional franchise charges.* Because perpetuating their name before the public is a big part of the franchise business, many companies charge a royalty or service fee or expect an advertising contribution. These are usually payable monthly or weekly and are based on a specified percentage of sales receipts.

Although some franchisors include training in the franchise fee, others do not. Tuition, room, board, and transportation must be paid by the franchisee as well as the costs of regional workshops and seminars later on. You should also check on the cost of a zoning license for your operation.

One all important question you'll want answered is *how much income you can expect* from the franchise of your choice. Since you will be your own boss, this will be largely determined by your own efforts. The more time and money you invest the greater the return you are likely to have.

A legitimate franchise company will be as concerned about your profit picture as you are. Most will give you a realistic estimate of the amount of money you will need to get going and will set exact standards to determine whether or not you can handle the financial burden. However, no ethical franchisor will specify how much money could be made with how much effort—as you will discover when you start looking into franchises. Many state laws prohibit this kind of "forcasting." However, just to give you an idea of the kind of return you can expect, later in this chapter we will examine the progress of a ServiceMaster franchisee.

Together with the establishment of a substantial income, *Profiting on resale* is another factor which must be taken into account when buying a franchise. You'll want to know what happens if you ever wish to sell out.

Usually you won't encounter any difficulty in selling a successful franchise at a profit. All the risks of opening and getting started have been taken and the public has shown that it will support the business. However, the franchisor will reserve the right to approve a new purchaser, understandably to control quality as well as to protect his image—both vital factors to the success of his franchise.

FINDING THE RIGHT FRANCHISE
BUSINESS FOR YOU

Just as in any independent operation, it is important in a franchise that you find the business that is right for you. One that you like and are capable of operating successfully.

According to a recent survey, the most outstanding successes were noted in franchises with well established brand names whose dealers had a background of operating and managing a business when they entered franchising. However, franchise owners come from all kinds of backgrounds and represent every social and economic beat of life. Many people in franchise businesses were not skilled in the particular field they entered. However, since most legitimate franchisors offer step-by-step training and careful supervision in the early stages, enthusiasm and hard work have brought them big profits.

Still, finding the right opportunity is never easy. It takes time and effort to investigate opportunities. Look about you. Do you see a service or product that excites your interest and enthusiasm? One of the best techniques for checking is to talk to a dealer about his franchise. What are the prospects of an ample income. Is the parent company stable and well recognized? Can you work comfortably within the framework of the company formula? Is the investment within your reach? Will you get help in financing from the parent company or must you go elsewhere?

Once you discover the franchise in which you think you can succeed, ask the franchisor for a copy of his franchise contract. Study it and show it to your lawyer. Only in this way can you know in advance if there are parts of this particular business that you will find difficult or impossible to fulfill.

There are many sources available for assisting you to learn about specific franchisors. *Where do you find franchise listings?* The latest information on opportunities can often be found in the business opportunities column of your newspaper. *The New York Times* and

The Wall Street Journal regularly run pages of advertising listing franchise opportunities. (See particularly *The New York Times* business section on Sunday; *The Wall Street Journal* on Wednesday.) By answering newspaper ads you will receive the kind of information you will need to have about individual companies.

Another source are the franchise shows. These are exhibits by franchisors which are held annually in every part of the country. Big city newspapers often advertise these as "Part-time Income" shows or "Start Your Own Business" expositions.

Your library can also be a helpful source of information in this area. Along with other material you might wish to see on franchise opportunities, is the *Franchise Directory* which is distributed annually. Or you might wish to write to the International Franchise Association, 1025 Connecticut St. N.W., Suite 906, Wash. D.C. 20036. This organization limits its membership to companies that subscribe to a code of ethics and therefore is a good indicator of the best in franchising.

After you've found several interesting franchise listings, you will want to check your findings. Suppose for example, that you find an advertisement in *The New York Times* for "Dunkin' Donuts," "Furn-a-Kit Inc.," and "ServiceMaster." Your first step is to mail a postcard to each of these requesting information about their franchise operations. The answers you receive will automatically eliminate the first two for you, since neither of these businesses can be operated from your home. The third, however, ServiceMaster, will fit nicely into a home operation.

Your next step is to seek out a ServiceMaster franchisee and ask him about the business. What does the parent company do for him? Was the training he received sufficient? Was it free? Was he paid to learn? Is he protected from rival franchise companies? How many hours a week does he work? How does he plan for vacations during the year?

These questions answered to your satisfaction, you will want to send for more information from the company. In most cases, this will consist of a personal letter from an executive of the franchise, pamphlets and brochures giving information of its operation, and a preliminary form to be filled in by you, which the company will use to evaluate your qualifications.

If you meet these basic qualifications, in most cases you will be interviewed by a representative of the company. Your application will then be submitted to a committee for routine credit and personal reference checks. If it is approved, you are ready to sign the franchise agreement.

Before you sign, however, be sure you know how to avoid schemes and frauds. In any line of successful endeavor there will always be unscrupulous people who will attempt to take advantage of the opportunity. This is true also of the franchise business. Many fraudulent promoters easily convince their victims that they can achieve financial success as a franchisee. Often they seize the name *franchise* to cloak their operations with a certain degree of acceptability and respectability, when in fact, what they offer is not a true franchise.

Even though you may be dealing with a *real* franchise company, you can't always be assured of their solvency. Some companies have invited law suits by advertising low-priced services, products that they couldn't deliver, by promising impossible net profits, or by accepting a franchisee who couldn't possibly make good in a particular franchise.

The Better Business Bureau warns against signing with companies that rush you for a quick signature. With a legitimate franchise company there will be no high promotional deals to *save* a territory for you.

You must also beware of schemes such as the one in which Charles Linden got "taken." According to his complaint, registered with the Bureau of Consumer Frauds and Protection in New York State, he had invested $24,000 in a stereo-tape-equipment deal. Although he wasn't actually told that he would receive high-quality, high-performance equipment, the promotional literature he received bore photographs of good equipment and implied that this is what he would receive. In reality, however, it turned out to be shoddy merchandise, worth little of what he had paid.

EVALUATING YOUR FRANCHISOR

Once you have decided on a franchise and been accepted as a prospective franchisee, there are several areas that should be gone over with your lawyer (one who is skilled in evaluating business contracts). You must consider not only the franchisor, but his reputation and business record, and his industry. You know best what you want from a franchise. Examine the one of your choice as it relates to your own competence and motivations.

National Better Business Bureau, Inc. has designed the following guidelines to help you in developing background information to lead to an informed decision before commitment.

How to evaluate the company:

1. How long has the firm been in business?
2. Does it have a past record of accomplishment?
3. Are its principals well regarded? Experienced?
4. What is its financial strength?
5. What are its plans for future development?
6. How does it stand with your Better Business Bureau or Chamber of Commerce?
7. How selective is it in choosing franchisees?

How to examine the product:

8. What is the product's quality?
9. Is it a staple, a fad, a luxury item?
10. Is it seasonal?
11. How well is it selling now, and has it sold in the past?
12. Would the franchisee buy it on its merits?
13. Is it priced competitively?
14. Is it packaged attractively?
15. How long has it been on the market?
16. Where is it sold?

How to judge the sales area:

17. Is the territory well defined?
18. Is it exclusive?
19. Is it large enough to offer good sales potential?
20. What are its growth possibilities?
21. What is its income level?
22. Are there fluctuations in income?
23. What is the competition in this area?
24. How are nearby franchisees doing?

How to check the contract

25. Does the contract cover all aspects of the agreement?
26. Does it benefit both parties?
27. Can it be renewed, terminated, transferred?
28. What are the conditions for obtaining a franchise?
29. Under what conditions can the franchise be lost?
30. Is a certain size and type of operation specified?
31. Is there an additional fixed payment each year?
32. Is there a percent of gross sales payment?
33. Must a certain amount of merchandise be purchased? From whom?
34. Is there an annual sales quota?
35. Can the franchisee return merchandise for credit?
36. Can the franchisee engage in other business activities?
37. Is there a franchise fee? Is it equitable?
38. Has your lawyer examined it?

How to evaluate franchisor assistance:

39. Does the franchisor provide continuing assistance?
40. Is there training for franchisees and key employees?
41. Are manuals, sales kits, accounting system supplied?
42. Does the franchisor select store locations? Is there a fee?
43. Does he handle lease arrangements?
44. Does he design store layout and displays?
45. Does he select opening inventory?
46. Does he provide inventory control methods?
47. Does he provide market surveys?
48. Does he help analyze financial statements?
49. Does he provide purchasing guides?
50. Does he help finance equipment?
51. Does he make direct loans to qualified individuals?
52. What assistance with financing is provided?
53. Does he actively promote the product or service?
54. How and where is the product being advertised?
55. What advertising aids does the franchisor provide?

56. What is the franchisee's share of advertising costs?

57. If a well-known personality is involved, does he assist you directly?

Now that we have gone over franchising, in general, let's take a look at two well-paying franchise businesses you can start and run from your home.

FINDING SECURITY WITH SERVICEMASTER

ServiceMaster International, Ltd., is parent to one of the oldest and largest network of franchised professional cleaning businesses in the world. Its licensees, now numbering over 1,000, provide one-step cleaning service to homes, offices, hotels, airlines, shipping lines, buildings, and institutions.

ServiceMaster was founded in 1929 by Marion E. Wade, now board chairman, as a mothproofing service for carpets and furniture. Since that time, the company developed the first on-location carpet-cleaning system, and special materials and methods that enable its licensees to perform 37 services encompassing over 100 interior surfaces.

The first step toward becoming your own boss with a Service-Master franchise is to write or call ServiceMaster International, Ltd., 2300 Warrenville Road, Downers Grove, Illinois 60515, or telephone 312-964-1300. Within a short time your mailman will bring you a large envelope containing a personal recorded message from Richard A. Armstrong, Vice-President and General Manager of the company. The record will tell you what ServiceMaster is and the kind of opportunity it offers. You will also receive a brochure explaining the business and an invitation to make a career with ServiceMaster.

This is exactly what David Kirkby, of Canton, Ohio, did back in 1956 when he turned theory into practice. Starting out in the carpet-remake business (cleaning and laying used carpet), Mr. Kirkby soon realized that he was equal to a bigger challenge. He wanted a business of his own. One in which he could grow, both personally and financially. He'd heard of ServiceMaster. Seen it in operation. His background in carpeting seemed to qualify him uniquely for a franchise. But together with performing the service of cleaning, a ServiceMaster franchise requires direct selling. Would he be able to make sales? Could he get customers?

His fears disappeared when he began the ServiceMaster training program. Having read several ServiceMaster manuals beforehand, he was able to pass, with flying colors, a series of open-book tests. Afterward, he had two weeks of on-the-job training with an already established franchisee. This was followed by still more training. For three days he was instructed at home in bookkeeping procedures, sources of business, and other management matters. He then attended a six-day "Academy of Service" at company headquarters in Downers Grove.

Ready to strike out on his own at last, he was nonetheless accompanied on his first calls by one of the company's regional directors, who showed him how to put the selling theories he had learned into practice.

David Kirkby began his new business cautiously, buying a limited-service franchise for carpet and furniture cleaning. He minimized the cost of his investment by using his car as a vehicle and storing his cleaning equipment in the trunk. Later, he traded the car for a station-wagon, and eventually a panel truck.

An investment of $4,500 purchases the license, training, promotional material, equipment, supplies and tools to allow the new franchise owner to immediately begin his business and create revenue. With hard work, in the first year he should be able to gross at least $25,000 of service sales. His income would be around 60 percent of this amount, approximately $15,000.

Usually for the first few years, the franchisee works from his home. Dave Kirkby found that this, too, helped to minimize his investment since his overhead expenses were almost nil. He was able to operate in this manner until his business began to grow. When it reached a $60,000 gross volume mark, he was obliged to move to an outside location—too many employees cluttering up the house.

Today, markets for ServiceMaster are no longer confined to carpet and furniture cleaning alone. They offer a housewide cleaning program which includes walls and floors, plus a wide range of other in-home services. Through special agreements with home furnishing retailers, thousands of the nation's top stores now offer Service-Master services and home care products. Customers can buy on the installment plan and charge the cost to their store account. A local franchisee provides the service and the products.

A special retail store program also enables the franchisee to act as an inspector for a retail store. He calls on new carpet owners, answers questions on the care of the carpeting and describes the retailer's full service program.

If he so wishes, a franchisee may also offer a post-disaster restoration service. This includes a complete one-step service for cleaning and restoring fire-and-flood damaged property, as well as smoke odor control, furniture refinishing, and carpet reweaving.

Another large market for ServiceMaster is professional building maintenance which serves the growing commercial building maintenance field. A franchisee operating in this field is given special training in servicing buildings, offices, and plants under contract.

David Kirkby's franchise operation encompasses the complete spectrum of ServiceMaster services. Even with a staff of 30-40 employees, he is ever busy and frequently late in getting home for dinner. However, he and his wife, Ruth, still find time to do things together. In pursuit of the latest knowledge research has to offer, they attend annual business and service-oriented seminars, sponsored by ServiceMaster, in various parts of the world. This learning experience has been shared with other ServiceMaster franchisees at luxurious hotels in San Juan, in Florida, and in Europe.

FRANCHISING WITH
GENERAL BUSINESS SERVICES, INC.

General Business Services is a business counseling franchise offering a variety of financial management and tax services to small businessmen across the country. Franchisees operate from their homes as independent business counselors, but deal with other small businessmen as clients exclusively.

To get started with GBS you would follow the same procedure as with any other franchise. After you have gone through the preliminaries of contacting the company, receiving their literature, filling out and returning an evaluation form, you will be contacted by one of their regional directors, who will make himself available to answer all questions regarding requirements and opportunities.

Thus far, the thread of similarity between GBS and other franchise companies is quite evident. Now let's take a close look. GBS has 700-plus franchisees now operating in the United States. Each is his own boss in counseling his clients and is free to charge whatever he feels is appropriate. His income is determined by his own efforts.

His market is the small business men in his area—doctors, independent stores, shops, gas stations, and the like. Among the many services offered is a record-keeping system which every business needs and is required by law to have. He also provides a tax advisory service, prepares income tax returns, and does counseling. Each franchisee also has the choice of offering optional programs such as a collection system, computerized billing service, and a computerized bookkeeping service.

Each territory assigned has enough potential clients to provide an excellent income with only 2 percent-5 percent market penetration. By adding associates, the franchisee can increase the market penetration of his particular area.

To succeed as an Area Director, GBS lists the following as an applicant's three most important qualifications.

1. Real motivation and desire for success.

2. Willingness to work hard and follow the program as planned for all Area Directors.

3. Have great respect for the independent businessman and desire to help him succeed.

To become a GBS Area Director it will cost you $10,500 ($5,250 for an Associate Directorship, where available.) Here's what you get for your investment.

1. An agreement to represent GBS on an exclusive basis in a given territory.

2. Prepaid services which, when sold, return over one-half the initial investment. You keep the entire proceeds of this initial group of sales.

3. Attendance at two separate training courses at GBS training institute in Washington, D.C.

4. Initial on-the-job training and guidance

5. Continued training and guidance as needed, including periodic seminars and group training sessions within your region.

6. Operating and advertising materials to start you off.

7. A $10,000 life insurance policy for a six-months period, after which you have the option to continue the program.

8. An opportunity to participate in group hospitalization.

9. Access to the Lending Library service.

10. The services of a dedicated and trained staff, working to help you develop a prosperous business of your own.

LISTING OTHER "AT-HOME"
FRANCHISE BUSINESSES

I have touched on two franchise businesses which can be carried on in your home. There are many others. Some can be conducted in your home indefinitely, while others can be started at home but will require more room as the business expands and grows.

WW Fleet Lubrication, Inc.
316 State Street
Hackensack, N.J. 07601
—provides truck preventive
maintenance service to
truck operators. Capital
required $16,000.

Edie Adam's Cosmetics,
175 Great Neck Road
Great Neck, New York 11021

Lawn King, Inc.
14 Spielman Rd.
Fairfield, N.J. 07006
—provides automated lawn
care. Total investment
$9,500.

Instant Mobile Powerwash Service, Inc.
117 Main St.
Little Rock, Arkansas 72201
—washes trucks, trailers, fleets—even
buildings. Minimum license fee $2,500.
IMPSmobile truck fully equipped $9,490.

The latest *Franchise Directory* lists all of the top money-makers plus new franchises. It describes each one and lists the approximate investment required. Ask for it at your library, or write Pilot Publishers, 347 5th Avenue, New York, N.Y. 10016. Enclose $2.

7

How to Make Money in Mail-Order

For many people, mail-order has been a gateway to success, and it can be for you too. It takes relatively little capital to start a mail-order business and it is easily operated from your home, whether that be in New York, Hawaii, or Waco, Texas. You can start by selling an inexpensive article from a newspaper or magazine ad, or you can sell a product you manufacture on your own. Big money has been made from both methods.

However, just as in any business, to be successful in mail-order, you need a good basic knowledge of business know-how. You must know management and record-keeping techniques, how to promote ideas, and particularly how to make your product available to the right people at the right time. A study of some of the big money-makers in the mail-order business can be of great help.

LEARNING FROM THE BIG MONEY-MAKERS

Although the Sears, Roebuck catalog business is probably the biggest thing in mail-order, in both sales and size, there is plenty of room for the small business person. Do you have imagination? Can you spot a bargain? Are you a pretty good judge of what the public will buy and what it won't? Can you predict the "big sellers" of tomorrow? If your answer is yes, and you are willing to work hard and persistently, you can make yourself a small fortune in mail order.

The secret of Hugh Clay Paulk's fantastic rise in the world of mail-order was timing and ingenuity. Perhaps you remember the man who, right after World War II, bought 50,000 surplus parachutes from the government and made a fortune selling them by mail at $13.95 a chute. He advertised them, not as something with which to jump from a plane, but as nylon cloth for sewing dresses, shirts, draperies, and curtains. His sense of timing and his imagination brought him $800,000 worth of orders from enthusiastic home-makers throughout the country.

Another mail-order "first" that netted its innovator thousands of dollars was a small Mexican burro. Remarkably, Max Adler of Spencer Gifts was able to sell live burros by mail! People boutht them for their children, for a novelty, or as a pet. Again, Max Adler was a perfect example of being at the right place at the right time with a "product" that captured the imagination of consumers.

Even selling rubber stamps can put you in business. Len Carlson of Sunset House invested his few-hundred dollars savings in this old mail-order standby and launched one of the business "biggies" of the mail-order world. He recently sold his company for millions of dollars.

KNOWING ALL ABOUT MAIL-ORDER

The three stories mentioned recount the success of highly prosperous mail-order operations, those who found a pot of gold at the end of the rainbow. But for every big money-maker there are hundreds of small failures. Before you enter into any action you should learn all you can about the various aspects of the mail-order business.

A strong product, advertisements with pull—these are the two chief ingredients of successful mail-order. Yet even possessing these, there is no magic formula for mail-order that will guarantee success.

The way mail-order works is simple. For instance, Pete Watkins sells a new type nutcracker by mail. He buys them in 12 dozen lots for $65.65 a dozen and sells them at a retail price of $9.95 each, making a profit of $4.48 on each one, minus advertising and mailing costs.

You can advertise your product through newspapers and maga-zines, as Pete does, or you may use direct mail to reach potential customers. They, in turn, will send orders to you through the mail, enclosing a check or money-order, together with your filled-out coupon. Upon receipt of the order, you then ship your merchandise to them. It's that easy.

Your mail-order item can be a product you manufacture yourself, or you can buy something wholesale from a supplier and sell it at a retail price to your customer. In some cases, your supplier will even ship the merchandise directly to your customer. This is called *"drop-ship"* and saves you the trouble of stocking and packaging the merchandise you sell.

Suppose you receive an order and a check for a novelty item, perhaps a fancy mirror, which sells at a retail price of $3. You address a mailing label for your customer, enclose it with a check (the amount you pay at your lower wholesale rate) and mail it to your supplier. He will then place your label on his shipping carton and mail the mirror to your customer.

BEFORE YOU START YOUR MAIL-ORDER BUSINESS

The opportunities in mail-order have made some people million-aires almost overnight, especially those people who developed and sold their own products, or who found a way to put an already established product to some new use. You can begin without your own product, or new idea, however, and it's really best to do so. Learn the business first, with an established product. For any beginner it can be a hobby, a part-time activity, or a full-time business venture. You can work your own hours—daily, evenings, any time you choose, and you don't come face to face with your customers. Your initial investment can range anywhere from a few dollars to thousands of dollars, depending on the scope of your first venture.

The least expensive and safest way to start your mail-order selling is to buy a quantity of some inexpensive but popular item you find in a supplier's catalog. The quantity does not have to be large, but be careful! There are a few questionable mail-order suppliers. Before you invest even the smallest amount of money, check the reliability of your tentative supplier with your local Better Business Bureau.

It is also wise to:

1. Read and understand the terms of any contract or agreement you are asked to sign.

2. Demand proof of earnings claims, and check by direct contact those whose earnings are quoted.

3. Before staking your reputation on the worth of a product, check evidence of its performance.

The surest way to get off the ground in mail-order is to start with a single product, or a group of closely related products. Jed Michaels began by selling home fire extinguishers at $3.98 each. Since his cost was $1.45 per unit, he made a $2.53 profit on each one he sold and was soon able to offer his customers other products for the home.

Because your product is the key to success or failure, it is essential that you choose carefully. Often an exciting new item becomes quite ordinary within a short time because more advertisers offer it for sale than the market can support. With all this competition then, where do you find a product that will pull in sales?

Unless you manufacture your own product, you must buy from a supplier, often the manufacturer. Names of manufacturers can be found at your library in trade directories such as *Thomas's Register of American Manufacturers* and *McRae's Blue Book.* However, many of these manufacturers are wholesalers and will not sell to small mail-order concerns. Then it is necessary to find small manufacturers or middlemen who are interested in handling small accounts, and who can provide adequate sources of supply.

An easier way to choose a product is to check the mail-order directories at your library. For example, the *Decorative Accessory Buyers Directory,* published by Geyer-McAllister Publishing Company, gives you a wide selection of items to buy and tells you where to send for them.

Mail-Order Business Directory, by B. Klein and Company, New York, is another complete guide to the mail-order market. It is divided according to states, for example:

ARIZONA

*OWL MAIL ORDER CO.   WILLCOX
P.O. Box 220, 281 W. Malley   85643
   Mrs. Clara Holland - General
   merchandise.

ARKANSAS

WILCO SPECIALTY CO.   BROOKLAND
Box 93, Route 1   72471
   Clarence B. Willey - Household
   and specialty items.

BLUE ACRES GIFT SHOP
   George Walker - Gifts,
housewares, Ozark crafts.

EUREKA SPRINGS
72632

MILES MOUNTAIR
   General merchandise

EUREKA SPRINGS
72632

GURDON GARDEN TOOLS
Box 22-P
   Garden tools and supplies

GURDON
71743

CALIFORNIA

EL MOLINO MILLS
3060 W. Valley Blvd.
   E.L. Vandercook - Specialty flours
bread mixes, cookies, health foods.

ALHAMBRA
91803

HARMON HOLDERS
1107 - 9th St.
   Burl Harmon - Telephone accessories,
toothpick dispensers (manufacturer -
drop-ship wholesale).

ALHAMBRA
91801

KRUGER CORP.
Kruger Bldg. - Box E51
   General merchandise.

ALHAMBRA

UNIVERSE CO.
Box 666
   Heinz W. Kirchner - General
merchandise, novelties, gifts,
sporting goods.

ALTADENA
91001

CALIFORNIA CRAFTS SUPPLY
531 E. Central Pk.
   Crafts supplies.

ANAHEIM
92802

How much money can you make with mail-order? The answer is not easily predicted. Come up with a "hot" new product and you may become a millionaire overnight. Start on a shoestring, adding new products as you go, and you can also pyramid your profits. There are one-man operations earning anywhere from a few dollars to $4 thousand a month. The range of products and services for sale is almost unlimited.

Suppose you buy 1 dozen "drinking birds" from a supplier for $7.80 and sell them to your customers at a retail price of $1.50 each.

You take in $18, of which you keep $10.20. Great? Yes, but you must not forget the cost of advertisements, postage, wrapping materials, and any other costs involved in this particular item. Naturally these costs will vary with different products.

The total cost of your mail-order merchandise will be the sum of the cost of your product delivered to the purchaser, and your advertising cost-per-order. To obtain the advertising cost-per-order divide the total cost of your advertising by the number of orders the advertising produces. For example, if a $50 ad produces 100 orders, the cost-per-order is 50¢.

Many beginners in the mail-order business start out by selling through a catalog. This can be one you produce yourself (Montgomery Ward started with a one-sheet catalog), advertising your own products, or you can buy a minimum number of catalogs (500-100) from a catalog house at 10 to 15 cents apiece. Postage to mail these out to your list of customers, brings the price up to about 25 ¢ each, or $250 per thousand.

When the orders start coming in, you merely pay the catalog house the wholesale price for each item, enclose labels addressed to your customers, and the merchandise will be drop-shipped to them. Your profit margin is usually 40 percent to 50 percent, which is somewhat less than it would be on a single item you produced yourself, or bought from a supplier. However, you have the advantage of offering an expert selection of merchandise which has been tested for its ability to sell.

To get started with a catalog, check out several houses, comparing product lines and mark-up offered and cost of the catalogs.

Gaylord's	Spencer Gifts, Inc.
North Summer Street	850 Spencer Blvd.
North Adams, Mass. 01247	Atlantic City, N.J. 08464
Fingerhut Products	Sunset House Distributing Corp.
3104 W. Lake Street	3485 S. La Cienega Blvd.
Minneapolis, Minn. 55416	Los Angeles, Calif. 90016
Mail Order Associates	Western Stationery Company
Montvale, N.J. 07654	242 Lindsey Bldg.,
	Topeka, Kansas

HOW TO SELECT THE RIGHT PRODUCT

Selecting the right product is the most important decision you, as a mail-order beginner, will have to decide. No one can make the decision for you or tell you what product or service will reap the biggest profits. In general, mail-order selling falls into these three categories:

1. Merchandise—this includes manufactured novelties, jewelry, foodstuffs, clothing, stationery, and such.
2. Information—this includes educational literature and "how-to" subjects.
3. Services—this includes any service which you can offer, such as typing, reweaving, and chair-caning.

A good bet for a positive start in the mail-order business is a product that is different from those you see on counters in department stores and gift shops. For example, Greg Dunne discovered small board games in a wholesale catalog. He ordered some and started selling the games for use in a car while traveling. He paid 75¢ for each game and sold it for $1.50, thereby permitting himself a good margin for mailing expenses and profit. His product also qualified for three other pluses for profit in mail-order. It was easy to handle. It withstood competition and provided opportunity for repeat sales. And the supplier offered a secure source of supply.

Perhaps that sounds like a difficult order to fill, but let's take a look at the mail-order market. Who will buy your merchandise through the mail?

Hobbyists come to mind first. They are always looking for do-it-yourself projects, kits or material and ideas for pursuing their craft or collection. Another ready market is made up of persons seeking gift items for birthdays, graduations, weddings, and other occasions. Still another group are those individuals who would rather shop by mail than go out into the bad weather and crowded stores, and those compelled to shop by mail because of rural living, age, or illness. There are also those who believe that because goods can be marketed by mail with lower service costs, they can buy less expensively than in a retail store.

Because your selection of merchandise is one of the most important principles in mail-order selling, you would be wise to test your product before you invest heavily in the promotion of it. You can give it a market test inexpensively by placing an ad in your local newspaper, or placing it in a local retail store.

Mark Gabin, a welder, whose small mail-order business supplements his regular income by about $150 a week, always trys to find an appropriate outlet for his product. For instance, because his latest product is a new type of baby carrier, he thought it might sell well in a children's clothing store. For an idea of its general sales appeal, he asked the owner to take a few samples on consignment. They were sold within the week.

For a test of the product's ability to sell through advertising media alone, he placed an ad in a local shopper's guide, using the same copy, photo, and dimensions he planned to use later in his national advertising. The ad brought orders for 17 carriers and several inquiries. More than enough, Mark felt, to warrant placing an ad in *American Baby* magazine.

The needs of a mail-order business are relatively small at the start. Keep them that way until your business begins to expand. It's not necessary to lay in excess supplies, or to invest in big expensive inventories, but it is important that you have lines of supply open. Suppose your test program proves you have a "hot" item and you decide to go ahead with a big advertising schedule. You'll want to be sure that you have unlimited access to the merchandise when orders begin rolling in. Aside from this, you will be wise if you use your money where it will accomplish most—in promoting your mail-order product, rather than in advance payment for stock.

Next in importance to the product itself is the advertising campaign. Those who make money with their product present a mail-order ad that catches the eye. It is concise, yet a complete sales pitch. It is attractive, easily understood, and convincing. But that's not all. The important thing is to find a readership that matches your product.

As a beginner you can use flyers, brochures, samples, and local advertising to promote the sale of your product. However, once it starts showing a substantial profit, you will want to begin advertising in national publications.

Magazine ad rates are based largely on circulation, meaning the more readers a publication has, the higher its rates. But don't let this be the basis of your selection. Mail-order doesn't work that way. For example, in a general interest magazine, your ad for a $150 teak-wood table from India, would be seen by thousands of readers. But only a small percentage would be interested. In a woman's magazine, the number of readers might be smaller, but the percentage of response would probably be higher. In a home decorating type magazine, the readership would be still smaller, but the percentage of response would be highest of all.

Now we can break that down even further. For instance, an ad in *American Home,* a magazine aimed primarily at families with a modest income, would probably not bring the same response as an ad in *House Beautiful,* a magazine read by a more affluent group who would be better able to afford your table.

Before placing an ad you might check *Standard, Rate and Data,* a directory found in most libraries. It lists all the publications in the United States and indicates their circulation and ad rates. You can also look over the ads in current magazines. Most of these publications will send you rate cards on request.

Your local newspaper and civic publications, as well as some national publications, can be a tremendous help in your advertising campaign. They often give free space to interesting new or unusual products. In order to qualify for this type of free promotion, your product must be something new and different, or you must have a new angle in your selling method.

In his hometown, a young man received a full-page spread in the local paper, describing how mail-order paid his way through college. His product was a simple automobile-sun-glass-holder. But think of the hundreds of dollars of free advertising!

If you don't have someone to write such a story for you, prepare one yourself. In a national magazine or newspaper you can hope for about two paragraphs. Therefore your copy must be informative and interesting, and must pinpoint newsworthy details. Be sure to include your mailing address, name and price of your product, instructions for ordering, and any special features. This brief description of your item should be written up exactly as you would like to have it presented, and should contain no more than about 22 words.

Type, double-spaced on standard 8½″ x 11″ typewriter paper, leaving a wide margin all around. Take your original copy to a typing and mimeograph service, where for about $3.95 you will be able to have 100 neat, clear copies made. Send a copy to as many publications as you are able to afford.

It would also be helpful to include a photo of the product. Most publications will accept glossy, black and white prints. In ordering your prints, seek out a photographic shop that specializes in quantity processing. For about $5 you should be able to get 100 prints, four 4" x 5", on a single 8" x 10" sheet.

Examples of magazines that accept such newsworthy ads are:

Mothers-To-Be/American Baby, 10 E. 52nd Street, New York, N.Y. 10021

The American Home, 641 Lexington Ave., New York, N.Y. 10022

Argosy, 205 E. 42nd Street, New York, N.Y. 10017

Family Circle, 488 Madison Ave., New York, N.Y. 10022

Mechanix Illustrated, One Astor Plaza, New York, N.Y. 10036

There are hundreds of others. Check them out in the periodical department of your library.

EQUIPMENT YOU WILL NEED

Your needs as a new mail-order operator will be relatively few at the start. Since all your business will be transacted by mail, your customers or suppliers won't even see your place of operation. Therefore, there is no need to set up an impressive looking office with expensive furnishings. It is more important that you use your money for advertising purposes and be ready for business when orders start coming in.

In the beginning, investment in equipment should be kept low. Along with other regular office materials, you probably already have a desk and chair in your home which can be used in your business. If not, any working table will do for awhile.

The most essential office requirement is a typewriter, but it need not be a new one and can be a standard or portable make. Good typewriters are often advertised for as little as $35 in the miscellaneous-for-sale column of your newspaper. Or you can sometimes pick up a good machine at an auction or garage sale. If you don't already own a machine and don't want to buy one, consider renting one as a temporary measure.

Can you type? If not, learning to type is another must. It's quite simple and you can easily teach yourself with a "how-to" manual, or check your local high school for evening classes, or a business school in your area.

Since your only contact with potential customers is through the mail, your most specific need is your choice of stationery and use of a letterhead. Choose a good quality paper with a neat-appearing letterhead. In the beginning you can order 100-500 letterheads, with envelopes to match, from your printer for a few dollars. As business increases, you can save money by ordering larger quantities at one time, thereby saving the cost of repeated type-setting. Your order forms too, should be printed on good paper which will take either pencil or ink without blurring and smudging.

Shipping labels for parcel post shipping are also a necessary investment. The customer's name and address should be neatly typed rather than written in long-hand. And when your venture shows signs of sustained life, a letterhead for these should be considered, as well as a couple of postal scales—one for letter mail, the other for parcel post.

Needless to say, even as you place your first ad and accept your first order, you will find need for a filing system and storage provision for supplies. If you have a filing cabinet in your home, clear out one or two drawers to use in your mail-order business. If not, make-shift files will do at the start. Press shoe boxes into use, loose-leaf binders, or corrugated boxes. As the business develops and expands more permanent equipment can be obtained. The important thing is to keep everything together and in its own place, so that you can find a letter or an order blank when you need it, without chasing all about the house.

The majority of mail-order beginners probably own cars and use them for trips to the post, freight, or express office. If your merchandise is too heavy or too large to transport by passenger car, a small utility trailer can be made quite easily.

Should you not have access to an automobile, your local postman can be of great help. Usually a rural carrier will pick up packages and deliver them to the post office for mailing for you. Or if, like an invalid friend of mine, you have a friendly postman who uses a vehicle in his mail delivery, you might ask him to perform this service for you. Check with the Superintendent of Mails at your post office to learn what accommodations can be arranged.

Building and maintaining your list of prospects are two of the most important operations in mail-order selling. The orders and inquiries you receive in answer to your first advertising will be the beginning of a list of high-potential future customers.

However, an inaccurate list can nullify an otherwise excellent campaign. Since people in the United States are constantly on the move from place to place seeking employment or being transferred, it is a good business practice to keep your lists current and accurate.

The post office will correct mailing lists for you, if individual names and old addresses are submitted on cards, at the rate of 5 cents per card, one name to each card. You can also request to be notified if mail is forwarded (1st, 3rd, and 4th class) or use the endorsements "Return Postage Guaranteed," or "Forwarding and Return Postage Guaranteed." However, a small fee is charged for these services, so check with your post office.

Another way to build your mail-order list is to buy or rent one.

However, not just any old list will do. As with any other advertising medium, direct mail has to be used in such a way that the material reaches the market toward which it is aimed. List houses can furnish names and addresses of prospects for any product. They are purchased at so much per name or per thousand; the more selective the list is, the higher the cost per name. Lists are always accurate when supplied, though there is no guarantee that they will remain so.

A complete current source of lists is available *free* from your SBA field Office or from the Small Business Administration, Washington, D.C. 20416. Ask for *Small Business Bibliography #29, National Mailing-list Houses.*

This is a sample of what you will receive:

ADAMS LETTER SERVICE, INC., 222 North Rockton Ave., Rockford, Ill., 61103.

Occupant lists for northern Illinois, Wisconsin, western Iowa. Local lists executive and clubs. Offset printing, addressographing, bindery, mailing.

AD-MAIL & ASSOCIATES, INC., 135 West Court St., Kankakee, Ill., 60901.

Occupant maps, special VIP list. Bulk literature distribution, addressing, mailing, catalog collation.

ADVERTISING DISTRIBUTORS OF WASHINGTON, 1726 17th St., NE., Washington, D.C., 20002.

Occupant lists of Washington, D.C. Mailing service, list maintenance, IBM and Speedaumat addressing.

ASSOCIATED LETTER SERVICE, 369 Robert St., St. Paul, Minn., 55101.

Local lists. Offset printing, multigraphing, mimeographing, folding, binery, and mailing services.

BUSINESS EXTENSION BUREAU OF HOUSTON, INC., 719 Anita or Post Office Box 66273, Houston, Tex., 77006.

Occupational, executive, and residential lists of Texas. Special Houston lists compiled daily. Complete mailing service.

CLEVELAND LETTER SERVICE, INC., 740 West Superior Ave., Cleveland, Ohio, 44113.

Professional and occupational, country club membership, occupant, and local lists. Duplicating, printing, personalized letters, and bindery.

CREATIVE MAILING SERVICE, INC., 1100 Stewart Ave., Garden City, N.Y., 11040.

National lists of business firms by financial ratings, general and specific businesses (catalog of lists by SIC numbers available). Geographical selections. Lists of realtors, attorneys, executives, accountants, and newly promoted executives.

EFFECTIVE LETTERS (PTY), LTD., Post Office Box 4564, Johannesburg, South Africa.

Car owners, farmers, teachers, company directors, professional groups, commercial and industrial classifications. Reply-O-Letters (under license).

THE E-Z ADDRESSING SERVICE, INC., 83 Washington St., New York, N.Y., 10006.

Specialists in financial lists, such as brokers, banks, investment advisers, security traders, etc. Complete addressing and mailing.

HARRIS PUBLICATIONS, 224 Market St., Newark, N.J., 07102.

42-page catalog of lists by SIC number. Addressing and automated mailing service. Dependable list maintenance.

JOE OTT ADVERTISING, 422 North Water St., Milwaukee, Wis., 53202.

Head of household in families in Milwaukee County and suburbs. Brides and grooms, widows, widowers, union workers, wealthy individuals, manufacturers, and professional people in Wisconsin. Catalog sheets, mailers, artwork and printing, lithographing, mailing.

LEWIS ADVERTISING CO., INC., 6 South Greene St., Baltimore, Md., 21201.

20,000 classifications for United States Income, executive, and specialized lists. Occupant mailing for Maryland. Direct-mail advertising, addressing, mailing, market research.

MAILMASTERS, INC., 460 Nordhoff Place, Englewood, N.J. 07631.

Residents lists, New Jersey. Automated addressing, all other mail services.

MARGIE FARMER LETTER SHOP, 101B Builders Exchange Bldg., Minneapolis, Minn., 55402.

Minneapolis Loop offices. Mimeographing, multilithing, folding, mailing, addressing, and bindery.

MARKET COMPILATION & RESEARCH BUREAU, 10561 Chandler Blvd., North Hollywood, Cal. 91601.

Business, consumer, occupational lists, occupant and credit prospect lists, and market research data. Mailing list compiler in excess of 1,500,000 names per week. Occupant coverage Western States, 44-page catalog. Marketing maps, research reports, and case histories.

NATIONAL BUSINESS LISTS, INC., 162 North Franklin St., Chicago, Ill., 60606.

Over 3,500,000 business firms on magnetic tape by SIC number. 42-page Marketing Guide with detailed list of statistics. Addressing only.

PROMOTION MAIL ASSOCIATES, INC., 120 Smith St., Farmingdale, N.Y. 11735.

Although keeping records is an important part of any business, it is particularly necessary in mail-order. Keeping special records will add to your profit, while neglecting to do so may cause your business to fail. Your records should include a file on customers, prospects, purchase data, correspondence, finances, and advertising.

The financial records discussed in Chapter 11 apply to mail-order as well as any other business. But let's take a look at these others.

Customers and Prospects:

These names can be filed alphabetically, last name first, on 3" x 5" index cards. Address, date, whether customer or prospect, and number of mailings should be noted. Also who or what led you to them and any personal information you may have on them. Both front and back of card can be used as in example.
Front of card

Smith, John			Customer
4112 Parker Ave.,			Referred by:
Colleen, W. Vir. 44709			Lloyd Smith
Date	1/23/73	4/12/73	8/6/73
Item	Pipe	chess set	candle kit

Back of card

Widowed invalid
Grandfather of two young girls about 4-8

Purchase data:

A file of all purchased products should be kept in order to determine costs. This gives you a type of continuing inventory. Use a card for each item, number and date purchased, number and date sold, and number on hand (see example). This reduces the chance you will run out of stock and gives you some idea of your turnover. If an item is moving slowly, it will be easy to spot and can be discontinued.

Item-Dog collar		Date purchased-2/6/73
Co.-Stow & Sons		No. purchased-60
Date sold	No. sold	No. on hand
Feb. 24	10	50
Feb. 28	12	38
Feb. 29	3	35
Mar. 2	8	27

Correspondence:

All letters should be kept. It might be wise to keep letters from customers and supply houses in separate files.

Advertising:

Many mail-order operators "key" their advertisements. This is merely a system of symbols which provides the operator with the source of all inquiries and orders. It is easy then to determine which methods of advertising are the most far reaching and the most effective for your product. The symbol can be a name change, an address variation, the use of a room number, department or desk number. Most operators find they get the best results when they keep the "key" as part of their address.

For example, suppose you insert an ad for an item in several publications. In one you would list your firm name, The William *S.* Bently Company; in another it would read, The William *T.* Bently Company; in yet another, The William *U.* Bently Company. Or you might prefer an address variation like *R*-420 Grand Street; *S*-420 Grand Street; *T*-420 Grand Street.

Keeping a record of your key advertising tells you which publications bring the most replies. Furthermore, such figures help you determine your cost per customer, per inquiry, or per dollar of sales. (See example.)

Key	Magazine	Issue	Ad Size	Cost	Item
R-420	Trader	June	¼ page	$100	ashtray
Wm. U	Golf	Aug.	4 line	30	"

KNOW THE RULES THAT REGULATE
THE MAIL-ORDER BUSINESS

Just as in any other venture, there are rules and regulations applicable to mail-order. Because you work from your home, you may not encounter all the problems your neighborhood grocer does. Nonetheless, it is wise to become acquainted with the various federal, state, and local laws.

Licenses and permits:

No permit or license is required by the Federal Government with respect to operating a mail-order business. However, occupational taxes are levied on the selling or retailing of certain items by some states. It would be best to check with your state or local officials to make sure this rule doesn't apply to your product.

Use of a personal or "firm" name:

Many mail-order operators make use of a firm name in their business, while others prefer to use their own name and mailing address. A personal name with home address can often inspire confidence in the customer, since most people like to deal with individuals. However, in order to sort personal mail from business mail, you might use a business title, such as *The John G. Hartville Company,* or *Hartville Mail-Order Company.*

Should you wish to use a name other than your own, check with your city clerk to learn what procedure is required by your state. Some states allow a company name even though the business is a one-man operation. Other states require that several partners control the business before a company name can be used. In some states, it is only necessary to register the business name with your city officials. Other states require you to register the name at your City Hall and also with the Secretary of State. Both procedures can be accomplished for a small fee.

Business address:

Some mail-order businesses use a business address, such as a post-office box. But for a beginner this is quite impersonal and not so effective as a street address in building relationships.

Glena Morrison, a young mother and a beginner in the mail-order game, feels that one of the big advantages of the mail-order business is that she can conduct the whole operation from her home. Using a business mailing address would defeat this purpose, since she would be constantly running to the post office. To avoid confusion between her personal and business mail, her advertising reads:

G.M. Morrison Co.
15306 Archdale Ave.,
Detroit, Michigan

On the other hand, Jim Reynolds, who has been in mail-order for several years, finds that a post-office box best suits his purpose. Not only does Jim live in a residential area with business zoning restrictions, but his home number, 222 Pony Tail Lane, hardly lends itself to a business address.

Postal rules and regulations:

One area in which the mail-order operator must be well versed is that of rules and regulations pertaining to the use of the mails. Fraudulent use of the mails is quite serious and it behooves the beginner to make sure he conducts his business with the utmost integrity. *Do not* make claims for your product which may be misleading. It can lead to loss of mailing privileges, and prosecution.

As a mail user, you are somewhat familiar with post office procedure. But let's review some facts. For example, there are various classes of mail.

1st Class—letters and other sealed materials. This mail will be forwarded if a new address is furnished. If a return address is provided undelivered mail will be returned. It is the most expensive class.

2nd Class—newspapers and magazines with notice of 2nd class entry.

3rd Class—miscellaneous printed matter and merchandise weighing 8 ounces or less. This class is your best selection for unsealed printed matter. Bulk mailing rates can be used. This is the least expensive class and used by most mail-order operators.

4th Class—parcel post mail and includes all parcels over 8 ounces in weight.

Book Mailings—this is a preferential rate given to packages containing books, and must be so marked.

To get acquainted with other mailing regulations ask at your local post office for guidance. You might also wish to subscribe to one or more of the postal publications mentioned further on.

Other Federal Laws:

In addition to abiding by post office regulations, mail-order business is subject to rulings of various other federal laws.

Federal Food, Drug and Cosmetics Act:

Standards of purity and content, and warnings involving dosage have been set and must be followed. Check with the FDA, Washington, D.C. 20250.

Federal Trade Commission

Advertisements which are misleading are a violation, and the Commission can prosecute the seller.

Federal Tax Commission:

Federal excise taxes are imposed on leather goods, jewelry, and cosmetics. Many states have sales taxes added to the retail price. They are applicable to merchandise sold in the state. Items sold outside the state are not usually included. Check with your State Tax Commission.

Your price list should indicate whether such taxes are included in your quoted price, or are to be added.

LIST OF PUBLICATIONS TO HELP
YOU GET STARTED

In this chapter, I have tried to give you a general rundown of the mail-order business. However, these pages merely provide guideposts.

You will also have to do some investigating and study on your own. The following list of publications should help you get started.

Government publications:

The following may be ordered from the Superintendent of Documents, U.S. Government Printing Office, Washington, D.C. 20402

> *Selling by Mail Order,* SBB #3, Free.
>
> *National Mailing List Houses,* SBB #29, Free.
>
> *Starting and Managing a Small Duplicating and Mailing Service,* S&M #8, 35¢

The U.S. Postal Service offers publications which supply general information on post office services, rates, and various office sizes. Some of those listed below are available in large post offices and local libraries.

> *International Mail* contains detailed information about postage rates, services available, prohibitions, import restrictions, and other conditions governing mail to other countries. $2.50.
>
> *Postal Bulletin* is issued weekly with supplementary issues. It covers changes in regulations, new developments and handling of mail. $6 a year.
>
> *Instruction for Mailers* contains regulations and procedures for public use. $3.
>
> *National Zip Code Directory* lists Zip Code for every mailing address in the United States. $10.

Non-Government Publications:

The following is a list of books, directories, and magazines which will be helpful to you in your new mail-order business. Most are available at your library.

> *How To Win Success in the Mail Order Business.* by Arco Publishing Company, Inc.—presents the basic principles and techniques of mail-order including organization, buying, merchandising, sales promotions, financing and legal requirements.
>
> *Direct Mail and Mail Order Handbook,* by Cartnell Corporation.
>
> *How To Start and Operate a Mail Order Business,* by J.L. Simon, McGraw Hill Book Company, Inc.
>
> *How I Made $1,000,000.00 in Mail Order.,* by E. Joseph Cossman, Prentice-Hall, Inc.

Salesman's Complete Model Letter Handbook, by F. Nauheim, Prentice-Hall, Inc.

Successful Direct-Mail Advertising and Selling, by Robert Stone, Prentice-Hall, Inc.

How to Start Your Own Mail Order Business, by Ken Alexander, Stravon Educational Press.

The directories listed below will be helpful to you in locating sources of supply and markets. You will find them in the business reference section of your library.

Mail Order Buyer's Directory, CoStar Enterprises,—lists sources of supply.

Mail Order Business Directory, B. Klein and Co.—lists firm names, lines carried, buyer's name, and other data.

Nationwide Mail Order Buyer's Directory, Machal Corp.—lists mostly drop-ship firms.

Mail-Order Shopping Guide, by Elizabeth Squire, William Morrow and Company.

Some business magazines offer marketing and management information on the various aspects of selling by mail-order. Check out the following in the business periodical section of your library.

Advertising Age, a weekly magazine.

Home Business Digest, a bi-monthly.

Mail Order Income, a quarterly.

Timely Tips Magazine, a monthly.

Income Opportunities, a monthly.

Guide To Earning Extra Income.

Salesman's Opportunity, a monthly.

Should you wish to subscribe to any of these you will find subscription rates and magazine address on the 2nd or 3rd page of each magazine.

Trade associations are usually excellent sources of information. Those listed below deal with some aspect of mail-order and most will send descriptive material of their services and publications upon request.

Associated Third Class Mail Users
1725 K St. N.W.,
Washington, D.C. 20006

Direct Mail Advertising Association
230 Park Ave.
New York, N.Y. 10017

Mail Advertising Service Association International
17th Street, N.W.
Washington, D.C. 20006

8

A Look at Party Planning

Each year men and women are earning handsome profits from the operation of a sales technique that only a few years ago was still in its infancy—party planning. Today the industry is growing rapidly. Literally billions of dollars worth of merchandise are being sold to countless millions who attend party-plan sales demonstrations in the homes of their friends.

MAKING MONEY THE HOUSE-PARTY WAY

Making money the house-party way is like giving a series of parties, and so much fun it's hard to realize that you're actually in a high-income business. So successful has this new system for making money become, that more and more companies are adapting their lines for party-plan selling. Some have deliberately come up with new products just to take advantage of this fast developing sales program, and each year more new companies are being organized to profit from the technique.

You can take your pick of lines. Housewares, clothing, cosmetics, jewelry, kitchen utensils, toys, wigs, and many other products—all are marketed at home parties. Some are offered by the largest and most famous firms in the country.

Who makes money from parties? Although the party-plan system is heavily weighted in favor of women, it is fast gaining advocates among men. A mother or father of small children, with no previous experience, can boost the family income without leaving home or neglecting the family. Few opportunities prove more rewarding or more pleasant. With party selling you can make a good profit and, in most cases, without any investment, collecting, or delivering on your part.

Some women have the neighbors in for mid-morning coffee, or a get-together in the afternoon while the children are still in school, or in the evening when she has completed her daily chores. Men usually fit party-planning into their schedules as a spare-time or full-time business. Then, too, many couples have succeeded in building highly lucrative husband-wife team enterprises.

With most party plans, in addition to regular sales income, you can earn extra cash bonuses, special premium awards, and valuable contest prizes. Successful demonstrators can become organizers, recruiters, and managers. The business is designed for fun and profit with your income determined only by your own energy and sales drive. If you advance and become a regional director, some companies will even furnish you with a car.

Take the story of Sara Hopkins as an example. Her career began when a friend invited Sarah to a sales party. At the two-hour long party, she found that she was one of ten guests gathered to view a demonstration of household products.

As the demonstrator (often called a "dealer") showed the products, guests marked their orders on order blanks. Then, at the end of the program, while the hostess served coffee and cake, the demonstrator tallied her orders. Based on the volume of orders received, and on future parties schedules, she offered the hostess a choice of special premium gifts.

Guests were then offered an opportunity to earn similar gifts by acting as hostesses at future parties to be held in their own homes. Sarah volunteered to be hostess for the demonstrator's next party. When she discovered that demonstrators often earn sums ranging from $25 to $50 per party, and more, her interest was kindled and she applied for a job as a demonstrator.

As a demonstrator, it was her job to make party arrangements with each of her hostesses. At times, her involvement consisted of nothing more than agreeing with them on a time and place. At other times, she was called upon to help in telephoning guests or sending out invitations. Sometimes she added a name or two to the guest list.

Once a party was set up, she demonstrated the products, trying to obtain as many sales as possible. At the party she also tried to recruit as many new hostesses for future parties as she could. This was easily accomplished, however, when she pointed out to guests the various prizes and rewards already won by their hostess. Since

Sarah worked on commission, it was naturally to her advantage to demonstrate her products at as many parties as possible each week. The more hostesses she had giving parties, the greater the amount of merchandise she could sell, and the higher would be her profits.

When Sarah had recruited six people who wished to become demonstrators themselves, and when she had sold about $2,000 worth of merchandise, she became eligible to become a district manager. As a district manager, Sarah held periodic meetings to inform her demonstrators about new products in the line, or to help them to give better demonstrations. Sarah also held training sessions for her new demonstrators, and sometimes would go out with them to a party, and take over demonstrations for them until they became familiar with the product line.

Within a short time, Sarah rose from district manager to become a regional manager, her present position. In this capacity, Sarah oversees five districts. Like the company's other district managers and demonstrators, she is an independent sales representative, receiving a commission and not considered an employee of the company. Although her company offers various special incentives such as gifts and awards to its sales people, Sarah also sponsors her own contests to foster competition between districts for sales.

Most people at the management level in party-plan companies are those who started out as hosts or hostesses. It is possible, however, to step right in as a manager if you have spent time as a door-to-door salesperson, of ir you have had party-plan experience with a different company.

In the same way that Sarah became interested, Jim Schulte discovered the possibilities in selling Celebrity Fashion Jewels. A friend invited Jim and his wife, Nora, over for an evening party. Although they determined beforehand that their purchases would be limited, they both enjoyed themselves. After having ordered a bracelet and a ring, the Schultes promised to host a future party. Shortly afterwards, Jim became a demonstrator, and then quickly made his way up to the position of regional manager.

Jim learned that demonstrators, or "fashion show directors," as they are dubbed by the company, are supplied with a basic kit containing over $300 worth of fashion jewelry. A reward for being a host or hostess is a choice of 20 percent of the evening's sales in jewelry. All the jewelry is loaned to the fashion show directors in a trim, tailored black case, together with catalogs and training materials, at no charge.

As in most party-plan arrangements, the longer Jim Schulte remains with the company, the more he is able to earn. As a manager, he receives 30 percent commissions on fashion show orders, and 40 percent commission on all other, direct orders, including re-orders from the catalog. The company took care of his expenses for management training, and he receives bonus gifts and recruiting awards.

HAVING A RUBBERMAID PARTY

According to William J. Gribble, Market Planning Manager for Rubbermaid Party Plan, his company started its party-plan operation as one of the first companies with an already established brand name to use this selling technique. Due to their brand identification, women recognize these houseware products and feel they need every item in the Rubbermaid line.

He says the first step a Rubbermaid demonstrator takes in setting up a party is to arrange a time and place for the demonstration with the hostess, usually of course, in her home. The hostess then invites the guests, calling them personally a week or so in advance of the party date. Those who are unable to attend are often invited to place an "absentee order" for products. As in the case of other party plans, Rubbermaid has a special catalog of gifts and added incentives for the successful hostess. The more guests who buy products at her party, the better the reward the hostess receives.

In addition to her gift, a hostess will also receive 10 percent of the amount of party sales in merchandise of her choice. For example, for a party with sales of $75 to $99, the hostess will receive an additional $2.00 in merchandise, and a $3.00 bonus in merchandise for party sales of $100 or more.

To display her products, the demonstrator will arrive about half an hour earlier than the invited guests on the day of the party. She will set up her products on a table belonging to the hostess, or on a table she has brought with her. Once everyone arrives, the hostess and demonstrator try to create a casual atmosphere, allowing guests to relax and be comfortable. The demonstrator then distributes a 26-page color catalog, and order blanks, with pencils. She shows how some of the products are used, with samples supplied by the company and accompanied by specific instructions for demonstration. As the demonstrator works, she asks guests to read about the product in their catalogs, where each item is pictured and described. Since it is impossible to demonstrate every product, she points out other items in the catalog.

The demonstrator instructs the guests about her method of taking orders and making sales. Order blanks have been given to the hostess for completion, and it is she who collects the money from her guests. She mails the money, together with the orders, to the Rubbermaid distribution center in her area.

At this time, the demonstrator tries to arrange future parties at the homes of the guests. Her hostess helps her, displaying the valuable prizes she has received for giving the party, and for each party which is booked as a result of her own. A demonstrator realizes she can't depend for very long on her personal friends. She tries to make each party lead to two or three additional ones. They in turn, lead to two or three more, and set off a "chain reaction."

A short time after the party, the filled orders arrive at the home of the hostess and she distributes them in whatever way she wishes. She may personally deliver the items, or phone to ask her guests to pick them up at their convenience.

INVESTIGATING OTHER PARTY PLANS

Before committing yourself to any party-plan company, you should investigate several. Although most companies follow the same pattern, there are differences of which you should be aware.

For example, some party-plan companies don't expect their demonstrators to do any collecting or delivering. The company does all the delivering and collecting from their home office. Other companies ask the demonstrator to make deliveries and collect funds.

To investigate party-plan companies and their opportunities, look in the Help-Wanted sections of your local newspapers. Many such companies advertise there. You will also find companies with party plans listed in the business sections of *The Wall Street Journal* and *The New York Times.* Various party-plans are described in magazines such as *Salesman's Opportunity* or *Income Opportunities.*

For an investment of about $35.00, Jane Ford became a demonstrator for Edie Adams' Cosmetics. She received a complete in-home demonstration kit of cosmetics, and has been successfully selling these at home parties. Her profit is 30 percent of all sales, plus an additional 10 percent whenever her sales reach $100 during any two-week period. This company has provided Jane with an exclusive territory in her area.

Another company in which demonstrators don't need to invest in large inventories is Stanley Home Products. This company markets cleaning products for the home, such as spot removers, along with a selection of mops, brushes, and brooms. Stanley, like Tupperware, is a name long familiar to party-planners.

After applying at Stanley as a demonstrator, Bill Thomas was supplied with a catalog and a good selection of products and was expected to conduct his parties in much the same way as a Rubbermaid demonstrator. Distribution, however, is somewhat different at Stanley. The company guarantees weekly deliveries to demonstrators, an order cycle which provides weekly profits for Bill since he collects when he delivers each order. This customer contact also provides him with another opportunity to recruit hosts and hostesses for his parties.

Mary Beth and Joe Totten are co-demonstrators for Spencer Fashions, a party plan line of women's apparel from outerwear to underwear. The line also includes fashion coordinates such as bags, hats, even jewelry to complement the clothing. They also offer some fashion items for men.

As demonstrators (fashion consultants, in this case), Mary Beth and Joe made no investment. They were supplied with a catalog and $300 worth of samples which they display on a rack at each party. They also carry swatch books so that guests can feel and see the fabric of any item they may wish to order from the catalog. Their demonstrations often consist of a "fashion show" in which guests have the fun of modeling the samples of clothing.

When orders are taken, they are mailed along with a small deposit from each guest to the home office. There are no deliveries made, or final collections or exchanges made by either Mary Beth and Joe, or their hostesses. Each order is shipped direct to the customers with the Tottens receiving profits each week up to $200 depending on orders received the previous week. In addition, they can qualify for as much as $800 per year in clothing and other party-line merchandise.

Another apparel-party plan is Town and Country Fashions, Inc., a 40-year old company offering the latest fabrics and designs in men's, women's, and children's clothing. Each hostess is given a handsome gift for having a party, and demonstrators of the line, or "stylists" as they are referred to in this company, make no deliveries.

As a demonstrator for Town and Country, Adele Watkins works from a full-color swatched catalog and displays her fashion samples during a party. She often averages about $220 of business per show, which gives her a commission of about $40. She usually has three or four shows a week.

Managers earn as much on each show they put on, and in addition, make an overwrite on stylists. Successful sales people travel each year and the person who can hire 20 qualifying people in one year gets a bonus of $2,000 or a new Ford Pinto.

To learn more of each company's party-plan program, write to the following addresses:

Town and Country Fashions, Inc.   Celebrity Fashion Jewels
983 Grafton Street   93 34th Street
Dept. op-12   Dept. 1-32
Worcester, Mass. 01604   Brooklyn, New York 11232

Spencer/Designers U.S.A.   Rubbermaid Party Plan
135 Derby Ave.   Box 7000
New Haven, Conn. 06507   Chillicothe, Ohio 45601

JUDGING A GOOD HOUSE-PARTY PROGRAM

As you can see, party planning offers innumerable product lines, commission arrangements, and methods of selling. It is up to you to select a product and program that best fit your interest and your time schedule. It is also important that you investigate a company before you invest your time or your money in the line of goods they offer.

In every type of successful business venture, you may find frauds and swindlers and party planning is no exception. To make sure you are dealing with a reliable company check it out with your Better Business Bureau before you make any commitment. However, since the Better Business Bureau will most probably not have a complete listing on all existing party plans, the company in which you are interested may not be on file. Therefore, you may wish to check with the Direct Selling Association, which sets certain standards for party-plan programs. A list of reliable companies, which have been given a seal of approval by the Association, can be obtained by sending a request to the Direct Selling Association, 1730 M Street, N.W., Suite 610, Washington, D.C. 20036.

Then too, as you study the various party-plan operations available to you, consider the following questions which must be answered to your satisfaction.

1. Is the company well known?

There are many companies taking advantage of the party-plan selling technique. Some are old companies with established names, just now entering the party-plan field; others have just been newly formed to take advantage of this booming business. Some sell brand name products; some don't. Some are legitimate; some aren't. Check them carefully before committing yourself to any particular party plan.

2. How much must I invest?

As you know, the amount of investment can vary from company to company. However, most companies try to keep a dealer's investment to a minimum. Some ask $25 or $35 for a demonstration kit and expect the amount to be paid right off. Others will allow you to pay on time by deducting the amount from your commissions. An investment of $50 or more should be approached cautiously. However, a company can usually be judged legitimate if it is putting out its own money in advertising and promotional support.

3. What profit margin is offered?

In each company offering a party-plan program, your profit is gained from commissions on sales made, plus bonuses for recruiting, plus contest prizes. Therefore, the amount of money you earn depends in large measure on the amount of time you are willing to devote to the business and on how hard you are willing to work. Party plan programs offer sales people commissions ranging anywhere between 15 percent-40 percent. However, before being swayed by a large percentage number, you will be wise to consider the price range of the product to be sold. In many cases, an inexpensive item will result in greater party-plan sales than will a costly item, and net you a greater profit.

A good indication of profit potential can be gleaned from the following estimate given to me by a company whose sales people average commissions of 21 percent-30 percent.

At the dealer level—$8,000-$15,000 per year

At the district manager level—$8,000-$30,000 per year

At regional management levels—$8,000-$50,000 per year

Divisional manager level—as high as $80,000 per year

4. Is the product backed by heavy advertising?

A legitimate party-plan program will be well advertised by the company. You will find ads in magazines and newspapers, even on TV, with the company frequently spotting ads in the areas where they have dealers. In addition to this, new products and items will constantly be added to the line, offering new incentives to make customers want to keep on buying.

5. Are products "repeat sale" items?

Most party-plan items are such that they will sell again and again. This is necessary since you must be able to book parties in your same area month after month, year after year.

6. What is the seasonability of the product?

Some products, such as housewares or kitchenware, know no season. They can be used all year round, as useful in the spring and summer as they are in the fall and winter. Toys, on the other hand, must be considered seasonal, since prime demand for these items is pre-Christmas, September to about mid-December, Clothes, too, are seasonal and the change of latest fashion product lines should be taken into consideration.

7. What is the price range of the product?

Most party-plan items are priced reasonably. At Rubbermaid, for example, merchandise is priced between $1.50 and $15. A demonstrator can be assured that guests will purchase enough to make her demonstration worthwhile and the party a success

8. What is the function of the demonstrator?

All demonstrators must demonstrate the company's product during a party and, in most cases, take orders from the guests. Many times, she is also expected to collect the money and make deliveries. On the other hand, if she isn't required to perform these last two duties, she can devote more time to setting up parties and demonstrating her products, and after all, that's what puts the money in her pocket.

9. How much merchandise will I have to carry?

Consider the size and shape of the products you will be handling. Jewelry, for example, will fit into a small compact case which can be carried under your arm. However, much merchandise offered in party-plan programs is large and heavy. Even lightweight material can be bulky and require two or three trips between car and house.

10. Are there extra incentives for demonstrators?

In most party-plan programs, dealers and managers can earn cash bonuses in addition to valuable contest prizes. Check these out to see how they compare with other companies.

9

How to Turn Dirt into Dollars

Being the owner of a tract of land, or even of a window-greenhouse, can put you in the money. But though gardening is still a popular business, today there are other ways, more profitable than the plow, to make money from the land.

Gib Taller owns a lot, 50' x 175' on Pamlico Sound in North Carolina, which nets him well over $500 per week. How? He operates a marina for small sailing craft.

In northern Michigan ski country, a small cabin situated on one-quarter acre is rented out during the skiing season and adds $150 per week to the income of its owner.

On a mountain road near Evergreen, Colorado, a potter sells her wares exclusively to tourists who can, if they wish, watch her at work in her backyard workshop.

MAKING MONEY FROM THE LAND

Expanding leisure time, growing interest in outdoor recreation, increased mobility of people, and a rising standard of living make it possible for more people to seek and utilize recreation areas.

For instance, Kings Island, a 1,600-acre tract in Warren County, Ohio, which opened for business in 1972, already threatens to become the Disneyland of the Midwest. People living in the area are using this huge amusement park to their advantage.

Pete Larkin, a young landowner whose home is adjacent to a newly established campground, operates a used paperback mart and book shop. His greatest profit has been about $250 a week and he knows he'll never get rich, but he finds the business interesting and it supplements his regular income.

In town, Mary Healy, whose husband is retired, operates an old-fashioned home bakery. She caters to tourists, particularly to campers, offering delicious breakfast rolls for $1.10 per dozen, and homemade bread for 60¢ a loaf. She sells all she can bake in her own kitchen which nets her an income of about $1,500 a month.

Being an imaginative businessman, a resident of nearby Lebanon took a different approach to cashing in on the land boom. Bruce Markling sized up the growth potential of the area and quickly bought up a 140-acre farm near Kings Island. Here he operates a tourist-trailer campground which is filled to capacity in season. He has installed electrical and water hookups, showers, an archery range and a playground area. A section of his grounds is maintained for those with tents who want to rough it for a night at $1.25 a person. Campers with recreational vehicles are charged $3.50 a couple. This rental income from 93 campsites is rapidly paying off his $60,000 investment.

To cash in on a land boom, you should be there before the boom starts. Otherwise, the prices of adjacent and surrounding properties will have skyrocketed. However, there are some unmistakable signs, and if you read them properly you can make large gains on an initial investment.

One important sign is the construction of new interstate freeways which make a town or area more accessible. Other signs include rises in local newspaper circulation and rises in the price of land. When big national motel chains start moving in, and the city fathers of nearby towns and villages start dusting off old landmarks such as hotels or forts, and begin restoration proceedings, you know you have a sure thing. Once you have found your land boom, there are hundreds of ways to set up a small business.

John and Betty Jo Tittle, retired farmers who live within a mile of Sea World, a water spectacular in Ohio, recognized the signs and immediately fashioned their lovely, old Victorian home into an antique shop. On an average, they sell about $60 worth of merchandise a day on a year-round basis.

When the city in which he lived began to mushroom, Harold Rigers started *a mini-bike park.* Seeing a need for a place where children could ride their mini-bikes in safety, he and his wife rented 40 acres of rolling terrain outside town. After weeks of clearing, weed-cutting, trash-hauling and track-marking, it was opened to the public at $1 a bike.

At first business was slow, but after some advertising in the local paper and in bike shops, the Rigers now have steady riders all week and up to 50-60 on Saturdays and Sundays. Because the children look forward to riding in the ice and snow, they are open in all kinds of weather, even though they live in a "severe winter" state.

UTILIZING LAND FOR RECREATION AREAS

One of the biggest potential areas of profit in real estate lies in the development or use of low-cost land. This can be acreage that you rent or buy for a specific purpose, or land that you already own. However, planning for any recreation development includes the process of gathering as much information as possible to minimize or eliminate future problems. The application of informed judgment and foresight will help you to insure a pleasant, healthful and safe environment for your project.

Today many people are making big profits from fun on their farms. City bred families find farm life diversified and delightful and are willing to come live with a farm family for a one-or-two-week vacation period. Some send their children to board for the entire summer. These paying guests are interested in such pastimes as fishing, hiking, hayrides, farm cooking, riding, swimming, scenic auto tours, picnics, making homemade ice cream, and campouts. They are even anxious to help with the chores.

Rates are usually on a weekly basis, $40-$90 for adults, and $25-$50 for children. Many states put out a brochure listing vacation farms. Check with your state Development Department at the state capital to see if they offer this service.

Or you might advertise through area newspapers and camping outlet stores. Your ad should include the size and location of the farm, activities and housing available, type of guest preferred, whether adults or children, rates, phone number, and the sex and ages of your own children, if any.

Another way to make big money is from campgrounds and picnic areas. If you are fortunate enough to own land that will lend itself to the operation of such a business, you can easily earn upwards of $15,000 per week. If your campsite is near boating, skiing, swimming, golfing or tennis facilities, so much the better.

However, you needn't own acres of land or operate a campsite to profit from today's vacationing public. From her home in Florida's Disneyland area, Maria Brightstar operates a small gift shop where she sells to the tourist trade. Most of her merchandise is supplied by local craftsmen, including Indian jewelry and leather goods. She sometimes clears as much as $200 a day.

A small bicycle rental business, operating out of his front yard in a New Orleans suburb, supplements the income of Josh Ritter. Campers eager to see the sights of the city rent his bicycles for 50 ¢ an hour.

Rex Nutter and his wife, Millie, who live next to a camping and picnic area on the banks of Lake Superior, frequently net over $100 a day by renting boats and fishing equipment by the hour, during the summer months. Rex also gives the newcomer a quick fishing course for an additional fee of $3.

Another recreational activity that can increase your income is horseback riding. If you know horses you can take advantage of this growing outdoor sport.

The primary income to be gained from the horse boom is not only the breeding and selling of pure-breds, but the stabling of privately owned animals. Boarding horses can mean anything from complete care, including feeding and exercise of the animal, to the mere renting of a stall. Prices vary according to location and services rendered, but the rental of even a small stall in some parts of the country can cost at least $30 per month.

Along with boarding privately owned horses, you might consider the rental of your own horses by the hour, day or week. A young couple who live on a five-acre "ranch" near a recreation area in Arizona, rent each of their four horses for $3 an hour. They also give horseback riding lessons for beginners—$6 an hour for group lessons; $10 for private. An average day's income falls between $80-$120.

Indirectly, there are other ways to make money from horses too. Because horse lovers want the best for their animals and are willing to pay for it, you might want to consider the operation of a tack shop. Or if you are fortunate enough to know the farrier's trade, you can command a healthy fee for shoeing the horses in your area.

Another business related to horses is manure disposal. Rather than chemicals, ecology-minded individuals prefer the use of horse manure in their gardens. John Rankin, a farmer friend of mine, who operates a riding academy on the side, has a growing market for all the 50-pound, plastic bagfuls he can fill. In the spring, monthly sales totaled well over the $300 mark for this waste material, and he has recently signed a contract with a local organic fertilizer company to supply them with all he has available.

Helpful information about horses can be obtained by writing to the American Saddle Horse Breeders Assoc., 929 S. Fourth Street, Louisville, Ky. 40203.

Swimming pools and outdoor bathing places are other ventures that can bring big profit returns. Even before Mark Spitz won his Olympic gold medals, swimming, and associated activities such as sun bathing and wading, were among the fastest growing recreational interests in the nation.

A young couple, who own an older home situated on a one-half-acre lot in the inner city, manage a wading pool for toddlers. It is within walking distance of several high-rise apartment buildings which house other young families. Mothers bring their children to the couple's yard, where for 50 ¢ an hour, they may rent a small, individual, plastic wading pool and fill it with water for an afternoon's splash session.

They also rent out folding lawn chairs for sun-bathing and sell homemade soft drinks on the side. Word of mouth advertising was all they needed to get started, but you might also try placing a notice in a nearby obstetrician's or pediatrician's office. This business won't make you rich, but a season's income can exceed $1,200.

Another couple dived into a big-business venture when they opened up their large, oversize back-yard swimming pool to the public. Covered by insurance which cost them $200 a year, they charged a daily fee of $1 per person for the use of the pool, grossing more than $1,500 their first month in operation.

Public health authorities are quite concerned with sanitation and safety problems involving swimming and bathing. If your pool is to be used by the public it should meet the standards outlined in the *Suggested Ordinance and Regulations Covering Public Swimming Pools,* which you may request from the American Public Health Association, Inc., 1790 Broadway, New York, N.Y.

Together with swimming enthusiasts, there will always be fishermen. If you have a small lake or a pond on your property and have a knowledge of fish, this can mean big money for you.

Today's fisherman has more leisure time to pursue his sport, and fishing now is a year-round occupation. But because of pollution in many of our lakes and streams, he has fewer natural places in which to fish. Many turn to fish farms.

To be suitable for fish farming, the site of your lake or pond or raceway should have a slope of 1 percent-3 percent. Your water source must be free of harmful gases, minerals, or other pollutants.

Most commercial trout farms, for instance, use raceways that have a reliable, year-round flow of high-quality water from springs, wells, or streams. Best growth and economic returns are obtained from water between 50°-65°F., having at least 5 parts per million of dissolved oxygen.

Income from a fish-farm can come from four sources:

1. A fish-out pond; people come to your pond or lake to fish. They pay for their catch by the inch or pound. You restock as needed to provide successful fishing.

2. Selling live fish for stocking fish farms, private ponds, lakes, and other waters.

3. Selling freshly-dressed fish to local markets or restaurants, or to larger operators for packaging and marketing.

4. Selling eggs: many operators start the season's production with fertile eggs bought from a commercial fish breeder. Fish eggs are easily air-shipped in special containers to almost any part of the country.

The U.S. Department of Agriculture has representatives in your area who can help you plan and establish a fish-farming operation. A phone call to the number listed under *United States Government, Department of Agriculture, Soil Conservation Service,* in the white pages of your phone book, will get you started. This department will not only check the suitability of your soil for fish production, but will help you design your pond or raceways and water-control system, and help you develop an operation and management plan for your fishery.

Government Price List #21, Fish and Wildlife, offers much information for the fish farmer. Pamphlets that can be ordered from the Government Printing Office, Washington, D.C. 20402, include:

Trout Farming S/N 0100-0244 10¢

Catfish Farming S/N 0100-0078 15¢.

National Survey of Needs for Hatchery Fish S/N 2410-0156 70¢.

Flounder S/N 2410-0239 55¢.

Two informative books available at your library are:

Fish Ponds for the Farm, by Frank C. Edminster, Charles Scribners' Sons, New York.

Homemade Fishing, by Verne E. Davison—explains bass and trout waters you can build yourself. The Stackpole Company.

GETTING A CASH RETURN ON
YOUR LAND INVESTMENT

Escapism is probably the fastest growing industry in the United States today. It is expected that in the next few years capitalizing on fun needs of the American people will become one of the most profitable enterprises in the country. Even today, the increasing amount of leisure time and extra spending power being enjoyed by more people is reflected by the increase in the number of recreational vehicles on our highways.

If you have land situated within easy access to superhighways, you can earn big money. How much depending upon the amount of land you own.

A large tract of land will support a travel trailer park—permanent, overnight, or destination. Managing a mobile-home park is a full-time job and requires good management practices. Parks of 100 spaces or less can generally be run by a husband-wife team, but those over 100 spaces may often require special management personnel, plus a maintenance man.

Small Business Bibliography #41, Mobile Homes, can be requested from the Superintendent of Documents, Government Printing Office, Washington, D.C. 20402. It will supply you with additional information including income and construction cost, directories and numerous publications endorsed by the Mobile Homes Manufacturers Association, 20 North Walker Drive, Chicago, Ill. 60606.

Even a small lot can be a source of income, allowing you to profit from those who travel our nation's highways. If you live in a large house, for instance, you can easily clear $1,000 for a 2 month period, *renting rooms to tourists.* All you need are clean sheets and comfortable beds.

If you live in a motel area, much of your business will come from vacationers. However, you can also build up a regular clientele of traveling businessmen.

Sometimes a tourist home will become so successful that it's owner will venture into the motel business and become a modern day inn-keeper. Before buying or building a motel, however, there are three important areas to investigate:

1. What is the economic profile of the community in or near your motel site? Is it stable, expanding, or shrinking?

2. Check the earnings of other motels in the same area. Markets should be evaluated on a 365-day basis by the count of *overnight* guests.

3. Make a study of actual and potential group business. A check of the site or location itself is also necessary. Will it meet the needs of today's market in a practical and aesthetic way? Will this be true 10 years from now? Fifteen? Remember, a change in highway or street location can affect your project.

Before determining whether the motel business is for you, you should do a great amount of personal investigating and check out the references listed below.

From the Government Printing Office:

Starting and Managing a Small Motel (S&M 7) 35¢.

Sm. Business Bibliography #66, Motels—lists directories, periodicals, and trade associations.

You can also obtain, *free,* an annual publication, *Trends In the Hotel-Motel Business,* which is a study of motels, covering occupancy, operating ratios, and business volume, by writing to Harris, Kerr, Forster and Company, 420 Lexington Ave., New York, N.Y 10017.

If your home is in a resort area, consider its use as a boarding house. In Miami, Florida, Mrs. Blevens, a widow, offers room and board to young people who work in local hotels and recreation areas. Because most of her clientele are students, her rooms rent for $35 a week and include breakfast, dinner, and use of her living and recreation rooms. Her operation brings her an income of almost $7,000 a year.

Another way to profit by living in a resort area is to make and sell something native to the area. For instance, on North Carolina's Atlantic coast, Vivian and Don Campbell use their home as shop and workshop for their seashell crafts and jewelry business. Starting out with shells they picked up on the beach and a knowledge of how to use them artistically, this retired couple now add about $1,500 to their regular annual income.

If you are fortunate enough to own property on a lake or river, you can put it to work and profit from "boat-campers." Today, more and more vacationers are being bitten by the camp-boat bug and are taking advantage of our 48,000 miles of inland beaches, more than 12,000 miles of ocean shore, and endless miles of streams and rivers. Although much of the land along these waterways offers free campsites for the boat traveler, he must first have a boat, which he rents or owns.

In Minnesota's Quetico-Superior land of lakes, rent for a canoe, tent, and food cost about $7 per person per day. Ron Dressler, a bachelor who has a year-round home on the shores of Lake Superior, makes his living operating such a rental concession.

Along the Missouri River, Aggie and Mark Prentice are engaged in a similar business. A family-sized inflatable boat rents for about $6 per day. On Lake Champlain, Bart and Mable Holmstrom rent houseboats for $150 to $500 a week. An oldster in Oregon rents his fleet of 50 canoes at the rate of $1.50 each per hour.

Then too, all privately owned boats need docking, launching, and storage facilities. In many areas marinas are being constructed to provide a center of activity where boats can be berthed, launched, repaired, fueled, and provisions obtained. Berth rental fees are usually charged by the season and can range anywhere from $3 to $12 per foot of boat for a 4-5-month period.

If you live in an area where boats are exposed to the rigors of the sea, you might set up a boat repair and painting business. Capt. Dan Flotea, who lives in a little inlet along the Atlantic coast, has all the business he can handle applying lacquer and paint to boats used for deep-sea fishing.

For information on boat-launching areas and boat-docking facilities, a book, *Environmental Health Practice in Recreational Areas,* is available from the U.S. Department of Health, Education, and Welfare, Public Health Service, National Center for Urban and Industrial Health, Environmental Sanitation Program, Cincinnati, Ohio 45202.

Other sources of information include:

U.S. Coast Guard Auxiliary
U.S. Coast Guard Headquarters,
1300 E. Street, N.W.
Washington, D.C. 20591

American Boat Association
P.O. Box 22
Ipswich, Mass. 01938

U.S. Power Squadron, District Office
2405 Millsboro Road
Mansfield, Ohio 44906

Other leisure time activities that can put money in your pocket include sky-diving, back-packing, rock-hounding, mountaineering, skin-diving, ice-skating, soaring, surfing, ice-fishing—all popular to-day. If you are expert in any of these fields, how about giving lessons? A young army veteran, living in a New York resort area gives on-the-spot sailboat lessons. For a two-hour lesson, he charges a fee of $20. During the season, this adds up to more than $500 a week.

Or perhaps you might own land that can be developed into a recreational area. Snowmobiles need lots of room in which to operate. So do dunebuggies. A gunnery range or a motorcycle track could provide a good income. Don't disregard a repair shop for these machines, either. In Iowa snow country, Nat Adams, himself a snowmobile addict, set up a small repair shop in his garage. Fixing broken machines and selling parts gives him an income of $300-$500 a week during the winter months.

People need hiking trails and bicycle paths and bird-watching havens. People also need recreational facilities in our cities.

One enterprising young man used his long, narrow, front lawn in Detroit's downtown area to build a miniature golf course. Catering mostly to teenagers, his net profit during the summer months averages about $1,000 a month.

An alert housewife, who erected a large tennis practice board in her backyard for the use of her own children, now rents it out to the entire neighborhood, children and adults alike, at a rate of 60¢ per hour. Another family gives a home to numerous wild animals within a large fenced-in, wooded five acres adjoining their small ranch home on the outskirts of the city. John, their business-minded young son began charging admission to amateur photographers who were allowed to take all the animal shots possible within a time limit of one hour. In Minnesota, a young couple erected an ice-skating rink on the vacant lot adjacent to their suburban home. Charging 50¢ admission, they often net $100 daily during the winter months. In the next block, a retired shop mechanic, operates a used-skates shop from his garage. Depending on their condition, skates sell for $2-$12 a pair. He also offers a skate-sharpening service.

In Oregon, a farmer made use of a magnificent hill on his property by installing toboggan equipment. People flocked to this new recreation site in droves and in three months the farmer had grossed $2,520.

Another farmer with more land than he could plant, decided that sand traps and putting greens could pay off big and used part of his land to build a golf course. Doing most of the work himself, he laid out the course and brought it into operational shape for $38,000.

He found that maintenance of a modern golf course requires a wide range of knowledge and experience. Not only must one be able to ensure the budgeting of sufficient funds for adequate maintenance, but a broad knowledge of all phases of turf culture is essential. It also helps to have a fair understanding of mechanics so as to be able to keep expensive equipment in repair at a minimum cost.

For helpful hints on establishing a golf course, write to the National Golf Foundation and Corporation, Rm. 804, The Merchandise Mart, Chicago, Ill. 60654, and to the O.M. Scott Seed Company, Marysville, Ohio.

GARDENING MEANS EASY MONEY

Owners of seed companies have seen an increase in sales over the past few years. They attribute this upsurge in demand to increased environmental consciousness, the economy, and a trend toward summer "vacationing" at home. But, for whatever reason, growing your own crops can put money in your pocket.

As more and more people turn to organic foods, organic gardening is becoming big business. There are now thousands of organic food stores in the United States, and more opening every day. New opportunities for profit are also available to those who operate roadside stands.

In the Midwest, Cal and Rita Burgess, a young couple three years out of agricultural college, sell all the sun flower seeds they can raise on their small farm to an organic food canning company. For their trouble they add about $4,000 to their annual income.

At their health food shop in front of their home, Peg and Al O'Connor, find that even though organic fruits and vegetables have blemishes on them that one doesn't find on chemically grown products, the organic food buyer will buy them. Their income from the sale of apples, peaches, and tomatoes alone, last year totaled over $2,400.

Exactly what constitutes organic food? According to the National Farmers Organization of Iowa, it is "food grown without pesticides; grown without artificial fertilizers; grown in soil whose humus content is increased by the addition of organic matter," and "food which has not been treated with preservatives, hormones, antibiotics, etc."

The market includes just about everyone—older people who have retired, young people looking for natural foods, and the average citizen concerned about chemicals used in the production, processing, and merchandising of food.

How do you grow organic food? Glenn J. Graber of Hartville, Ohio has one answer. His secret is the use of pulverized, dehydrated seaweed as a soil conditioner. This seaweed, which he obtains through the SeaBorn Mineral Division of Skod Company, Norway, contains minor elements which are depleted from the soil by ordinary farming, but which are essential to healthy disease-resistant plant growth.

Mr. Graber estimates that one acre of ground should produce $1,000 worth of vegetables. This could be achieved by one person working hard. However, the demand for his produce is so great that 70 persons are employed on his 400-acre farm. In season he airships 400 baskets of bibb lettuce a day to restaurants in California that feature organically grown foods. He also ships vegetables to outlets in Cleveland, Cincinnati, New York, Boston, Chicago, and cities in Wisconsin and North Carolina.

Information on organic gardening and ways to control garden pests are available from books on your library shelf.

Peacock Manure and Marigolds, by Janet Gillespie.

Gardening Without Poisons, by Beatrice T. Hunter.

The Bug Book—Harmless Insect Controls, by John and Helen Philbrick.

The organic food list is no longer limited to wheat germ and soy beans. It now includes such items as fresh eggs, baked goods, milled and whole grains of all types, seeds, oils, jams and jellies, and all fresh fruits and vegetables. Tops on the list of homegrown products, organic and otherwise, are tomatoes, beans, sweet corn, cucumbers, peas, lettuce, radishes, squash, melons, and beets.

Long before the organic food craze, a young woman got her start in business by selling her home-made preserves. Friends and neighbors were her first customers. Local stores clamored for all she could make. Today she sells on the national market grossing over $8,000 a year.

Another interesting avenue to organic profit is through grapes and mushrooms. A grape farmer in Oklahoma worked hard for three years. In the third year, his 10-acre site produced enough grapes to net him a $7,000 income.

Information can be obtained by writing to the following organizations:

The American Concord Grape Assoc., Inc.   The American Mushroom Institute
900 Jefferson Road   P. O. Box 373
Rochester, N.Y. 14623   Kennett Square, Pa. 19348

Although pumpkins and squash may need large areas in which to grow, there are big profits to be made from mini-gardens. Your garden can be a small plot in the backyard, a home greenhouse, or even a box on the windowsill. Crops that will net you big money with the least amount of work are herbs. A miniature herb garden might include parsley, basil, marjoram, thyme, sage, and summer savory.

Sell your herbs, packaged in small cardboard boxes or plastic containers, on commission at grocery stores, delicatessens, organic-food and health stores. One enterprising young student boxed and sold miniature herb gardens via mail-order to help pay his tuition. You might try offering them for sale in florists shops and cookbook departments.

If you get a headstart on the growing season you stand to gain additional profit. A tomato grower planted his garden very early, then on cool spring days, he placed a stiff plastic cover over each plant, and over this a bushel basket. His tomato crop was ripe long before his competitors and he made a killing on the local market.

Another lady, who runs a small florist shop from her home, has a lean-to type of greenhouse built against her house. This makes her a master of all seasons. Profit from her orchid plants alone, which she sells for $11-$35 apiece, often approaches $4,000 a year.

If you are interested in growing trees, shrubs, and plants, you can probably succeed in the nursery business. Landscape planting is of concern to homeowners, environmental improvement has become increasingly important, and many owner-managers decorate their commercial buildings with plants. Most of this work is done by nurserymen.

A retail nurseryman may not have to be a specialist in horticulture, but he must know about the types and care of the nursery stock he handles. As a nurseryman you will have to compete with variety stores, discount houses, and supermarkets. You can beat them by offering your customers quality and service.

Your plants can be sold to landscapers, retailers, or directly to a customer. If you can offer economical delivery service, so much the better.

Helpful government publications include:

Starting and Managing A Retail Flower Shop #M 18 (55¢).

The Nursery Business—Small Bus. Bibliography # 14.

Both are available from the Superintendent of Documents, U.S. Government Printing Office, Washington, D.C. 20402.

From the same source you may also request the following booklets:

Selecting Shrubs for Shady Areas, S/N 011-0804, 10¢.

Plant Hardiness Zone Map, S/N 011-0434, 25¢.

Trees For Shade and Beauty, Their Selection and Care, S/N 0100-0795, 10¢.

Transplanting Trees and Other Woody Plants, S/N 2405-0144, 35¢.

Magnolias, growing magnolias, S/N 0100-1300, 10¢.

Hollies, growing hollies, S/N0100-0793, 5¢.

Dogwood, growing the flowering dogwood, S/N 0100-1011, 10¢.

RAISING AND SELLING ANIMALS FOR PROFIT

Many people have discovered that breeding animals can be an interesting and profitable business. There is money to be made from both large and small animals. Your choice will depend on space requirements, housing, food, and the climatic conditions required. Before you invest in any animal raising business, however, local markets and convenient facilities for shipping should also influence your choice. Study them.

In a lifetime, almost everyone has a pet of some sort or other. Today this can be anything from a common dog or cat to the more exotic jungle animals. Even snakes have become big business in the pet category.

If you are an animal lover, the work is not arduous, and the list of potential pet owners is long. City and apartment dwellers are buying both large and small dogs, for protection as well as pets. They are also ideal customers for cats, gerbils, hamsters, tropical fish, parakeets and other birds, snakes, small turtles, and lizards.

You can sell direct to the public or through pet shop owners or dealers. If you are selling from your home, place a small classified ad in your local paper, and an attractive sign in front of your house.

How much can you make? It depends on what kind of animal you sell. In Rawlins, Wyoming, the residence of Gerry and Jim

Hacklow, both high school teachers, is over-run with Cairn Terriers. But each dog represents a profit of $125-$150 dollars.

On the other hand, Cris Templer's backyard on the coast of North Carolina, is the base of his business operation. He sells hermit crabs for $1.25 each.

From the Superintendent of Documents, Washington, D.C. 20402, you may request the following:

Selection and Care of Common Household Pets, S/N 0100-0665.
Pet Shops, Small Business Bibliography, #76.

The sale of *small animals* for other than the pet market, can also earn big profits, and set you up in a money-making business. Pharmaceutical houses, laboratories, hospitals and research centers use vast numbers of small animals for vital medical research and testing purposes. Schools, universities, and day camps need them for educational purposes. Zoos, reptile exhibits, and animal farms need them as food for larger animals. Small animals in this category would include guinea pigs, white mice, white rats, and hamsters.

A colony of any of these animals can be started with a single male and three or four females. Female guinea pigs should produce 4-6 litters a year ranging from 2 to 6 young per litter. Hamsters produce about 4 litters a year, with 3-14 offspring in each litter. Rats and mice can be expected to produce about 8 litters a year with about 6 young in each litter.

All may be easily raised in homemade cages of wood and wire, although all-wire cages are best for hamsters, since they are likely to gnaw through wooden walls. Wood shavings or excelsior can be used for nesting material. Water should be available at all times, preferably by means of an upside-down bottle, with a dispenser tube leading into the cage. Food is inexpensive and should consists of mouse or rabbit pellets, plus regular feedings of fresh green vegetables and fruit such as raw apples.

For additional information from the United States Department of Agriculture, Government Printing Office, Washington, D.C. 20401, ask for:

Raising Guinea Pigs, List #5, L466.

Raising Laboratory Mice and Rats, Leaflet #253.

Another way to sweeten your money-pot is with bees. It is estimated that approximately one-half of each year's honey production is sold by the producer direct to consumers through roadside stands, by house-to-house selling, through mail-order sales, or from the producer's home.

Honey, beeswax, and "comb honey" are always salable commodities and the bees themselves can bring big profits. They can be sold to others who wish to start a hive, or you can rent your bees to farmers and orchard growers for pollination purposes.

Bees are the most efficient and dependable pollinators because they visit flowers methodically to collect nectar and pollen and don't destroy the plant by feeding on it as do other insects. Some seed and fruit crops that show definite increases in yield or quality as a result of the pollinating activity of bees include: Alfalfa, clovers, garlic, leek, onion, cotton, okra, radishes, melons, celery, and most fruits and berries. In fruit orchards, one colony per acre will provide adequate bee visitation.

When Mary and Pete Whitol decided to go into the bee business they started out with two hives, which they purchased for $25 each from the bee inspector in their area. Each hive contained frames and beeswax comb foundations for the storage of honey, plus a queen and about 20,000-30,000 bees.

Placed in a partly sunny, secluded spot in the backyard, the bee colony developed rapidly and soon there were new queens with which to start additional hives. Today, the Whitols package bees and queens and ship them to beekeepers in all parts of the country. Although keeping bees requires no license, a registration fee of $1 must be paid each year.

Several booklets are available from the United States Department of Agriculture.

> *Beekeeping for Beginners,* G 158.
>
> *Controlling the greater Wax Moth, a pest of honeycombs,* F 2217.
>
> *Identifying Bee Diseases in the Apiary,* AB313.
>
> *Protecting Honey Bees from Pesticides,* L544.
>
> *Selecting and Operating Beekeeping Equipment,* F 2204.
>
> *Shade and Water for the Honey Bee Colony,* L 530.
>
> *Using Honey Bees to Pollinate Crops,* L549.

Other information may be obtained from books in your library.

> *A Living From Bees,* by Frank C. Pellett, Orange-Judd Publishing Co., Inc.
>
> *Beekeeping—The Gentle Craft,* by John F. Adams, Doubleday, 1972.
>
> *Beekeeping in the United States,* U.S. Dept. of Agriculture, Handbook # 335, 1971.

Associations are also centers of helpful information.

American Honey Institute
111 East Wacker Drive
Chicago, Ill. 60601

American Beekeeping Federation
Rte. 1, Box 68,
Cannon Falls, Minn. 55009

It is a known fact that rabbits multiply rapidly. Used as a basis for a business venture they can multiply your dollars. Although they require considerable care, their breeding for commercial and scientific uses is an established business in many parts of the country. Some breeds of rabbits are best for meat, others for fur. Their benefits include high nutritional value, low investment cost, high productivity, as well as sales of pelts and other byproducts.

Marlo Graying, a student who lives with her parents in Newark, New Jersey, began raising rabbits as a 4-H project. Today, she raises them for profit. Her beautiful show rabbits sell from $6 to $150 each. However, if you want a stable income, breeding rabbits for meat can net you more than $100 per week.

From the government: Department of Agriculture.

Raising Rabbits, F 2131, free.

Commercial Rabbit Raising, S/N 0100-1376. Government Printing Office, Washington, D.C. 20402, 35¢.

At your library, look for

Rabbit Raising For Profit, by Marvellus A. Meek, Greenberg, New York.

If you live in a rural area, the breeding of large animals can bring large profits. In addition to horses and dogs, which we discussed earlier in this chapter, there are numerous other large animals that can be bred and sold at a profit.

One of the biggest animals in demand today, particularly in the West, is the buffalo. Many butchers and traders want to market buffalo steak, hides, and rugs.

A Colorado rancher got into the buffalo breeding business six years ago with two animals. He buys new ones whenever he can, and now has 300 bisons roaming his 850-acre fenced in area.

A bred cow (one carrying a calf) sells for about $750, a 2-year-old bull for $500. If you are getting started, it would be best to start with some bred cows rather than young calves. A calf will not be able to produce offspring for at least two years.

A buffalo raiser in Medina, who also operates a hardware business, sells buffalo meat at a counter at the rear of his store.

Before the meat crisis, a buffalo T-bone cost $3.50 a pound as compared to $2.65 for beef T-bone. Round steak, $3 as compared to $1.99 for beef round. Also on sale is buffalo sirloin at $3.50 a pound, buffalo liver, $1.75 a pound, and buffalo tongue and heart at $3 a piece.

For more information, write to the National Buffalo Association, which has 200 breeding members (Box 995, Pierre, S. Dakota 57501).

Another animal that can help you make money is the goat. Goats are hardy creatures and easily adapted to all climates. They thrive on rough pasture and other wastelands and are happy to call an unused garage or shed home, providing it is clean and dry.

Because of the interest in organic foods, goat's milk is of special value today. A local health food store or organic food shop would make a good selling center. Too, many elderly people drink it for health reasons, and you could have a ready market at local nursing establishments and senior citizens homes.

Then of course, there are all the usual farm animals—sheep, hogs, cattle, plus poultry farming, which includes chickens, ducks, geese, turkeys, and guinea fowl.

Booklets from the U.S. Department of Agriculture, *free*:

> *Raising Ducks,* F2215.
>
> *Raising Guinea Fowl,* L 519.
>
> *Housing and Equipment for Sheep,* F 2242.
>
> *Raising Livestock on Small Farms,* F 2224.
>
> *Breeds of Swine,* F 1263.
>
> *Improving Your Dairy Herd,* F 2132.
>
> *Beef Cattle,* F 2142.

Books from the library include:

> *Sheep & Wool Science,* by M.E. Ensminger, Interstate Printers and Publishers, 1970.
>
> *Aids to Goatkeeping,* by Carl A. Leach, Dairy Goat Journal.
>
> *Goats,* by Will L. TeWalt, Orange Judd Publishing Co.—a guide for breeders.
>
> *Why They Call Him the Buffalo Doctor,* by Jean Cummings, Prentice-Hall, Inc., 1971.

Associations:

American Goat Society, Inc.	American Assoc. of Sheep Practitioners
1606 Colorado St.	520 Railway Exchange Bldg.
Manhattan, Kansas 66502	Denver, Colorado 80202

American Dairy Goat Assoc.
Spindale
North Carolina 28160

American National Cattlemen's Assoc.
P. O. Box 569
Denver, Co. 80201

Fur farming for profit is a highly specialized business in the United States today. Because it is not considered chic to wear clothing made from the fur of many "threatened species" wild animals, there is a greater demand for the furs of those animals that can be raised in captivity.

Although successful business operations in this field require capital and expert knowledge, the animals can be raised outside on cheap land, or indoors in a garage or basement which meets climatic conditions required for them. Animals whose pelts are salable include: mink, chinchilla, rabbit, racoon, and fox.

To check out licensing and fur farming in your locality, write to your state college or your county Agricultural agent.

Books from the library which will be of help to you include:

Mink Raising, by L.H. Adams, A.R. Harding, Publishers.

Mink Farming, by J.L. Edwards, Fur Farms Publishing Company.

According to statistics, worms are worth more than a wiggle. Some people are making over $10,000 a year in the worm business. For a business that can be started with an outlay of about $10, that's not bad.

Many worm dealers export worms to other states by mail, as well as delivering them to local bait and tackle shops or to fishing camps. Anywhere in the United States is a good place to raise worms, though a warm climate is preferable. If you don't live in an area which is good for fishing, you can ship them to an area where there is a demand.

Each month a worm is capable of dropping four egg capsules containing from two to 20 worms apiece. Worms start breeding when they are about 3 inches long, and they are bisexual. When the breeder worms grow to six inches long they are "bait size."

A good place to find big dew worms is on a golf course. Some big-time bait distributors pay a golf course between $3-$10 thousand a year for the dew worm rights and crews of pickers, outfitted with miner's lights on their hats and cans strapped to their legs go out at night and collect the worms. On a still, moonless night, a good picker can collect as high as 7,000 worms. When distributing, most dealers use a plastic coated paper cup with a perforated lid which holds about 50 worms and the peat to keep them alive. On a good week he will sell more than 2,400 cups of worms at an average of 4¢ each worm.

It takes a little capital to get started. A novice breeder can begin with 10,000 African night crawlers, which can be bought for about $10 per 1,000, or the more desirable Red Worm, which costs about $5 per 1,000. Sales of breeding stock are frequently advertised in leading sports or fishing magazines in the classified sections.

Consult your local agricultural agent for information on raising worms in your area. Write to Shields Publications, Box 472, Elgin, Illinois 60120, for a complete list of how-to booklets on raising worms for profit.

Library books which will prove helpful are:

The Million-$ Earthworm, by Jim Newton, Fort Hamilton Press.

Earthworm Buyer's Guide, Robert L. Shields, Shields Publications—lists over 1,000 sources for breeders.

10

Setting Up Your Home-Bound Business

Before the industrial revolution, most businesses were centered in the building in which the craftsman lived. The potter, the cabinet-maker, the glass blower—each had a trade-sign hanging outside his door, and a workshop in his home. Today the home-operated business is enjoying a resurgence of popularity. This chapter will tell you why, and explain how you can go about setting up your home office or workshop.

ADVANTAGES OF A WORKSHOP IN YOUR HOME

Every business mentioned in this book can be started in the home, and most can be maintained there indefinitely. Although friends and relatives may voice concern when you tell them of your plans, the good things in setting up a shop at home far outweigh the bad. Let's take a look at some of these important advantages.

Probably first on the list is money. Over the years you've paid Uncle Sam a lot in taxes. Right? Well, now it's your turn to *get a tax break,* and at the same time help your business to become a success.

If you can prove that you work at home, and have a place set aside in which you do it, you can qualify for various tax deductions. For the person who owns or is buying his home, deductions can be made for taxes, mortgage interest, and depreciation. Let me give you an example.

Suppose you use one room of the seven-room ranch house, in which you and your family live, as a studio for your ceramic creations. According to government regulations, you are allowed to deduct one-seventh of all home maintenance expenses. This includes light, heat, taxes, and mortgage interest.

If, however, the room is divided between your work and your family's activity, you can deduct only half of the one-seventh use, or one fourteenth of the expenses.

A good savings can also be affected by listing equipment used in the course of your business. This pertains to investment credit and depreciation deductions for desks, filing cabinets, typewriters, and other business machines as well as those used in the manufacture of your product, or the maintenance of your service.

Telephone bills can likewise be a source of savings, since the portion of your bill attributable to business calls is deductible.

If you pay for cleaning and maintenance of your home, this fee too can be deducted on a pro rata share basis. Electric bills can also be deducted. If you use an electric typewriter, have need of extra lights, electric tools, or other electrical equipment, the deductible proportion of what you are charged can add up to half of your total bill. This would also apply to gas-powered equipment.

To make sure you are allowing for all the deductions allotted to you, don't hesitate to seek professional advice. Your tax consultant will also be able to tell you which expenses are best deducted from your personal income tax and which should be deducted from your business expenses.

Working from your home gives you the advantage of saving money in other ways too. Transportation costs, for example, are completely done away with. And although a neat, clean appearance is a must during working hours, a choice of clothing is another advantage gained over the individual who must dress up and march off to the office every day.

In this area, you save in *two* ways—in comfort and in cash. Not only do you erase the expense of buying numerous suits and outfits, shoes, and hose, but you can relax in sports and casual clothes, even work in your bare feet if it pleases you.

Another advantage to operating a business from your home is that it helps you save time. Again we can mention transportation. For you are exempt from the greatest time consumer of them all—that dreary every-day trip from home to business, and from business to home.

At home, no one stands guard as you punch a time clock. Lunch is as close as your kitchen, and when you feel like working until late in the evening you are your own master. If your daily quota of work is finished at noon instead of the prescribed 5:00 P.M., you needn't hang around for the rest of the day looking busy. You are free to spend your time in the pursuit of whatever you wish.

It is an acknowledged fact that time used in the pursuit of a goal we set for ourselves is better spent than that used to accomplish a task set for us by someone else. We all know, too, that no one operates at peak efficiency all day. Each of us has a time when we function best. For me, it is the early hours of the morning. For you, it may be later afternoon. With a business at home, you can set your schedule to take advantage of your best work capacity hours.

Having a home workshop or office can also help you to avoid business world pressures, and the depersonalizing aspects of today's business society. Every day interruptions, demands, meetings, put-downs, luncheons—all can be kept to a minimum when you work at home. Also, because many of us are psychologically geared to perform more productively in the secure and familiar environment our home gives us, we are less threatened by stress, headaches, and ulcers.

Frequently, your family can be helpful in reducing your work load, although having them constantly underfoot cannot always be termed an advantage. However, since they will be around and about while you are pursuing business matters, why not put them to work for you?

Children love to play office. Take advantage of this. Filing, stuffing envelopes, licking stamps, stapling papers together, and affixing return address stickers are favorites.

And what teenager isn't looking for an excuse to drive the family car? Let them run errands for you. To the post office, to pick up supplies, or to deliver your product. Older children can also earn extra pin money by helping with office work, such as typing your letters for you, or keeping books.

A husband or wife can be helpful in many ways too. Accept their aid whenever it is offered.

STARTING OUT WITH KNOWLEDGE

Before you set up any sort of home business, it is essential that you have a good working knowledge of that business. We have discussed this before, I know, but it is important enough to bear repeating. Without sufficient manufacturing, selling, management, or advertising know-how, your business may be doomed to failure.

Many times a small business doesn't even get off the ground because the owner is deficient in knowledge of one or more of these operations. And he won't take the time and effort to learn.

One way to insure yourself of a successful business is to operate efficiently. To do this you must follow two principles of organization. The first encompasses the attitude required toward the development of your long range goals. [We will discuss this in a later chapter.] The second involves the thoughtful planning of each day in accordance with its particular needs and requirements.

Without proper application of this second principle, you will have a business studded with confusion, delays, frustration, duplication, and wasted effort. On the other hand, every minute you invest in sound organization and planning can pay you back, quite literally, in money and hours saved.

Be prepared to judge a home-oriented business by asking yourself, "Do I get an adequate return for the amount of time I spend at my work?" Your answer will be "no," if it takes you five hours to do a job that is usually done in two hours time.

This negative answer could be prompted by one of two reasons. 1. You may not yet be skilled enough at your job, or 2. You're not doing the work for which you are best suited. In the latter case, it might benefit you to consider some other line of work. In the former, give yourself time to master the business. Remember, people are inclined to work hard at what they enjoy doing. They also like doing what they do well. If you like your work, given time, you will eventually do it well.

But perhaps you don't have difficulty in either of these areas. You are most knowledgeable and proficient in the techniques of management and production. You like your work. But you still don't have a money-making business because you fall down when it comes to daily organizational office chores.

For you then, an important factor in successful home business operation will be *knowing how to schedule your work.* Not only is it essential that you accomplish a planned amount of work each day, but that you do this without disrupting the rest of the family's daily activities, or allowing them to disturb you, or interfere with your work day.

A noisy marble-saw in the basement, for instance, won't be conducive to baby's nap. Nor will a child's trumpet lesson add to your concentration in getting out that important report. If situations like these are not handled right, many domestic crises can arise.

Your best defense is to *set up a routine* and stick to it. When you work at home, you are always handy to perform numerous jobs that contribute to daily family living. Running errands are a large part of this. Someone must drive the children to and from lessons and school activities. The cleaning woman must be picked up at the bus stop. Shoes must be taken to the cobbler, and clothes to the cleaner.

Since you're at home you can easily fall prey to this kind of trap, plus many other distractions.

Another trap for the home-worker is the telephone. Friends who wouldn't think of calling you at a "regular" office, won't hesitate to bother you at home. But even if you enjoy talking to them, remember—they're cutting in on *business* time. You may also find yourself taking telephone messages for other members of your family.

A strong, simple statement to your family and friends concerning your hours may be sufficient to diminish these problems, but you will probably find, in the beginning at least, that this admonition must be given frequently.

The following suggestions will help you to set up a daily routine that is right for you and your particular situation.

1. Start work on time. Don't let a second cup of coffee or a neighbor's phone call interfere with the start of your work.
2. Tackle the crisis. Every job has work that is critical. Do it while you are mentally and physically fresh.
3. Do the necessities. Every day finds things that are necessary to the success of your business. Don't leave them dangling.
4. Perform the routine. There are many daily chores that don't require you to think. Since they can be done almost automatically, it doesn't matter that you aren't functioning at your "peak" performance level.

Although schedule and routine are important to the success of an efficient home operation, don't neglect to *take time off.* This applies to time away from your work on a daily basis as well as vacation time.

Frequently, people working at home become so enmeshed in business matters that they seldom leave the house. This is not good. Go out for lunch with friends once in awhile. Occasionally meet with others in the same line of business through a trade organization or guild. Try playing a game of tennis or handball on your lunch hour. You'll find that such activities will help relieve daily tension and stress, and keep you mentally stimulated.

Most businesses have a slack season and you will probably plan to take your vacation during this time. What happens to your business while you're away? This depends on the type of operation in which you are engaged. However, much satisfaction can be obtained by use of the two following suggestions.

1. Engage an answering service to tell your clients that you'll be away for whatever length of time, and that you will call them when you return.

2. Contact your post office and ask that your mail be held until you call for it, or that it be forwarded to you at your vacation address.

SETTING UP YOUR OFFICE

When you are just beginning in business, it isn't likely that you will need a large, elaborate office. Some businesses which are flourishing today, and making thousands of dollars for their owners, started out with a drawer for an office or a shoe box as a filing cabinet.

It matters little whether you have an entire floor of the house to yourself, or merely a corner of the grape arbor, but it is important to have an office. Why? There are two reasons.

1. Even though your business may be conducted through personal contact alone, you will need a place to keep records.

2. Psychologically an office takes your venture out of the hobby or experimental stage and allows you to view it in a true businesslike manner.

Since you must have an office then, how do you *decide where to put it?* Three factors will determine the answer to this question.

1. The size of your home.

2. Your type of business.

3. The amount of business you expect to have, and the potential growth you expect it to reach.

For some, an after-dinner dining room table can become a sufficient desk, and a drawer of the kitchen cabinet an effective file cabinet. Others may set up their office in an attic alcove or a basement laundry room. In areas with a warm climate, your office could be a screened-in porch or patio.

However, the ideal office is a separate room with space enough for all needed office equipment and record-keeping facilities. Many people use an extra bedroom or utilize all or a portion of a recreation room. An older writer friend of mine took over her child's abandoned, backyard playhouse, where she can bang out stories free from even the jangle of the telephone.

Once you've located your office space, it will be necessary to determine how much office equipment you need. This too, will depend on your type of business. For a tax consultant, an accountant, or the owner of a business counseling company, a complete office setup may be necessary immediately. However, many who sell a product or service, such as pet-sitting, find that they are able to start out with the very minimum amount of equipment.

You must judge for yourself which pieces of equipment will get you started. Go slowly at first. Others can be added as your business progresses. For example, you may want to invest in several pieces of equipment all at once—a duplicating machine, an adding machine, a dictating machine, a copy machine, a tape recorder. But be sure you need what you buy and that you get the best buy for your money.

This can often be accomplished by watching the "For Sale" columns of your newspaper. Large offices turn in their older machines when they buy new ones. A good used piece of equipment can often be a better buy than a cheaper make in a new model.

Sometimes a desirable desk or lamp is advertised in a furniture-for-sale column, or an auction offers a piece you can use. A young wife and mother I know, who writes short stories for women's magazines, picked up an antique roll-top desk, with loads of drawer space and all those interesting little pigeon holes. When she is finished writing each day, she rolls down the top, locks it, and her manuscripts are safe from her toddler's destructive little hands.

In considering what you should buy first, be assured that for almost every endeavor you engage in, a typewriter will come in handy.

If you are a writer, as I am, it is an essential piece of equipment which will be in constant use, and therefore should be the best you can afford. I recommend an office, or compact, electric model with automatic carriage return. If you shop around, you can buy a good, used, reconditioned model with up to a year's guarantee for around $175.

Should your business require only an occasional letter to be typed, however, a manual, less expensive model will serve you nicely. You can often pick one up at a garage sale for as little as $15.

Next on your list of office priorities, I suggest a filing cabinet. Though you may start out with a makeshift filing arrangement, each business day will bring you closer to the need for a regular filing system. A metal two-drawer cabinet would be a good starting investment. You may even end up with two of these, as did a friend of mine who is a breeder of AKC registered German Shepherds. He placed a plain, flush door over them and voila! He had a desk. Later, when he purchased a regular desk, he cut up the door and used it for shelves.

Along with the desk, you will, of course, use a chair. If you plan to do much sitting, you'll need one that is comfortable and gives your back proper posture control.

Also be sure that you have proper lighting. A good desk lamp is a prerequisite for your office, while fluorescent lighting is easily installed in your work-shop area.

As you progress, you will learn to develop techniques for storage. You must do this yourself, since what works for one individual and one type of business will not necessarily work for another. However, there are a few rules, which if followed, will result in a neat and efficiently run office.

1. Keep only current work on your desk. Everything else should be filed or put in its proper place.

2. Keep material which you are currently using in marked file folders.

3. Set up a good filing system and discipline yourself to use it.

4. Be careful not to misfile material. You may never find it again.

5. Keep your files current. Go through them on a semi-yearly basis.

6. Keep outdated material in a file set up specifically for that purpose—or destroy it.

7. Use your round file (waste-basket) frequently. Keeping irrelevant material can overload your filing system and be confusing.

MAKING PHONE CALLS AND MAILING LETTERS

No one need tell you how important the telephone and the postal service are to the success of your business. There are few businesses in existence today that could continue to operate efficiently, if at all, without them. Knowing how to take advantage of all they have to offer in the way of service will save you time and money.

First, let's take a look at *how to get the most for your telephone money.* As a beginning business person, you must first decide how many phones are necessary. Many people do well by using only their local number. However, if there are teenagers, or long-winded adults in the family, or if a telephone is an integral part of your business, you'd be wise to have a business phone installed.

Color phones are in these days, but a black one will cost less, and also be easily differentiated from the family phone. It will also lessen confusion if the ring of one phone is different from that of another.

Aside from convenience, there is another advantage in having a business phone. You get *free* listing, using the name of your company, in both the white and yellow pages of your telephone directory. You are also eligible for various free telephone-education services. For instance, telephone companies have trained personnel to explain phone service, to teach telephone manners, and to help you make the most of other handy telephone devices and equipment.

Perhaps you are already familiar with the following money-savers. Remember to use them in your business.

Use direct dialing whenever possible.

The cost of long distance phone calls varies within a 24-hour period. Take advantage of this by placing your calls during the least expensive time.

Check on the lines into major areas where you do a lot of business.

Check on conference calls, an arrangement which allows three or more persons to converse together at the same time.

Always ask to have your call returned, when the party you call is not in.

A section devoted to *how to answer your phone* may seem

needless to you. But the manner in which a caller is greeted can reflect on your business.

Perhaps, in the beginning, your home phone will also serve as your business phone. In this case, it would be helpful if your family could remember to answer each ring with a businesslike greeting. Even if you have two phones, and the family has been instructed not to answer (or use) the business phone, chances are there are times when they will.

What's wrong with "hello?" Nothing when it is a greeting in answer to a call from a friend. However, a better opening to a business conversation might be one of the following:

> Good afternoon, Green's
>
> Good morning, John's Cycle Shop
>
> 483-3972, John Green speaking
>
> John Green Company
>
> Green's, Lisa speaking

Any of these is highly acceptable. Anything, in fact, that will fulfill the three objectives listed below.

1. The caller knows he has reached the right number.

2. You give him the courtesy of telling him to whom he's talking.

3. Your approach should immediately lead him to tell who he is and why he is calling, which in turn gives you the information you need to determine the course of the call from that point on.

While we're on the subject of telephones, you might wish to consider an answering service. This service is beneficial whether you step out of your office for a few minutes, take an hour for lunch, or are gone from home on a two-weeks vacation. It will report the names and phone numbers of all incoming calls. Some services will dispense simple information to the caller and accept simple messages from customers. Others will even screen your calls for you, advising you of a caller's identity, and giving your business a more professional touch.

Your needs will determine which kind of service is best suited to your business. A veterinarian, for instance, will require constant service, whereas a lawn-care operator may be happy with an eight-hour service coverage. However, you may pick up a new customer and derive other additional benefits from late-hour coverage. A phone unanswered could mean the loss of a customer.

I've already mentioned something about knowing how to use your post office in the chapter on mail-order. However, since this can be a definite advantage for the person engaged in a home business, there are additional pointers to be considered.

One such, is the fact that most home mail deliveries are made only once a day, twice at the most, whereas the post office itself receives mail several times daily. This means that the order you received in your 2:00 P.M. mail delivery today, could have been sitting at the post office since early yesterday morning.

Sometimes, if you have an agreeable postmaster, he will accommodate your need for a more frequent mail delivery by allowing you to go to the post office and pick up your own mail. If you enlist the help of someone else to make the pickup for you, call the postal authorities ahead of time and request that they release your mail to that person. Or perhaps you will want to rent a post office box where you may check your mail as often as you wish.

Another area that can cause concern is outgoing mail. Try to locate a mail deposit box near your home with an hourly pick-up schedule. This will aid you in getting out those last minute letters and can often save you a day in delivery. If you aren't aware of the location of such a box, a call to your postmaster will provide this information.

You can also save time with postal equipment—money too, if your business utilizes the mails to any great degree.

Always keep a good amount of postage on hand. This, plus having a postal scale to weigh your mail, can cut down on the time you might spend waiting in line at the post office. Instead, with your letter or package already stamped, you need only to drop it in the correct mail slot and it's on its way.

Typing time can be saved by the use of window envelopes whenever possible. Other time savers are airmail and regular post cards, and pre-stamped envelopes.

DECIDING ON A WORK AREA

Earlier we discussed the importance of having an office, even though it be nothing more than a drawer of your dresser. It is equally important that you have a defined work area—a place where you can leave your work out, and then return to find it exactly as you left it. A place that is off limits to the rest of the family.

How do you select a site that affords you these luxuries when you work at home with family and friends constantly underfoot? Perhaps, like writer Jean Kerr, you may have to resort to locking yourself in the garage in the front seat of the family automobile. Ideally, however, your workshop should be close to your office (or vice versa), in the same room or general area, if possible. This puts everything at your fingertips and eliminates time-wasting trips back and forth to check on orders and other records.

Again, your type of business, the size of your home, and the circumstances under which you must work will determine, in part, where you set up shop. A 48-year-old man with a heart condition found it necessary to locate his découpage shop on the first floor of his home to reduce walking and stair-climbing. A mother of young children will want her workshop in a location where she can keep an eye on the activities of her toddlers.

When you've decided on the proper place for a work area, how do you provide for storage? The answer will depend on your business needs. If you are in pet-sitting, your need for storage space will be comparatively small. Room for a few grooming tools is all you'll need. A desk drawer or filing cabinet may be all the space required for an office-oriented business. However, should you be in the house-party line, or in some phase of manufacturing, you will need more room in which to store supplies and materials.

Most people I've talked with solved the storage problems of a beginning business by utilizing whatever they had at hand. An old cedar chest can be cleaned out to make room for knitting and other needle-work yarns and patterns, or be taken over for the storage of just about any craft materials you can name. Sometimes, the shelves of an old cupboard can be used for small machine storage as well as for parts and pieces of some manufactured item.

In Illinois, a small-car mechanic partitioned off half his garage for a workshop, using a built-in workbench and the shelves above it for storage of small parts and tools. Large parts, such as fenders and doors, he had hanging from walls and rafters.

Another young man, who operates a wrought-iron shop, had material to store in such large quantities that he rented a neighbor's garage. So you see, much will depend on your need.

With storage for materials and supplies provided for, you will want to think of other ways to equip your workshop. This is the way some business people I know have done it.

One enterprising woman, who has children of grade-school age, operates a secretarial service from her home. Her office workshop is a portion of her kitchen, which is equipped with a small metal desk, a comfortable chair, and a typewriter. This space affords adequate light, electrical outlets, is within reach of the telephone, and allows her to be aware at all times of the comings and goings of her family.

A photographer friend, who lives in an ancient house, took over a basement room that had once served as a coal bin. His first step was to build a partition which divides the room. On the windowless side, he created a photo-developing workshop, complete with darkroom. On the other, fluorescent lighting supplemented natural light from one small window, providing cheerful office space for a desk, filing cabinet, and other necessary equipment.

A man in Detroit, retired and with grown children, has taken over the entire recreation room for his woodworking shop. Large saws and a drilling machine occupy one end, together with a workshop bench and a host of small woodworking tools. On the other side of the room he has set up a complete, but compact, office.

Along with efficient equipment and space in which to keep it, one of the chief requirements for the home business person is *family cooperation*. Without this, your business doesn't have much chance of succeeding.

Few people are prepared to believe that you really work at home. You might have a hobby, or putter about a bit in your basement. You might spend a few hours each day at your desk, poring over papers and writing letters. But conduct a business that makes money? Not likely! If you are married and have children, even these people will need time to get used to the idea that the work you do at home can be as financially rewarding as that done by the person working out in the "regular" business world.

Until your work-at-home routine has been established and accepted by the members of your family, you will undoubtedly have to put up with interruptions and distractions—even resentment that you are within reach, yet unavailable. On the other hand, once they accept your home business and the work it entails, they can be of help with many activities as well as discouraging visits and phone calls by friends, while you are working.

Remember, you won't be able to get away from husband, wife, children, in-laws, and other relatives. They know you're there. So rather than trying to hide from them, solicit their understanding and cooperation.

Another area which must concern the home business person is

how to avoid accidents. Since it is a well known fact that most small accidents occur in the home, consider how much greater that percentage can become when you have a workshop in your home. Not only can an accident cause pain, even death, but it might also result in grave financial loss to you and your family. A customer may decide to sue merely because he broke his little toenail while falling over a loose board in your back steps.

Most injuries and law suits can be avoided, however, if you will but take a few safety measures beforehand. Such an approach would include three things.

1. Find and remove physical hazards. Do you exercise care in your home that guests don't trip on ragged carpets and children don't get into poisonous medicine bottles? Then do the same in your shop. Keep harmful material locked up and dangerous machines disconnected when not in use.

2. Set rules and stick to them. Make your workshop off limits, especially to children. Try to impress people with the danger of what can happen to an inexperienced person in your work area.

3. Use preventive safety maintenance. Always be on the alert to new areas of danger and try to eliminate them as soon as possible. A nail protruding from a wooden table, for example, should either be hammered down or removed before it causes an accident.

CONSIDERING SOME DISADVANTAGES

In the beginning of this chapter we considered some of the advantages of having an office or a workshop in your home. Although low overhead, tax deductions, and being with your family may sound rewarding, I would feel remiss in my responsibility as an author of this book, if I neglected to point out that there are also some disadvantages.

Since working at home, then, can also have its drawbacks, you will have to learn, among other things, *how to handle distractions.* These may appear in the person of family, friend, cleaning lady, mailman, garbage collector, and various other visitors who will have a tendency to interrupt you in the course of the day. You may also find yourself intrigued with a neighbor's dog giving birth to puppies, or the artistic bent of the tree trimmer on your street.

Your best defense is a rigid resolve to stick to your work at all costs, plus a firm power of concentration. You are, however, entitled to an occasional coffee break and a liberal lunch hour. During these times you might wish to stretch your legs in the backyard, to help Johnny build a sand castle, or to visit with friends and family.

Another disadvantage that you must learn to overcome in a home business is loneliness. This is particularly true if you happen to be a painter, a writer, or are skilled in some other art or craft which keeps you isolated from people day after day.

One of my writer friends, who is a widow, overcomes this problem by getting out in the evening as often as possible, and by making definite dates with friends to meet for lunch, see a show, or do something together, even though it be nothing more exciting than a downtown shopping trip. Another way to make sure you get out with people, is to join a club or a sports league which has regular meetings, and will depend on your being there.

Checking on expansion now, before you start your own business, may save you grief later on. Sometimes a business is so successful it surpasses its owners original plans. As his venture builds, he soon runs out of office or workshop space in his home. He needs more room in which to operate effectively, but finds that he has no place to go, no room to expand. And he is forced to move into a business location somewhere else, unless he wishes his business to remain static.

This happened to a "young" 64-year-old man, who started an antique business in the basement laundry room of his small ranch home. As the business grew, he took over one basement room, then another, until there was no place left that wasn't cluttered with sleigh bells and hump-back trunks. He finally had the choice of moving to a larger home or renting a shop. He chose the latter, but it was a difficult decision for him to make.

Another disadvantage to be considered is the lack of business facilities available to a home business. We have already mentioned the values to be gained from multiple mail deliveries, the advantages of mailing out-going letters early in the day, and the inexpediencies incurred with one-day postal delivery and pickup. But even though you find a way to cope with these difficulties, there are others to be faced. You will also be somewhat removed from offset and printing shops, libraries, and other in-city located routine services of benefit to any thriving business.

In some instances, your home address might be classified as a disadvantage. Suppose, for example, you live on a street in one of those newer developments—1220 Robin's Egg Blue Lane, or 64 Clover Circle Grove. Who's going to be fooled into thinking that this is a business address? And might not some people rather deal with a "big" business concern rather than a one-man, home-centered operation? But perhaps you can get around this by using a post office box. If you're lucky, your postmaster may even agree to automatically forward your box mail to your home address.

11

How To Finance Your Home Business the Money-Making Way

As a fledgling business person, you probably have the basic knowledge needed to keep records which separate your gains from your losses. These are elementary essentials. However, no matter how clever you are about money matters, it is likely that you will need financing at some stage of your business.

It takes money to expand, to grow, to enlarge your base of operation. But don't let the word finance scare you. Borrowing money isn't the awesome and frightening process some people have painted it. In this chapter you will learn some general techniques to help you borrow money and profit right from the beginning.

EXPLORING YOUR SOURCES OF CAPITAL

As I stated in an earlier chapter in this book, there are some business ventures which can be started with no investment whatsoever, utilizing instead, a talent, a skill, or materials which you already possess. There are also those endeavors which require some small amount of capital, and there are those for which thousands of dollars are required. However, even for those ventures which require no money outlay at the start, as the business progresses, availability of money sometimes becomes essential. Now where do you get the money you need?

Your first source of capital could be *your own pocket.* If you are starting out on a small scale, you might possibly have enough money on hand to buy the materials and equipment you will need to put yourself in business. This can be money from a personal savings account, from stocks and bonds, or from an insurance policy. However, you will need more than this "starting" money. It is wise to keep in mind that every business needs capital for two reasons.

1. You need money for your initial business plunge.

2. You need money to use as your business progresses.

The first will take care of fixed assets, such as equipment or tools. The second, classified as working capital, will be needed for supplies, paying wages, extending credit, and other day-to-day operating expenses, plus marketing and advertising expenses.

Because it is very important for you as a new business person, to have sufficient capital on hand, if you aren't able to finance yourself, there are several other places to turn for financial help. One is *the pocket of a friend.* This doesn't mean, however, that you approach him with the idea of a handout or a personal loan. You must be prepared to offer a percentage of your business, perhaps a partnership or a corporation deal. Such an arrangement means that you must work with someone else and share the control of the business with him. Even though he may be a "silent" partner, you must be prepared for his recommendations and offers of advice in every aspect of the business. However, if you're not willing to take someone into your business just to obtain capital, there are other places to look.

One such source is the government. Perhaps you qualify for one of the government programs presented earlier in this book. Aside from those previously mentioned in Chapter 2, there are also economic opportunity loans available from the government. This type of loan makes it possible for the disadvantaged, who have the capability and the desire, to own their own business and to become part of the economic life of their community. Both prospective and established small businessmen may receive assistance under this program. It provides both financial and management assistance, with a maximum amount of $25,000 for up to 15 years.

To qualify for this program, an applicant must demonstrate the ability to operate a business successfully. There must be reasonable assurance that the loan can be repaid from the earnings of the business, and the applicant is expected to have some of his own assets invested. It is also required that his total income not be sufficient for his basic family needs, and that due to social or economic disadvantage he is denied the opportunity to acquire business financing through normal lending channels.

If you think you might qualify for this program, contact your SBA field office, or write to Small Business Administration, Office of Public Information, Washington, D.C. 20416.

Another area you might wish to investigate as a source of capital are the venture capitalists. These are individuals or organizations who are willing to lend money as an investment for themselves. If you deal with these people you might expect to pay a higher interest rate than on money obtained from a commercial bank. To ensure protection for yourself as well as the lender, make certain that all papers are drawn up by a reliable attorney.

You might also consider the sale of company stock as a source of capital. Usually, however, the sale of stock through a public offering is not available to the small business beginner. The company is not large enough nor does it have a history of sufficient earnings to enable it to pay dividends and thus is no real attraction for people who would not have a share in control of the operation of the business. But once your business reaches a stage of development whereby it can offer investment advantages to the stockholder, you have a good built-in source of capital.

For example, when Green Thumb Enterprises, a nursery owned by Jon Maxwell, was offered the landscaping contract for a complete urban renovation program, the need to expand the business was quite apparent. John couldn't take on such a big job contract with only the two men he employed or the tew machines he had on hand. To obtain the needed capital for more equipment and a larger payroll, his banker suggested he sell stock in his company. Because John's records showed sufficient earnings and assets in the past, and the business now had a most promising future, he felt there was an adequate market for its securities.

Offering stock in his company quickly brought John the necessary capital he needed. Contracting for bigger and better jobs caused the company's gross annual income to skyrocket from $12,000 to $30,000 within a short time.

Another source of capital for the advanced business is a loan through an insurance broker. A few insurance companies, such as the Prudential Insurance Company of America, make mortgage loans on commercial properties and others offer term loans such as you might obtain from a bank. This type of financing involves rather high interest rates, usually on a 12-year basis and the companies which offer it are extremely selective, looking for businesses which return 20 percent or better on equity, and almost always requiring warrants or conversion privileges to obtain stock of the borrower company. However, it might pay you to investigate this source, if you can offer adequate security.

The business opportunity columns of your newspaper are another source of capital that can't be overlooked. For instance, the following ads appeared in a single recent issue of the New York Times.

> Private investor financing consultant has clients with unlimited funds for worthwhile solid business proposals.
>
> Are you endowed with the ability but lacking sufficient capital or encouragement to proceed on your own? I can help finance and actively participate in a joint venture.
>
> Immediate cash available. Any worthwhile project anywhere in the U.S.

Advertised operations of this type range from the highly respectable down to outright loan sharks, so be especially careful with whom you deal, and what you sign.

Of all the sources frequently used by the beginning business person, *bank loans* still remain most popular. You will be well advised to consider bank financing, particularly since your local bank is anxious to provide financing for businesses within its service area and will tend to be liberal and helpful. The amount your bank can or will lend, depends to a large extent on what you, the borrower, have as capital.

WHAT YOU SHOULD KNOW ABOUT BORROWING

Some beginning business people can't understand why they are turned down when they apply for a loan at a lending institution, when others have no problem in obtaining a loan from the same source. They are also surprised to discover that there may be strings attached to their loan. It is important that before you approach anyone for a loan you know something about borrowing money.

One of the most important factors in obtaining a loan is to make sure your business is credit worthy. A bank or any other lending source wants to make loans to businesses which are solvent, profitable, and growing, or have the potential thereof.

A lender will also hesitate to lend money to you if you are vague about *how much you need* and for what purpose it is needed.

When seeking funds for a small business, bear in mind that your request or proposal is competing with all other applications. The attractiveness of any particular type of proposal depends on many factors in addition to the figure analysis. Some are personal, regional, or institutional preferences. There are also factors akin to fashion cycles.

Here are some questions to ask yourself before you ask for a loan.

1. What sort of person am I? As far as my business is concerned, am I reliable and do I have the knowledge and ability to make a go of it?

2. What am I going to do with the money and how much do I need? When starting a new business, one doesn't have the advantage of estimates based on previous inventories and accounts receivable. Therefore, your needs must be fairly accurate estimates.

3. Am I borrowing for the purchase of fixed assets or working capital or both? Be sure to allow ample cash for your working capital; for instance, giving yourself leeway to do special promotion work at the right times, and to keep your credit rating high.

4. When and how can I pay back the loan? Your business ability and the type of loan you are able to obtain may well be determined according to your answer to this question.

5. What is the outlook for business in general and for my business in particular.

Aside from answers to the above questions, there are other *questions the loaner will want answered.*

As we have discussed, your business can acquire capital from private and public financing. There are advantages to both. If your company is already of significant size in earnings and assets so as to be able to sell stock, some of the advantages of public financing are:

1. More lenient terms and less direct interference in the operation of the company.

2. The publicity that a registered public offering brings can be beneficial.

3. A lower cost of acquiring money.

However, if your business is just getting started, the largest source of financing available to you is private. It offers these advantages:

1. Money can be obtained more quickly than through stock issue.
2. It costs less because there are no registration and underwriting expenses.
3. If you wish to change business practices or make adjustments in your business, you have only yourself or a partner to deal with, rather than needing the vote of all the stockholders.
4. If your first source of capital is satisfied, a second loan can be easily negotiated.
5. There is no need to disclose your operating figures to the public and your competitors.

MATCHING THE SOURCE OF YOUR CAPITAL
WITH YOUR NEED

When you set out to borrow money it is important to match the source of your capital with your need. The purpose for which the funds are to be used and the way you intend to repay the debt are important factors to be considered. Therefore, be sure you choose a lending institution appropriate for you. Each has its own policies and standards. Don't borrow from your old family banker, for instance, just because your family has been banking with him for years. Do a bit of scouting first to see where you can get the best deal.

Suppose you need *a short-term loan* for inventory purposes. You intend to repay the debt as soon as your inventory is complete and has been converted into salable merchandise. In this case, the lender expects his loan to be repaid within a short period of time, as soon as its purpose has been served and usually no longer than three to six months. Such money is granted either on your general credit reputation with an unsecured loan or on a secured loan—against collateral.

The *unsecured loan* is the most frequently used method of obtaining funds and represents a loan from a commercial bank. You are not required to put up any collateral, but are granted the loan on your credit reference.

A *secured loan,* on the other hand, involves a pledge of some or all of your assets. This is the largest source of financing available to you and can be obtained from banks, individuals, and insurance companies. Acceptable collateral would be real estate, stock, capital equipment, inventory, and accounts receivable.

Using private stock as collateral, Ted O'Keefe secured a loan of $1,500 to enlarge his small cement sculpture business. With the loan he was able to buy new molds and another cement mixer (used), and thereby take advantage of a large order placed by a local seed store owner. This exposure led to more and bigger orders which enabled him to pay back his loan in 90 days.

Term-borrowing is another way to acquire money. This is money which you plan to pay back over a long period of time. It can be broken down into two forms:

1. Intermediate, which consists of loans longer than 1 year, but less than 5 years.

2. Loans for more than 5 years.

Most people pay back a term loan in periodic installments from earnings. For example, four years ago, Sophie Lewis borrowed $8,000 from her banker to expand her arts and crafts business operation. The loan was to be repaid in monthly payments over a 10-year period. Now, in her enlarged building, she not only offers classes in arts and crafts, but has many "home crafted" articles for sale which she imports from all parts of the country. Because this new attraction adds greatly to her income, she feels confident that her debt will easily be paid off in accordance with her agreement.

Equity capital is money you don't have to repay. But you must sell a part interest in your business to obtain it. If your company is a going concern, people will be willing to risk their money in the purchase of stock. They are interested in potential income rather than in an immediate return on their investment. However, as I mentioned earlier, this is not a feasible route for the beginning business.

KNOWING ABOUT BANK LOANS

New business people often feel ill-at-ease when dealing with banks. Frequently their experience with them and their knowledge of how they operate is limited to the use of a personal checking or savings account. However, most banks offer a wide variety of services of value to the business person. Aside from business loans, these can include:

Credit references on customers,

Check certification

Payment of freight invoices

Payroll accounting services

Discounting customer's accounts and notes payable

Safe deposit boxes

Night depositories

Perhaps the bank you deal with at present is as good as any other, and can offer you the services necessary for your business. However, before making a final decision, here are 12 pointers to help you choose the right bank.

1. If possible, choose a bank with knowledge of your type of business. Such knowledge can better help them understand and evaluate your business needs.

2. Choose a progressive bank. Some banks are more interested in loans for new products and services than are others.

3. Choose a bank convenient to your business. This not only lessens the risk involved in transporting cash, but acquaints you with another businessman in your neighborhood—your banker—who has faith in the future of your community and will be willing to invest in it.

4. Check the size of a bank. Usually a convenient branch bank can offer you all the services of its main office, or a small bank can draw on the resources of a larger bank.

5. Choose a bank whose officers are available for consultation when you need it. Your choice of a bank is best made when you first start out in business. However, if you discover, as Sophie Lewis did after she had been in her arts and craft business for several years, that your current bank doesn't offer you all it should, it's time to change. Mrs. Lewis visited several banking establishments in her vicinity and talked with the president of each one. In locating the one that best fulfilled her needs, she used the five pointers listed above as well as those which follow.

6. Choose a bank used by a number of potential customers, where check clearance will be quickly available to you.

7. Choose a bank that is willing to furnish you with the information you need concerning customer credit.

8. Choose a bank that makes all types of loans available.

9. Choose a bank that doesn't take long to have a loan approved.

10. Check on the type and amount of collateral required for loans.

11. Check on repayment terms.

12. Check to see if you must maintain certain balances before the bank will grant you a loan.

Figure 1 is an example of a personal financial statement, similar to that which you will be asked to fill out when applying for a bank loan.

When you have satisfied yourself that you have found the right bank, there are certain things your bank will want to know about you. On your first visit you might bring a prospectus estimating expected sales, expenses, and anticipated profits. Don't try to pad the financial facts about your business. They are best placed out in the open for you and your banker to examine. This mutual frankness will help to build your reputation for good character integrity, and since bankers, like lawyers and doctors, have a code of ethics, the information will be kept confidential.

The three pointers listed below will help you to get faster and better service from your bank.

Explain your plans freely, even inviting your banker to your home to show him your place of operation.

Tell him about your source of materials and other supplies.

Explain your business experience and the operating techniques you plan to use.

In building a strong relationship with your bank, *getting to know your banker pays off.* Jon Maxwell's banker, Fred Hanns, is not only a business associate but a friend as well, a relationship which began when the two men served together on a civic affairs committee. As a friend, Fred was in on the ground floor of Jon's nursery business, taking a personal interest and steering him to many shortcuts when he was in need of service from the bank. For instance, when Jon needs a quick credit reference, he can ask Fred for information over the phone.

Once you have established a rapport with your banker, it is important that you *keep a good credit rating.* The following pointers will help you.

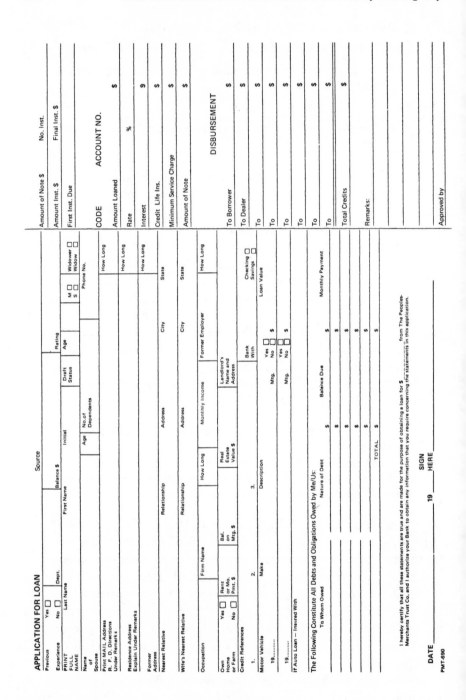

Figure 1

1. Make sure your accounting system is accurate.
2. At all times know the cost of offering your product or service to the consumer, of selling, and maintaining it.
3. Don't allow your bank accounts to become accidentally overdrawn.
4. Don't skimp on the amount of money you borrow to run your business, but be sure to pay it back with interest when it is due.
5. Don't abuse your credit by using money borrowed from the bank for any purpose except that for which it was loaned to you.

CHECKING ON YOUR COLLATERAL

When it comes to lending money, there are few individuals or institutions that are willing to take unnecessary risks. This is especially true of banks. Therefore, even when dealing with a bank at which you are well known, don't feel offended if you are asked for some type of collateral.

When requesting a loan from a bank where you have maintained a long standing account, your signature as security, may be the only necessary requirement. However, in most cases, the bank will expect you to put up something else of value as assurance that the money will be repaid.

A *chattel mortgage loan* is one way to obtain the money you need. Sometimes you can get a loan by assigning your *life insurance policy* to the bank. Another kind of collateral, which can be assigned to the bank, is your savings account. In such cases, an assignment statement must be signed by you and your passbook held by the bank. If your savings are in a different bank, it will be noted in their records that the account is being held as collateral for the lender bank.

Real estate is another form of collateral which is acceptable for loan purposes. If you own property you wish to use in this way, your bank will need the following information.

Location of the real estate

What it consists of as regards buildings and land

The foreclosure value

The type and amount of insurance you now carry on the property

If you don't wish to offer any of the above as collateral, there are other ways to avail yourself of a loan. Perhaps you might make use of a co-maker, an endorser, or a guarantor. These are people who can bolster your credit by signing a note with you. They make themselves liable for the note they sign should you fail to pay your debt.

Established businesses often obtain money on their accounts receivable, although this is not a probable source of collateral for the person who is starting a new business. However, if you have advance orders for your product or service it is not impossible.

A bank may take accounts receivable on a notification or a non-notification plan. Under the first, the customer is informed by the bank that his account has been assigned to it and he is asked to pay the bank. The other plan allows your customer to continue to pay you, and you in turn pay the bank.

If you own stocks and bonds, these can also be used for collateral, but they must be marketable. As a protection against declines in the market value, banks usually lend no more than 75 percent of the market value of high grade stock. On Federal Government, or municipal bonds, they may be willing to lend 90 percent or more of the market value.

HOW LENDERS' LIMITATIONS CAN
AFFECT YOUR BUSINESS

A lending party, whether an individual or a bank, is not just interested in having a loan repaid. It is also interested in the borrower who has a healthy profit-making business. Therefore, even though they may require collateral for a loan, they set loan limitations and restrictions to protect themselves against unnecessary risk and against poor management practices by their borrowers. Sometimes these lenders' limitations can affect your business, although not always adversely.

Why are you required to sign *a loan agreement?* This is a document which covers or refers to all the terms and conditions of the loan. The reasons for such an agreement are twofold.

1. They protect the lender's position as a creditor.
2. They assure the lender of repayment according to the terms.

Negative covenants in the agreement restrict the borrower from acting in certain capacities without the lender's approval. For example: he can't add to his debt, such as applying for another loan from another source.

On the other hand, *positive covenants* spell out things the borrower must do. Examples:

He must maintain a minimum net working capital.

He must carry adequate insurance.

He must repay the loan according to the terms of the agreement.

He must supply the lender with financial statement and reports.

Be sure to thrash out the lending terms of an agreement *before you sign.* Although loan agreements can be amended from time to time, or certain provisions may be waived from one year to the next with the consent of the lender, it is always wise to check them out carefully beforehand. Ask to see the papers in advance of the closing date and get the advice of your associates and outside advisors. Try to get terms that you know you can live with a year from now as well as at the present time. Often a legitimate lender will give some if you point out that a certain term or terms will be difficult to fulfill.

Banks and other lending institutions ask that you sign a loan application, in duplicate, before advancing you a loan. Some applications are more detailed than others, necessitating more knowledge about the applicant. Figure 2 represents a simple statement such as might be required by most banks.

For more information on financing your beginning business, the following booklets can be obtained *free* from field offices and Washington headquarters of the Small Business Administration, Washington, D.C.

Loan Sources in the Federal Government—Management Aid #52.

The ABC's of Borrowing—Management Aid # 170.

Building Strong Relations with Your Bank—Management Aid # 107.

Is Your Cash Supply Adequate?—Management Aid # 174.

THE PEOPLES-MERCHANTS TRUST CO.

LOAN APPLICATION

Date _____

OFFICE: 01 · Canton — 02 · Massillon — 03 · Brewster — 04 · Belden — 05 · 30th Street — 06 · North Canton

☐   New   ☐   Renewal

BORROWER	COSIGNER (S)
NAME:	NAME:
ADDRESS:	ADDRESS:
TELEPHONE:	TELEPHONE:
OCCUPATION:	OCCUPATION:

Amount applied for _____ Rate _____

If Renewal:
Original Date: _____

Total (including this application) owed Bank _____

Original Amt.: _____

TYPE OF LOAN:

☐   Secured Demand   ☐   Unsecured Demand
☐   Secured Time (30, 60, 90 day)   ☐   Unsecured Time (30, 60, 90 day)
☐   Secured Term (Over 365 day)   ☐   Unsecured Term (Over 365 day)
☐   Secured (Minimum Charge)   ☐   Unsecured (Minimum Charge)

PURPOSE OF LOAN: Business ☐   Purchase Securities ☐   Personal ☐

_____

_____

PAYMENT PROGRAM: **PAYMENT FREQUENCY:**

☐   Pay in Full at Maturity   ☐   Stated Payments to be Made Monthly
☐   Renewals Permissible at Maturity   ☐   Stated Payments to be Made Quarterly
☐   Renewals Permitted with Reduction of Principle ☐   Stated Payments to be Made Annually
☐   Disposition to be Discussed with Loan Officer ☐   Stated Payments to be Made Irregularly

Payment Amount _____   Includes Interest ☐   Excludes Interest ☐

Description of Security: _____

_____

Statement Date: _____   Maturity Date: _____

APPLICANT ALSO HAS: Signature of Borrower and Cosigner:

☐   Time Deposits   Amount _____   Mr. _____

☐   Demand Deposits   Amount _____   Miss/Mrs. _____

☐   Installment Loans   Amount _____   Mr. _____

☐   Other Commercial Loans Amount _____   Miss/Mrs. _____

☐   Trust

☐   Safe Deposit Box   Officer _____

☐   Master Charge   Additional Comments on Reverse:

☐   Computer Application   ☐   Yes   ☐   No

☐   Other (Explain)   Committee Action:

PMT-622 Rev. 7/72

Figure 2

12

How to Make Big Money
Right from the Start

The whole purpose of this book is to help you find the right business, and once you have found it, to help you make big money from its operation. This is truly possible if you are dedicated enough and go about it by learning the practices that lead to big money and eliminating the bad habits that keep you from this goal and result in business failures.

SELLING SECRETS TO START YOU OFF

Let's assume that you have selected your business carefully. You've studied your community and its needs. You've decided how best to fill these needs with a business in which you have a basic working knowledge. All that is needed now is for you to follow through with good salesmanship and you're on your way.

Selling isn't difficult. You don't need previous experience. You needn't be a genius. There are techniques that can be learned. But there are many selling secrets practiced by experienced businessmen that may escape notice by the beginner.

Therefore, you'll need to make a study of how to promote sales. This is an area as vital to your business as production or marketing plans. Perhaps more so. For you are in business only as long as you have someone who is willing to buy what you have to sell.

Before putting a sales plan into operation, you will already have identified your market and have a marketing plan in mind. You must then consider all of the market opportunities that exist for your product or service. Will you sell retail or wholesale? To a boutique or to a jobber? Will you do the selling yourself or contract it out?

Experience has shown that direct mail, mail-order, or catalog selling can be used to approach a very minute segment of the market, or to sell large quantities of goods. Will your sales be through one of these outlets, or will you sell from a home shop, a chain store, or door-to-door? In determining which way is best suited to your purposes, you must also take into consideration the needs of your potential customers.

For "Red" Stevens, salesman for a solid-state electronic security system, "crime" paid off. His product was a set of sensors, placed throughout a home, which alert authorities at the first moment of intrusion or fire. In just ten months, "Red", who is 28, advanced from a salesman to regional sales director for his company. As a beginner, his method of tapping the extremely security-conscious market was to watch local newspapers for burglary and fire locations. Next day, visiting homes throughout the neighborhood, he would demonstrate his product at every opportunity. In his first two months "Red" sold 17 full security systems, at $4,000 each, and recently he closed sales totalling $14,500 for one week.

An entire book could be written on the subject of sales promotion alone, and indeed many are. You'll find those mentioned at the end of this chapter most helpful. You, of course, will have to develop your own sales plan. Once you know what the job you want done is, you can devote your time to the study of those particular sales promotion ideas which will work best for you.

One way to promote selling is to use *positive sales language.* Think about your product or service in terms of what it can do for your customer. He, or she, will be drawn to an item that can promise one or more of these four things.

1. Something that will help him to attain popularity, health, riches, or prestige.

2. Something that will save him time, money, or effort.

3. Something that will lead to self approval or accomplishment, such as friendships or knowledge.

4. Something that will strengthen his self image by making him more attractive, more successful, or more effective in some area.

When it comes to selling, another technique not to be overlooked is *word-power.* Whether you place an ad in a magazine or newspaper, use a direct, door-to-door selling approach, or tack up posters in strategic locations to make your business known, the kind of words you choose will have a direct bearing on your sales.

According to research done at Yale University there are 12 English words regarded as persuaders, which pinpoint self interest.

YOU	MONEY
HEALTH	EASY
NEW	SAVE
PROVEN	GUARANTEE
RESULTS	LOVE
DISCOVERY	SAFETY

Whether or not you plan to sell by mail, look at the advertisements in any mail-order catalog. How many times do you see phrases like: Save money; New discovery; Big savings; Fast results; Money back guarantee. And don't discard the word FREE.

Listen as a professional salesman talks to a prospective buyer. Count the times he uses the word *you.* A noted sales psychologist tells me that people don't always hear the words we speak. Let me explain. While you're using the word *you,* your customer is hearing the word *me.* A question such as, *What is your opinion?,* brings your customer into the conversation and is an indication on your part that you recognize him as an educated and well informed person. Other phrases are: *What do you think? You're right. Do you have any thoughts on this?*

Using the right word at the right time became part of the Jack Powers sure-fire selling method. Jack is a top salesman for one of the country's leading encyclopedia publishers. His clients consist mainly of parents, teachers, and students. However, his approach to selling can be advantageously adopted by anyone having something to sell. Jack claims that a salesman's strongest tool is knowledge. Because he constantly implements this tool in his business, he seldom loses a sale to his competitors.

Let's take a look at Jack's approach.

1. He knows his product thoroughly and can answer any questions put to him by his clients.
2. He knows what his clients want—the best education for themselves and their children.

3. He knows how his products will deliver this *want,* or need to the client, and he communicates this to them.

MAKING PEOPLE'S WANTS WORK FOR YOU

If you plan to make big money right from the start, your product or service must fill a need. And, in every instance, a customer has the need that your business is going to satisfy—either a customer who returns again and again or a new one you are trying to reach. Today, people's wants and needs are many. Some want to live better, to be more successful, to acquire more efficient tools and household appliances, to have more money. Others want to have more leisure time, or to look younger, or to be more attractive.

It was with this last premise in mind that Davis Factor invaded France. This young man carried a suitcase containing the feminine aids to beauty which were manufactured inexpensively by his father's relatively unknown cosmetic company in the United States. Thus "Max Factor" arrived in France.

It was his belief that women were the same the world over and that he had something that every woman wanted. Women in the U.S. were eager for something to make themselves more beautiful. So too would be the women of France. French cosmetics were expensive luxuries for the wealthy; Max Factor cosmetics would be available at low cost.

His phenomenal success, not only in this country and in France, but throughout the world is legendary. Today, Max Factor and Company is one of the best known and most respected business names in the cosmetic industry. In fact, growth abroad has an even greater potential than in the United States. And it all began because a young man saw a need to satisfy women's desire to look more attractive. Whatever your business, this "Max Factor idea" will apply—give the people what they want at a price they can afford to pay.

It's easy to make people's wants work for you when you know your customer. But how can you know what will motivate your customers to buy? You might practice sizing up the customers you meet in your business. What are their tastes, temperament, background? You don't need to do an in-depth study or ask pointed questions to do this. Friendly interest and casual conversation, in which you *listen,* will bring about responses which will uncover attitudes and discover needs of the buyer.

Aside from getting to know your customer, it is always good practice to *demonstrate your product's worth.* The best way to do this is to show reasons why your product or service will be of benefit and, when possible, demonstrate this to your customer. If you can offer a good reason for him to buy, or show how your service can be of help, you'll have a sale.

For even though a potential customer wants your product or service, he also needs to be told or shown reasons why he should have it. A housewife wants to be able to explain to her husband that having the carpets cleaned by your service will not only prolong the life of the carpet and save the cost of buying new, but will also save her, or her husband, the time and energy required to do it. The man about to purchase a new puppy for his family wants to be able to tell them that they not only have a protector, but a pet which will provide an interesting and educational experience for them.

This is the time to use the basic rules of persuasive selling. These are simply ways of persuading your customers that they really need your product or service. Let's take a look at them.

1. Know your business. Be prepared to answer any questions the customer may raise. What is your product or service all about? What benefits are to be gained from using it? What qualifies you as a business person in this area? How have others gained from your offering?

2. Counter objections. Objections to your product such as, "I already have one," "I don't need one," "My husband wouldn't want me to buy it," or "It's too expensive," can be sales-stoppers. Be prepared for them.

3. Have confidence in your business. Whether you're manufacturing plastic toy-model-kits, or offering a typing service, be convinced that your venture is the best. This confidence and sincerity will come across.

4. Use sales psychology. Remember to make people's desires work for you. A student's desire to make the track team can sell him on the idea of eating organically grown "health food." A manufacturer of rubber gloves sells his product to women by suggesting them as an aid to beautiful hands.

5. Don't oversell. When you've reached a point where the customer is ready to buy, stop and sell. From this point on, anything else you might add will only be anti-climatic and serve to weaken your former presentation.

You can also increase your profits by adopting the following "do's."

1. Do be careful of the way you look. Personal cleanliness and neatness of dress are big selling points.

2. Do be polite. People won't tolerate rude or discourteous remarks or attitudes.

3. Do empathize with your customer. By putting yourself in his shoes you can better understand what approach will cause him to buy your product or service.

4. Do tailor your selling technique to his specific needs.

5. Do remember to follow up your customer contact by sending samples, brochures, newsletters and the like.

6. Do try to find out something about your customer. Does he have a family? What are his hobbies? Other interests?

7. Do acquaint yourself with your customer's business organization. Secretaries and other employees can frequently be helpful.

8. Do emphasize value. As a lasting feature, value or performance of an item or service over a long period of time is often a main selling point.

AND BE SURE TO OBSERVE THESE "DON'TS"

1. Don't run down your competition. Instead, stress the good points of your own business and the advantages the customer will have in availing himself of it.

2. Don't confuse your customer. Present facts and figures about your business clearly, step by step.

3. Don't neglect visual aids. Whenever possible use sales displays and literature.

4. Don't hesitate to ask the buyers for an opinion of your product or service. Often their constructive criticism can help you in building a better business.

5. Don't do all the talking. Stop occasionally and give your customer a chance. You can learn much if you are willing to listen.

6. Don't antagonize your customer. Disagreeing or arguing with a customer will gain little satisfaction for you, but it can lose sales.

7. Don't be a bore. Talk about your product or service only as it relates to your customer, rather than concentrating on the business as it relates to you personally.

8. Don't be a tattletale. Passing trade gossip on to a customer is bad business.

PLEASING YOUR BOSS—THE CUSTOMER

As I mentioned before, your business—any business, large or small—can exist only if it has customers. You can have the finest product, or offer the most needed service; you can have all the financing you'll ever need; you can have the most expensive and up-to-date equipment and the best educated employees working for you. But until you have a customer you don't have a money-making business.

Suppose you are selling an organic product such as honey. In the beginning your customers could be friends and neighbors to whom you sell directly. Or you might sell through club and church affiliations. Later you can sell to food stores, with your list of prospects being made up of wholesale grocers, buyers for food chains, and food brokers.

Or perhaps you might wish to go into mail-order selling. In that case you will want to obtain a list of people most likely to be interested in buying honey. Homemakers and health food addicts come first to mind.

Once you have established yourself, it is necessary that you *understand your customer's needs.* This means being on the alert to his buying habits, his likes and dislikes, and his demands. Aside from offering your customer the product or service which he needs and wants, you must offer it in such a way that he prefers doing business with you rather than one of your competitors.

If you expect your business to flourish and make money, knowing *how to deal with your customers* is equally important as understanding their needs. But to do this effectively, you must know why your customers buy your products or service, and particularly, why they buy from you.

People buy something for three principal reasons:

1. They need it.
2. They can use it.
3. They want it.

Suppose a young woman comes into your candle shop for the express purpose of buying four candles to decorate her table for a dinner party she is hostessing that evening. She needs the candles and they are her primary purpose for coming to you. However, while in your shop, perhaps she sees an attractive candle holder, just right for the large, fat candles she uses during the holiday season. She buys the candle holder because it is something she can use. Browsing further, she comes upon a very large, very expensive, hand-carved "art" candle. She doesn't need it. She most certainly isn't planning to burn it. But just having it in her home will give her a pride of ownership. So she buys this candle too—because she wants it.

Knowing the reasons shoppers buy from you can also be an advantage in learning how to keep your customers coming back for more. Why did the young woman choose your shop? Perhaps it is close to her home, or your hours are convenient for her. Maybe you offer a wider variety of candles than your competitors. Perhaps she likes the idea of having a choice of related objects from which to choose—candle holders, incense burners, and table decorations. Or perhaps it is because you offer credit buying and allow your customers the freedom to browse about among your merchandise. Maybe she knows that your shop is clean and neat and that she can always find the newest line of candles on display.

Whatever her reasons, she will keep coming back as long as they exist, and as long as your shop and service continue to please her. To help you do this with all your customers, you might ponder the answers to the following five questions

1. What is their income level?
2. What is their age level?
3. How do they react to new merchandise?
4. How do they react to promotional material?
5. Who buys more often—men, women, children?

Knowing the answers to the above questions can help you to turn complainers into satisfied customers. Remember, a customer is not about to adjust his buying habits to conform to your way of conducting a business. In fact, quite the reverse is true.

EXTRA SELLING POINTS THAT WILL
TILT THE SCALES IN YOUR FAVOR

What you're trying to sell—the product you make, the service you offer—will determine your selling technique. You may have to try several different methods before you arrive at the one which is best for you and will lead to the greatest profit. Therefore, it might be wise to experiment a bit on a small scale before you commit all your resources to one way.

This is an area where selling research pays off big. Many benefits may be gained by looking ahead. On the other hand, if you introduce a product or service without any idea of which course to follow in moving your idea into the hands of a consumer, you can find yourself with very serious problems.

In this same area you will want to consider which type of advertising will work best for you and which marketing procedures you should follow.

If you are planning to sell through retail sales methods, or if you plan to have a shop in your home, you can take advantage of "impulse buying." I'm sure you have noticed that many people buy "on the spur of the moment." You've probably done it yourself. That's what impulse buying is all about—getting the customer to buy something that he didn't plan for. Something that he happens to see and wants, and decides to buy in a few minutes.

A man may go into a fishing and tackle shop to buy a new reel and impulsively lay out money for a hand-tied fly. Food items such as honey and special home-made preserves will be picked up on impulse by the housewife doing her routine shopping. Many craft items are bought on impulse. Novelties of all types can be classified as impulse items.

A successful impulse item is attractively presented and usually priced between $3-$5. It is a brand name or something that the customer already knows about. It is easy to store or can be consumed quickly and is usually small or lightweight. Because people thrive on change, there is always a ready market for impulse buying.

Another method of selling in this same vein is *suggestion selling.* Again someone enters your shop or place of business with the intention of buying a needed or wanted item. It then becomes your job to try to interest him in purchasing a more expensive item than the one he had intended. You might also suggest additional items for which he hasn't asked.

Make a habit of showing your higher-priced items first. Many of your customers can afford them and will buy if they are encouraged. Suppose a man comes into your picture-framing studio asking for a frame to fit a small water color. You point out the features of one of your better frames and he buys it. Before letting him walk out of the shop, try to interest him in another frame, or a side line which you carry, such as picture hooks, wire, or small miniature paintings.

At all times it is important to *stress the personal touch.* To keep original customers coming back, and also to cause them to spread the news of your business by word of mouth, which is good advertising, you will want to encourage them to identify with you.

In stressing quality and taste, you should especially *cater to young customers.* There are three reasons for this.

1. Teenagers between 15-19 years of age have terrific spending power in our society. So too have the young marrieds, 20-24 years of age. They are also our fastest-growing group of adults.

2. Because of their age, these young people have a longer customer life. As they mature, they will need more and more of the product or service you have to offer.

3. Because, in general, young people are intelligent, they are constantly moving up the economic scale. They often buy on the basis of their aspirations and future expectations rather than on their present incomes. They are attracted to high quality, the new, and the different. True, they are just getting started, but their futures are promising. Check out their credit ratings, to be sure, but don't shun them.

Once your business is established, another way to tilt sales in your favor is record keeping. Any business will benefit from keeping records on customers and prospective buyers, on advertising results and correspondence. These can be handled in the same manner as was discussed in Mail-Order, Chapter 7.

A good *financial* record-keeping system is enormously helpful to your success in business. These are your accounting records and have to do with money—that which goes out and that which comes in. As a beginning business person you can keep adequate accounting records yourself, in a journal or ledger from a stationery store.

You'll need an account of:

Cash receipts—cash which the business receives

Cash disbursements—amount of business expenses

Sales—summary of monthly income

Purchases—purchases of merchandise or supplies bought for processing or resale

Payroll—wages of employees, including yourself

Inventory—investment in stock

Accounts receivable—the balance which customers owe

Accounts payable—the amount you owe to creditors and suppliers

If you don't wish to undertake the task of keeping your own books, there are others who can do this for you. Perhaps a member of your family can help you. Another possibility is a certified public accountant. He will, of course, charge considerably for his time, operating expenses, and profit.

To my mind, a free-lance bookkeeper best serves the beginning business person. You will find them listed in the yellow pages of your telephone directory.

She or he will sit down with you and decide, first of all, what type of financial records will be most helpful in your particular business. You will also be advised on cash requirements, borrowing, business organization, budget forcast, and taxes. Your bookkeeper will meet with you twice monthly to collect your raw sales receipts and bills. From these she will prepare your financial statements. This will include a profit or loss statement which will show what profit or loss your business had in a certain time period.

ADVERTISING YOUR PRODUCT OR SERVICE

A planned advertising program can help you to start selling right from the start and keep profits on the increase. Still some people feel that it will cost too much money. Or they don't want to be bothered with it.

But the only real way to build your business is to keep telling people about it. That means a steady, skillful advertising program set up with careful planning and a wise use of the media best suited to your needs.

First off, let's examine the purpose of advertising. It is essentially your way of communicating with the public. As a seller of a product or service you are out to persuade potential buyers to become active purchasers. This you do by informing them about your offering and giving them reasons why they should patronize your place of business.

Jane and Art Crawford, a young San Francisco couple new to the antique business, feel that even with a limited budget, they must use advertising. During their first year, a small, moderately priced ad placed in the yellow pages of the phonebook proved a most effective weapon in the competitive struggle with other antique dealers, and built up public recognition. Later, inexpensive business cards, distributed at antique shows and sales, helped to give their business an identity of its own, and earned them an annual income of over $14,000.

To *obtain maximum effectiveness from your advertising,* your ad must do four things.

1. It must attract attention. This can be done by leaving ample space in your ad so that it doesn't appear crowded; by the use of color or attractive pictures; by distinctive borders and eye-catching word-pictures; by relieving an otherwise monotonous effect with distinctive type face and varying type sizes.

2. It must persuade the customer. This can be done with pictures or with words, or both, but it must lead the viewer to want your offering and move to buy it.

3. It must outline a need. It must show why the product is necessary and what it can do for the customer.

4. It must invite purchase. A limited time offer or a special price, will induce the customer to buy *now,* at this particular time.

When deciding upon your advertising copy, keep in mind the *basic rules of advertising.* 1. Simplicity 2. Credibility.

When planning your advertising campaign, don't overlook free advertising. Junp at every chance to get your name before the public, whether it be the subject of a feature article in a business publication or the story of your prize rose garden in the local newspaper.

Elaine Young, operator of a miniature furniture craft shop, did this very thing by letting her local newspaper know all the details when she caught a second-story burglar by using an old hobby—roping. The tale made the front page news, and though people may no longer remember her name, they still associate her shop with the lady who "lassoed a bandit," and this has helped business.

She still continues to avail herself of free publicity at every opportunity. Newspaper people remember her and this is helpful when she submits items about herself or her business.

Perhaps you are a member of a club, a fraternal organization of some kind, or a church group. Try to get your name before the public by being active on committees and becoming involved in various club functions. This too helps to spread your name.

And don't forget trade journals or company newsletters. They are always anxious to receive material. If you've discovered a new display technique or a clever time-saving plan that works for you, let others know about it.

Along with free advertising, you will want to get started with *classified ads.* For the beginning business person on a shoestring budget, those found in the daily classified section of your newspaper will probably be the least expensive way to go. A 15-word ad, run for 7 days, will cost about $9.45 in most newspapers. Magazine rates are usually somewhat higher.

If you inquire about larger advertisements, you will discover that the advertising departments of these publications often offer assistance in copy preparation, art work, and layout. They may also be willing to advise you on your sales promotion planning.

SELLING YOUR PRODUCT—WHERE?

You have a product or service and you want to sell it. Where do you turn? Place it on consignment in a near-by gift shop? Try to place it in a special section of a large downtown department store? Offer it over local radio or TV? Or perhaps, as discussed above, you will want to use the classified ad section of your newspaper.

Maybe you are a maker of macramé leaded glass, jewelry, flowers, knits, wood sculptures, tinware, or some other handcraft. Perhaps you offer a service such as baby-sitting, lawn-care, home cleaning, pet-walking, or tool-rental. No matter what business, you'll want to let people know about your selling market.

We've already discussed classified advertisements, both here and in the chapter on mail-order. But there are various other ways to sell your product or service.

Let's first investigate how direct selling works. As the name suggests, this medium brings the seller in direct contact with the buyer—either in person or through the mail. It is through your own hard work, your perseverance, your aggressiveness, your selling ability, that your service or product will sell and will move your business toward bigger profits.

Direct selling is a method of merchandising in which you sell direct to the consumer, either yourself or through a personal representative. It enables you to render a personal service to your customer and to eliminate the middleman, the retailer, the jobber, and the wholesaler.

As a direct seller you have the advantage of the undivided

attention of the customer. You show your product, demonstrate its merits—and write your order.

There are also advantages to selling through cooperatives and exchanges. Markets for needlework, leather goods, and crafts of all kinds, as well as foodstuffs, can often be found at bazaars and women's exchanges. Paintings and sculptures are frequently sold through cooperative exhibits, as are gems and cut stones. Many antique dealers depend wholly on the sales they make during an antique show. Because people are attracted to displays of this type, the seller has the advantage of drawing upon a much larger customer potential than he would were he the only person selling in this field.

However, you may wish to try selling through small retail boutiques. These small shops, often located in the most populated shopping areas, provide an excellent outlet for the home crafter. Even though he may specialize in the sale of one particular item, the shop owner may not be adverse to selling your product. He may even welcome the opportunity.

A perfume boutique owner in Detroit, for instance, was delighted to display the scented candles of a home craftsman among his own merchandise. In a little town in Indiana, a wedding boutique accepted a line of homemade jewelry. A small interior-decorating boutique in New York City made room for a selection of home-crafted paper weights. In each instance, the boutique owner deducted a percentage of the selling price as payment for the use of his shop as a "showcase" for the product.

This same approach can be used to sell in department or chain stores. Simply try to match up your product with the section of the store that sells complementary merchandise. In this case, however, instead of obtaining permission to display your product from the owner, you will seek out the manager of the department. He, in turn, must abide by the policy of the store, but in many cases that includes taking merchandise on consignment.

You may also wish to take advantage of other sales media. One method might include selling through jobbers or wholesalers. In this arrangement, you sell your product to a middleman. You allow him an agreed-upon discount from your price to the retailer, and he assumes the credit risks.

Another outlet for your product is a mail-order house. These companies often contract to buy your entire output over a given period of time. They will buy at a low discount price, in exchange for which you are relieved of all credit risks, plus the problem of selling.

A direct sale to a large store or chain organization would be enacted the same way and would net you the same benefits. There is one drawback, however. Since you would be selling your entire stock to only one customer, your business could find itself in difficulty. Suppose that one customer, for one reason or another, should decide to drop your product? Things might be a bit tight until you could secure another outlet for your goods.

SELLING AT THE BEST PRICE

"Buy low, sell high," has long been a sure-fire formula for making big money. But, these days, the consumer is ever watchful of his pocket-book and not always willing to pay what you ask.

How then do you determine the best selling price? The *best* for your product or service is not always the price that sells the most Nor is it always the price that brings in the greatest number of sales dollars. NO. The best price is the one that will maximize the profits of your business.

This means that it will be high enough to cover your costs and help you make a profit, but low enough to be in line with competition, attract customers, and build sales volume. Volume produces profit. For it is only with volume that materials and supplies can be purchased in quantities large enough to warrant wholesale prices. And it is only with volume that employees can be kept busy enough to prevent your paying for idle time. Without volume you cannot expect to make *big* money.

How then do you set your price to insure volume? The first move is to *estimate material costs*. What price must you pay for the supplies required to put together your product or operate your business? Be sure to include every last penny you spend, for to overlook some small factor—a telephone call, even a postage stamp—may be the difference between profit and loss.

Another important area to consider when pricing your offering is *the worth of your labor*. Even though you may enjoy making or creating an item, or feel that your service is beneficial to you in other than a monetary way, remember, you're not in business for fun and frolic, but to make money. Place a fair hourly or daily rate on the actual time you spend in the pursuit of your work.

Don't forget to *include overhead costs*. There are costs in this area other than those associated with manufacturing and advertising. For example, in determining your price, don't forget to include the cost of electricity, heat, insurance, and equipment depreciation as well as other maintenance costs.

Because your product or service will only be considered by the buying public if it is worth its price, market awareness can help you. As a business person with something to sell, you need up-to-date knowledge of market conditions. The right selling price for a product under one set of market conditions may be the wrong price at another time.

Marketing research is broad in character and the best selling plan varies with product and service. It would be impossible to outline them all in this short space. You will need to experiment and study until you reach the approach suitable to your particular situation.

However, you might wish to start with the "direct costing" approach, outlined in a government pamphlet (see below).

Suppose, for example that you are considering a price for a ceramic ashtray, whose direct cost—material and direct labor—is $4. Suppose further that you set the price at $6. We'll call the difference ($6 -$4 = $2) "contribution" or working money. For each ashtray sold, $2 will be available to help absorb your manufacturing overhead, such as depreciation of equipment and building mainte-nance, and your non-manufacturing overhead, such as selling and administrative expenses, plus making a contribution toward profit.

Any price above your direct cost will serve toward paying your overhead costs. The amount of this "contribution" will depend on the selling price and on the number of units you sell at that price.

If you are interested in making big money right from the start of your business venture, the references listed below will be most helpful.

From the government: address the Superintendent of Docu-ments, Washington, D.C. 20402.

Free booklets from the SBA:

> *What is the Best Selling Price?* Management aid #193.
>
> *Developing a List of Prospects,* Management aid #188.
>
> *Accounting Services for Small Service Firms,* Management aid #126.
>
> *Advertising—Retail Store,* SBA Bibliography #20.
>
> *Record-keeping Systems,* SBA Bibliography #15.
>
> *Building Good Customer Relations,* Small Marketers' Aids #120.

Others include:

> *How To Build Your Sales Volume,* in Management Aids, Annual #2, $1.

Pricing Your Services for Profit, Marketers Aid, Annual #8, 35¢.

Color Can Stimulate Sales, No. 85, Marketers Aid, Annual #7, 50¢.

Understanding Why They Buy, No. 73, Marketers Aid, Annual #7, 50¢.

Financial Recordkeeping for Small Stores, SBA Management Series #32, 50¢.

Your library is also a source of much helpful material. Books include:

Successful Retail Salesmanship by O. Preston Robinson, C.H. Robinson, and George H. Zeiss, Prentice-Hall, Inc.

Planning and Creating Better Direct Mail, by J.D. Yeck and J.T. Maguire, McGraw Hill Book Co., Inc.

Advertising Proceedure, by Otto Kleppner, Prentice-Hall, Inc.

Secrets of Overcoming Sales Resistance, by Albert Goldstein, Parker Publishing Company, Inc.

Secrets of Closing Sales, by Charles Roth, Prentice-Hall, Inc.

13

How to Build Extra Profit into Your Business

More than likely, when you start out in business, you will operate by yourself. But as you grow, your organization will grow. It is wise, therefore, to think of yourself as an organization and to operate accordingly right from the beginning. From the day you declare yourself "in business," you must begin to think of your company's growth, its image, its goals, and most of all, its profits.

Ask any businessman, "Why are you in business?" He may tell you that he wants to be his own boss; that it gives him satisfaction; that it is a rewarding experience. But, if he is truthful, he will also answer, "To make money." To be successful he has to make a return on his equity. It is a risk element that must be paid for. He must receive compensation for his time and his capital.

SETTING GOALS FOR BUSINESS GROWTH

To achieve success in your business you must set goals for return on your equity. Everything you do should be directed toward contributing to the attainment of that goal. If your business is to grow it has to make money.

Since business is for profit it is important that you be in control of what you are doing. Making plans, setting goals and budgeting for those goals are the best efforts that you can make to control the future of your business. But you must also set up ways which will let you know at all times how your plans are progressing. Should you fall short of your goals, these controls will help you to discover why and to take action to change.

Keeping a small business on target involves watching trends, anticipating changes, and acting at the right time. It means keeping products and services beamed at customers and prospective customers in a combination of looking backward and forward. Examination of present and past records is needed if you are to successfully determine your weaknesses and strengths. Your resulting action may involve making changes in products, in channels of distribution, or both.

A case in point is the story of Thomas Rousseau who, to meet the challenge of the change in hair fashion, switched from barber shop to poodle parlor. When his barber business got so bad he was obliged to look for a second job to maintain his income, Tom decided to give it up in favor of something else. In searching for a new business, his barbering background led to two choices: hair-styling, a way in which many barbers found employment—or dog-grooming. He chose the latter, and after a six-weeks course which cost him $350, he celebrated the opening of his new venture—K-9 Styles by Tom. In his new venture, Tom grooms on the average of 4-6 dogs daily, giving him a monthly income in the $1,200 range.

In coping with trends and anticipating changes, it is wise to examine the life cycle of your product or service. New technologies are bringing about such an increasing number of new products that what was a big seller last week is a drag on today's market. Because of these rapid advances in technology, your product may become obsolete within a short time of its introduction. Likewise, a new trend or technique can render a former well-paying service no longer necessary.

The typical product life cycle has four stages:

Stage 1 is a testing or introductory period, In it your product will have a low consumer awareness, low consumer acceptance, and as a result, small sales.

Stage 2 is a growth period. In this phase your product becomes better known and sales gains are rapid.

Stage 3 is a leveling off period. Product sales are stable.

Stage 4 sees your product on the decline. Sales decrease.

The end of a product's life cycle, however, may not always be the reason for sales decline. It could be a weakness in your business. How you correct a product or service weakness depends on what's causing it. It could be that your competitors have offered a better product for the same money. Perhaps they give the customer some fringe benefit that your service does not. To meet the competition you will have to follow suit.

Your marketing channels should also be checked for weaknesses. In our fast changing world, distribution channels can lose their effectiveness. Your customers' buying habits may change. New competition may develop. As a result, what you once considered an effective way of distributing your product, or selling your service, can become totally inadequate.

In setting goals for business growth, you don't want to neglect *setting production goals.* Logically, production objectives would start with your customers because they are the reason you're making a product or selling a service in the first place. You have something to sell that they want to buy.

Since your customers set your production goals, your planning of production should start with a sales forecast. How much do you expect to sell in a week, a month, a year? When do customers want their orders delivered?

For example, if your business is making and selling Christmas candles, you will probably have to make your products several months ahead because all of your customers will want them at the same time—the start of the season. On the other hand, if your product is handmade leather clothing, perhaps you will want to wait until you have definite orders for certain items before you start making the garment.

In the beginning, accurate sales forecasting may be difficult, but the task becomes less chancy after you've been in business for a while. You can then predict your next year's sales by analyzing your past sales and adding a reasonable amount for expected growth of your business.

CHECKING YOUR DISTRIBUTION SETUP

Probably your first way of distributing your product will be through local shops, department stores, or buying offices. And you will probably take your samples around yourself in trying to make your first sales. However, greater sales, higher dollar profit, and lower distribution costs can be yours if you are willing to take the time to do a little marketing research. A list of sources and procedures can be obtained *free* by writing to the United States Department of Commerce.

Several years ago when Bernice Crowley decided to sell hand-made quilts, she test marketed a twin size, double wedding ring pattern in her local dry goods store. Weighing customer reaction to her product alerted her to ways of increasing its sales appeal. For example, for promotional purposes she learned that the quilts best characteristics were its bright colors and its "handmadeness." She also discovered that because customers found the quilts most appealing, "just like grandma's," they were willing to pay more for them than she charged—she had grossly underpriced her product. Today Bernice sells through retail stores as well as mail-order. Her quilts bring $80-$160 each and the phrase, "just like grandma's" has become part of her advertising technique.

Flexibility means greater profits. Even though you may start off by offering the customer a product or a much needed service, it is a good idea, as the old cliché reminds us, not to "put all your eggs in one basket." Sometimes the sales of an established product or service decline and it is necessary to come up with a substitute in order to keep your business going. To offset the lack of sales which the decline of a product or service can cause, try to get in with a new idea as soon as possible. Perhaps you might come up with a new application for an old product. Even while your original product or service is riding the crest of popularity, you can add to your profit by offering associated products and services.

At the same time you can be working to *improve your channels of distribution.* Sometimes the sales yield from an existing channel can be increased by working more closely with your distributors. Providing tools, such as counter cards and displays, can help them to promote your product. You might also get better cooperation from small shops and other distributors by offering them help in inventory control and technical aid, if your product warrants it.

Detroiter, Daniel Gutenberg, found that something as simple as a more efficient delivery service resulted in more products sold. A cabinet maker with his own home workshop, Mr. Gutenberg's part-time specialty was a round, solid oak game table with pedestal foot. But although many admired his workmanship, he made few sales, averaging about one during a six-months period. However, when he advertised "free delivery," business perked up. Today, his tables add over $3,900 to his annual income.

Even though you may be pleased with your present distribution setup, sometimes the only way to keep sales building is by seeking and using a new channel of distribution. For example, Ginny Perkins, a homemaker who added adult ski caps to her line of children's knitted headgear, couldn't get proper distribution from children's clothing stores, her established channel for her children's wear. She had to seek new channels. Adult clothing and sports shops were able to provide greater opportunity for sales of the new item. This year with an anticipate gross volume of 3,000 adult caps, Mrs. Perkins is looking forward to an income of more than $20,000.

Another man, Fred Floto, producer of a cut-out wood product, was dissatisfied with an independent hardware store in which his product was displayed and sold on commission. He felt he needed broader distribution than the small store provided. By changing to distribution through a local variety chain, he got his product in many more stores and obtained a much larger coverage. Last year he also grossed a much larger income—$9,000.

In keeping your sales on a high level, looking ahead pays off. Planning that involves product or channel changes can't be rushed into at the last minute. It requires time. As your business expands and grows, you will want to add more products or additional services. You will want to find bigger and better ways of distribution for your product.

Keep in mind that new technology has shortened the life expectancy of many products, and negated the need for many services. The Small Business Administration tells us that of today's products, 60 percent came on the market as "new" within the last 10 years. In the future the rate of change will be even faster. Timing is most important in keeping your product's sales high or your service profit up. Know when to make changes and be prepared to make them.

JUDGING THE SUCCESS OF YOUR

BUSINESS OPERATION

A sound net profit is probably the most important indication that you are carrying on a successful business operation. However, many small businesses fail because the owner thinks he is getting a reliable profit picture, when, in truth, his information is not giving him a complete profit story.

To judge the extent of your profit it is necessary for you to adopt a questioning attitude in the areas where you might be fooled about profits.

1. In calculating profit, are you taking into account such items as depreciation and inventory?

2. Comparatively, can your profit be considered sufficient for your size and type of business?

3. Even though your total operation shows a good profit, are there areas or departments which are actually losing money?

4. Does your trend of profit show steady progress or is the tendency towards less and less profit?

In order to know your profit, an accurate and meaningful accounting system is necessary. As an example, let's take one of the most critical areas in the false profit picture—that of depreciation. Because he didn't check it out beforehand, Bill Jackson, a tree and shrub trimmer, judged depreciation of his new lightweight $300 chain-saw over a period of one year, based on daily use. Actually, it fell apart and had to be replaced at the end of six months. It seems like a small matter, perhaps, but for six months this wrong judgment was allowing Bill to get a false picture of his profits.

On the other hand, in calculating profit of her novelty gift shop operation, Grace Howell not only took into account such depreciation items as showcases and store fixtures, but she also set a sales deadline for her inventory. For instance, on an order of 100 pewter mugs, only 78 sold within her three-month-deadline. Therefore, the remaining 22 were immediately reduced in price and placed "on sale."

Grace Howell and other successful business people know that inventory alone does not mean profit. To produce a profit, a product or service must be *sold,* even at a reduced price.

1. Cash method

2. Accrual method

The cash method shows actual receipt of income and the actual expenditures of expenses. The accrual method, on the other hand, reflects business transactions which took place during the reporting period whether or not any money actually changed hands.

Since credit transactions may account for a large part of any business, I would suggest the accrual method. The cash method doesn't give as accurate a picture of where you stand, whereas the accrual method accounts for all activities, cash or credit, completed during the period.

In reading your profit and loss statement, it is also necessary that you consider maintenance and upkeep expenses for facilities and equipment. These are often forgotten because they occur only on a six-months or annual basis. However, when these bills come due, they can sometimes be large enough to wipe out profits for several months.

Another fooler for people who start a home business, and one which should, but seldom does, appear on their profit and loss statement, is their own salary.

Another item on your profit and loss statement which can distort your profit picture is the *cost of goods sold*. For example, suppose in your candle business, the closing inventory of your merchandise available for sale was valued high. The cost of goods sold would be lower and profits would be higher. Since the cost-of-goods-sold figure can be easily distorted by any change in the method of inventory valuation, it is a good idea to review your inventory procedures to determine if the basis used reflects the most realistic value of the stock on hand.

Controlling cash in a small business is also necessary for a profitable operation. But before you can make efficient use of your cash balances, you need to know your firms *cash flow pattern*. How much cash comes into your business each month? How much goes out? How much, if any, is left

Knowing how, when, and why he spends money in his home-painting business, assured Ted Stokes of its financial health and business growth. In the beginning, income from paint jobs didn't always cover Ted's capital expenditures such as drop-cloths, brushes, and ladders, and he frequently found himself in the red. Now, however, he keeps a sufficient quantity of working cash to pay incoming bills for materials and daily expenses. He finds that this approach not only preserves his good credit rating with the companies from which he buys, but it makes a favorable impression on his banker, who is always happy to lend him capital when the need arises.

Grace Howell admits the same to be true of her gift shop business. She also feels that cash flow records come in handy when trying to estimate future cash balances. Her simple budget technique involves two steps:

1. Adding to her cash balance at the beginning of the month her estimate of income expected for the next month.

2. Subtracting her estimate of expenses for the next month.

Doing this for 12 consecutive months gives Grace her expected cash balance for each of the 12 months, knowledge which she finds most handy when planning ahead to Christmas, her busiest time of year. It allows her to have cash on hand, or arrange for a loan to take care of the increased merchandise and increased accounts receivable which she expects in her peak season.

Knowing your cash flow ahead of time will allow you to use your excess cash to produce income. For example, let's suppose that you've been in business for two years. During that time you've kept a close watch on incoming and outgoing cash and you are aware of the months when your cash inflow is greater than your business needs. This is the time to put that excess cash into something which will earn income.

You may want to invest it in new lines or products which can increase sales and profit. Or perhaps short-term securities appeal to you. Whatever you decide on, it is important that you keep your investments fairly liquid so you can turn them back into cash quickly should the need arise.

MEASURING THE RESULTS OF YOUR ADVERTISING

How much good is your advertising doing? It should be doing the job you intend it to do—bringing you more buyers for your product or service. If it isn't, perhaps you aren't using the right media or going about it the right way.

Basically there are two types of advertising available to you— immediate response advertising and attitude advertising. Each is designed for a particular purpose.

How do you use attitude advertising? Ted Stokes thinks of this type of advertising as "image building." Grace Howell calls it her "reputation builder." Actually, it's both. With it, you remind people day after day, week after week, about your product or service, or tell them about new or special services or policies. Such advertising should create in your customers the feeling you want them to have about your business—its products and services.

Because attitude advertising is spread over a long period of time, it is sometimes difficult to measure results. The sales it promotes can be created long after the ad has appeared. However, to some degree all of your advertising should help to build your image, even your immediate response advertising.

This type of advertising is used to cause a potential customer to buy a particular product or service from you within a short period of time—today, tomorrow, on the weekend. Ads of this type should be checked for results daily or in a few days after their appearance. It is also a good idea to check at the end of 2-weeks and 3-weeks periods, since all advertising has some carry-over effect.

When analyzing ads in relation to response, there are several devices which can prove helpful. For immediate response ads, a coupon is often used to represent the sale of a product. It can be used in various ways.

1. Coupons brought in. These can represent the sale of an item, or the request for additional information. If the coupon is dated, you can determine the number of returns for the first, second, or third run.

2. Hidden offers. Such a coupon offers further information upon request and can cause people to phone or write to obtain it. Results should be checked over a 1-week through 6-12 months period because this type ad may have long reaching effects.

3. Test ads. These are run on the same day in different parts of the same publication and each ad differs from the other in some way you would like to test. They can be identified by the message or by a code number so you can tell them apart.

As an example, Don Risher, owner of a household-cleaning business, placed two ads in the classified section of the Sunday edition of his hometown newspaper. They differed only in lettering. Pertinent information in the first ad was set in boldface type, while the same information in the second ad appeared in regular newspaper type. Don's objective was to determine which ad would bring in the most new business. Results proved the second ad as equally effective as the first. However, since placement at cost was one-half that of a boldface-type ad, in consequent advertisements, Don was able to save money in advertising expenses by using the ad with smaller type.

OPERATING FOR PROFIT

Once you have established your home business you must subject it to periodic checkups if you wish to make money and build your operation. Keeping your business pointed toward success means never losing sight of your goal to finish each year with a profit. This can be achieved in many ways. For instance, reducing waste increases profit. Everyone salvages obvious waste materials. We save paper clips and rubber bands for office use, and gather up excess materials from product production. But frequently waste in other areas goes undetected. What about waste of time? Leisurely telephone calls or errands unrelated to your business can cause as great a profit loss as the waste of materials.

In any business inefficient use of manpower also means waste. If a conveyor or a machine can do a job properly and inexpensively, you and your employees can be freed to do something that a machine can't do.

Wasted space can also reduce your profit. To work in a makeshift atmosphere can be debilitating to an individual. It also results in poor space utilization which in turn can necessitate excessive handling of material. Even though it may cost a little to rearrange your working space, it could mean a substantial profit in the long run.

Wasteful design can also be a way of throwing away profit. Sometimes a product uses material which, in fact, has no advantage over a less expensive material.

Sometimes even *throw-aways are worth money.* Take Mrs. Bessie Scott, an elderly widow who sells indoor plants to supplement her social security check. Instead of throwing away the broken-off leaves from African Violet plants, she uses them to start new plants. And she plants these slips in "used" paper cups.

Always be on the lookout to salvage discards such as cardboard boxes, paper bags, bottles, jars, anything that you can use in your business to cut down on the cost of buying new.

Aside from the waste that can curb your profits, some pricing practices lose money for you too. If you are in the habit of pricing new merchandise from products you already have on hand, you can easily cheat yourself. All new items should always be priced from the invoice costs, especially in these times of rising prices. You must also remember to change the price on "old" merchandise to reflect rising costs. If you mark down an item for a sale, be sure to re-price it after the sale is over. Another tip from the experts is that items found on sale too often can quickly lose their customer appeal.

Analyzing your records can also reduce costs and help your business stay aimed toward profit. However, unless adequate records are maintained through a proper accounting system in the first place, there can be no basis for ascertaining and analyzing costs. You can't reduce costs by attempting to slash your expenses unmethodically.

You must understand the nature of your expenses and how they interrelate with sales, inventories, cost of goods sold, gross profits, and new profits. Only then can you take effective cost-cutting action.

Your profit and loss statement should be a summary of expense information and be the focal point in locating expenses that can be cut. The Small Business Administration gives us a useful method for making expense comparisons. They call it a break-even analysis.

Break-even is the point at which gross profit equals expenses. It is the time that sales volume becomes sufficient to enable your operation to start showing a profit.

Another way to keep operating for profit is to *avoid bad checks.* Granted it is sometimes difficult to distinguish a bad check-passer from an honest customer. However, if you are constantly on guard and know something about checks, you won't often get stuck with a bad one.

In their position as owners of a large shopping center art gallery, Lillian and George Ellis take in a lot of checks. They have found that the following system helps to reduce losses from bad ones.

1. They never accept a check that's not properly dated; that is written illegibly; that is more than 30 days old.
2. They never give a customer change for a check, but ask that it be made out for the exact amount of the purchase price.
3. They always require identification to be sure the person holding the check is the right one.
4. They require that the check show the person's address and phone number as well as the location of the bank.
5. Although they always remain smiling and friendly, they're firm in refusing to cash checks for persons they know only slightly or not at all.

Mr. and Mrs. Ellis also feel that it helps to be familiar with various types of checks. Let's examine those you may be asked to cash or to accept for your merchandise or your service.

1. Personal checks. These are made out to you and signed by the person offering them.
2. Two-party checks. These are issued by one person to a second person who endorses it so that it may be cashed by a third person.
3. Payroll checks are issued to employees by a company. Usually the name of the employer is printed on it, it has a number, and it

is signed. The word "payroll" is also printed on it. Beware of cashing a payroll check that is handprinted, rubber stamped, or typewritten.

4. Government checks. These can be issued by the federal government, a state, a county, or a local government. Be particularly careful about government checks. Often they are stolen.

5. Blank checks. These checks don't carry the name of a bank. The buyer fills this information in, along with his name, address, and bank designation. The risk in cashing such checks is great.

6. Traveler's checks. These are signed when they are purchased by persons who don't want to carry large sums of money. The purchaser must counter-sign them in the presence of the person who cashes them.

7. Although a money order isn't a check, it can be passed as one, and is usually bought to be sent in the mail.

Although accepting bad checks is one type of loss you are likely to experience in your business, there are others more far-reaching. Fires, thefts, and injuries, for instance, make insurance a necessity.

Take Ray Bell, for example. Ray is still solvent and in business today because he took his lawyer's advice and covered his small welding operation with adequate insurance. At first Ray balked at casualty insurance. He had no employees and, since he picked up and delivered, no customers came into his shop. Fortunately, however, his lawyer, Dick Anderws, convinced Ray that such coverage was a good safety measure. A point that more than proved itself last year when a delivery man, coming too close to the welding activity, was the victim of a freak accident which put him into the hospital with third degree burns on his face and neck.

The following checklist for business insurance gives you an idea of the many forms available to you.

1. Casualty insurance. This protects you, your customers and your employees against loss from an unfortunate occurrence which happens without plan. A customer falling on a slippery floor, for instance, or an employee losing life or limb.

2. Burglary and theft insurance. This covers you for loss or damage to property resulting from burglary, theft, larceny, robbery, forgery, fraud, vandalism, wrongful conversion, and loss or damage to money, securities, and other valuable papers resulting from any cause.

3. Credit insurance.This covers you from loss resulting from the extension of credit or from customers non-payment of debts.

4. Fidelity bond. Should you have employees, this insurance guarantees you against loss caused by dishonesty.

5. Fire, lightning, and windstorm insurance. This protects you against financial loss because of damage sustained by fire, lightning, or windstorm. It also covers loss by smoke or water accompanying a fire.

6. Bodily-injury and property damage liability insurance. This covers you for bodily injuries and property damage while riding in a vehicle owned by you.

7. Business life insurance. This covers loss by your business from t.. death of someone associated with it.

These are but some of the many insurances available to the beginning business person. To be sure you are carrying all necessary coverages for your particular business, get the advice of a competent, reliable insurance agent.

Sharing information not only keeps you pointed toward profit, but in many cases helps to increase business. Any technical or "know-how" information about your business can frequently be of help to someone else. At the same time you share this knowledge, publicity in trade papers, technical publications, professional journals, magazines and newspapers, makes your company and its product or service better known to suppliers, customers, potential customers, and others in the business world. Such articles can enhance your business reputation, familiarize readers with your company, and result in greater sales for you.

Together with the points mentioned thus far, having a "success attitude" is yet another way to build extra profit into your business. You know by this time that you have the determination to plan ahead and the talent to reach the goals you set for yourself. This belief in your own ability can quickly transmit itself to your customers, inspiring their faith in you and your operation. You will find that with such a positive attitude, and by keeping an eye on details, your business success can easily be achieved.

14

How to Jump from Home Business
to Small Business

Every year, a sizable number of people become millionaires; about 5,000 more each year, according to prominent authorities. Many, like you, start out with a business in their home. As it becomes known, profits grow and continue to grow until the time comes when the venture reaches its limit of expansion in the home. For some, it remains at this same level for years, but for others, the big step toward making a fortune comes when they move from their home to a business location.

MOVING INTO A BUSINESS LOCATION

In this chapter we will deal with those businesses which, although they may be started in your home, have the potential of snow-balling so quickly that you may soon feel the need for more space than your house affords. When this happens, you will find yourself face to face with a new set of problems. Where to set up shop? Should you buy, build, or lease? How will the move affect the legal structure of your firm? These questions and others will be examined as we go along.

But first let's take a look at the *advantages a shop can give you.* For Patty Clark, a job placement consultant, the most welcome aspect of a shop location is more room. Ms. Clark rents a small suite of three 2nd-floor offices in the downtown district of Port Huron, Michigan, for which she pays $160 per month. These afford her ample space to interview clients, to consult with applicants, and to set up an office. Her central location has brought more business her way, plus the added advantage of knowing that her entire operation is enclosed in one area and therefore, no longer interferes with other members of her family, or they with it.

The latter also holds true for Clem Roberts, who recently moved his home upholstery business to a shop location. For $125 a month, a once-upon-a-time auto-display building offers him a large workshop area with a small adjoining office. Here he can leave his hammer and tacks lying about without fear of his small children hurting themselves. Another advantage, one which Mr. Roberts feels is partially responsible for the 10 percent increase in his $20,000 annual income, is the easy, drive-in availability of his pick-up and delivery service.

Having a business near other shops and stores is the chief advantage which Bob Edwards credits with boosting his candle business to an annual income level of $23,000. Customers from nearby shops make up a large part of his business, buying not only his original "homemade" candles, but many commercial varieties as well, plus numerous gift items he added as a new line when he moved. Bob also finds that being in a business location affords him the added advantage of proximity to mailing, receiving, and delivery services.

Once you have decided to move from home to shop address, you must decide whether you should lease, buy, or build. Building your own shop today can be very expensive, both for materials and labor. A strike by carpenters or electricians can delay your opening for weeks, sometimes months, and result in unforeseen expenses.

Buying could place you in a financial bind. If your financial position is not such that you can meet the terms of your purchase, you may find that you must spend business capital that you had set aside for needed equipment and operating costs.

Leasing seems to have the most advantages. Your initial investment is lower, leaving you ample cash to operate your business. Most lease and rental rates are such that you won't even need a bank loan. And you're not saddled with ownership risks such as fire, tornadoes, or value depreciation.

In estimating the costs of opening a shop, the amount of capital needed for each of the following should be considered: legal fees, licenses, advertising, fixtures and equipment; and post-opening operating expenses.

Rent will be one of your major items of fixed expenses. It must be paid each month regardless of whether or not your business is showing a profit.

Legal services can be most helpful at this time, both in site selection, lease provisions, and financial planning. Should you sign a lease for one year or longer? If building alterations are necessary, who will pay for them, you or the property owner? What about responsibility for maintenance of repairs to the building? When should you give notice to renew your lease? Before signing anything, you would be wise to seek the advice of your legal consultant who can give you the answers to all of the above questions.

When you do finally settle in the location of your choice, your "store image" will affect business just as it did in your home location. Don't try to change it without careful thought and planning. Prices, quality, and service are just as important now as before because the flow of your customer traffic depends on them.

What people see as they pass by your store is another important element in its image. Even people who never enter a store form an impression from its outside appearance. That impression causes them to walk through your doorway, or to pass by without a second glance. Customers base their opinion of your store on the image it projects, both inside and out, and their opinion can mean the difference between repeat or lost business.

To help keep your image sharp, the inside of the store must reflect quality and service. Fixtures, layout, and displays should create an atmosphere in which your customers will feel "at home." It should present an inviting appearance, with aisles kept clear and clutter avoided.

The experience of Dick Little, whose New York clothing shop caters to teenagers, is a good example. In the beginning, Dick's shop looked like any other young men's store—clean, neat, good quality merchandise at good prices. But he was barely making ends meet. On the advice of a friend, he borrowed money and re-did the entire shop. Mod colors, "black lights," and rock music made all the difference. Now the young people flock to his door. He is out of the "red" and earning an income of more than $40,000 per year.

Ask customers what they like about your new location and why they prefer it to others. Also invite customer complaints. These can frequently help you to determine which course to take in changing a poor image.

Try to see your store as your customers see it and use this

approach in periodic image reviews. This can help you spot defects and give you indications of how well you are obtaining your goals.

Sometimes the business you operate from your home gets along quite well without a formal name. But when you move from home business to small business it is necessary to *select a business name.*

Probably the chief reason you will have for moving into a business location is that of an expanding business. In fact, that's how baby-sitting became "Mrs. Irwin's Day Care Center."

Married and with children of her own, Glenda Irwin began early in her marriage to supplement her teacher-husband's income by baby-sitting in their home. Glenda's dream was to open a nursery school someday, but for a black couple like the Irwins achieving the goal seemed difficult. If you are determined, however, you can still make a dream come true, and Glenda did just that.

With a master's degree in early child development from Detroit's Wayne State University, Glenda is well qualified to direct the school. It is a thriving business, with 65 children enrolled five days a week. The school building is a renovated older home. Fulfilling school needs and meeting city requirements to convert it into a "school building" cost $29,000 and took almost 3 months. The installation of a 2nd-floor fire escape, and other fire code laws had to be met; outside play areas had to be fenced in; and the kitchen had to be remodeled to meet city health regulations.

Financing, one of the Irwins biggest problems, was resolved by the Detroit Area Chamber of Commerce's "Resource Bank." Not a money lending institution, but an advisory service, the bank is similar to those found in many cities. They are run by businessmen who donate their time and talent to help struggling small business operations. The bank steered Glenda to an accountant who helped her draw up a detailed forecast for her business. With that in hand, she applied to a city bank for a $40,000 loan, and the Small Business Association agreed to guarantee 90 percent of the loan.

MAKING MONEY WITH YOUR OWN MACHINE SHOP

The successful machine shop owner knows that hit-or-miss methods in any area of operation seldom succeed. Before moving from his home-based business and committing his funds to start in a shop location John Talbot investigated several areas. His first concern was to *choose a location.* Because he wanted to offer greater service (fabricating electrical components, such as capacitor banks, plus cleaning, repairing, and rewinding motors up to and including 400 horse power) to local factories, he looked for a building equipped to handle these operations. For example, a wooden floor might be acceptable for someone manufacturing tiny precision parts for microscopes, but only a cement floor could withstand the grease and oil and bear the weight of his large machines. Also, because of weight, mileage, and freight considerations, it was important that he locate near his customers and his source of supply. On the other hand, he didn't want a trading area that was overcrowded with competing shops.

Once a satisfactory location was found, John's next step was to *select the right building*. Keeping in mind that good light from windows cuts down electrical bills, and that fire escape routes are important, his chief concern, nonetheless, had to do with the type of machine shop he wished to operate and the type of orders he intended to solicit. Again, weight was a consideration. Ceilings had to be inspected and exposed beams examined to see if they were strong enough to support a hoist and other lifting equipment. The size of entrances to the building was also important. Doors had to be wide enough to allow large trucks to enter. When all of these things were checked out and approved, John was ready for business, and was able to obtain a year's lease, at $400 per month, on the building of his choice. Today, he employs three men on a five-day-week basis. His annual income, before taxes, averages $160,000.

If you are to make money with your own machine shop, you must *use space effectively*. Every square inch counts, especially if space is limited. Many owners of shops, both large and small, find themselves headed for trouble because of problems resulting from inadequate space. There comes a time when they realize that they must either use their space better or build new facilities. The latter can prove most expensive and even improving space utilization costs money and eats into profits. Better to set up effective space for your operation in the first place.

As a guide to the effective use of space in your shop, the following checkpoints will come in handy.

1. Keep aisles clear.
2. When possible, use conveyors and lifting devices to move materials.
3. Keep articles clearly labeled.

4. Keep areas well lighted.

5. Store items in the most easily handled unit.

6. Make full use of overhead and wall space.

You might also wish to check the following sources for further information:

From field offices and Washington headquarters of the SBA,

Effective Use Of Space In Your Shop—Technical aid #77—free.

Plant Layout Planning and Practice, by R.W. Mallick, published by John Wiley & Sons—discusses planning and determination of the efficient layout of job shop and production plants.

Another factor to be taken into account in setting up your machine shop is the *use of effective lighting.* When putting together your lighting system, installation costs, light renewal, maintenance, and energy cost should all be considered, as well as monthly payments to the electrical company.

IES Minimum Standards of Lighting

AREA	FOOTCANDLES ON TASK
Fine bench and woodworking machine work	100
Printing press	70
Jewelry and watch manufacturing	500
Wrapping, packing, and labeling materials	50
Loading and trucking	70
Service garage repairs	100
Fine hand painting and finishing	100
Sheet metal machines	50
Store showcases and wall cases	200
Upholstering	300
Candy making	100

For example, when Ruby Collins set up shop to manufacture her ceramic jewelry, she asked her electric company's power sales engineer to determine the proper quantities of illumination necessary for her various operations. At her two work tables, for instance, the lighting level required a minimum of 500 foot candles. To achieve this quality and quantity of light, fluorescent lamps, drop chains, and other shadow diffusing equipment was used. Initial installation cost about $350, but Ruby feels it more than pays for itself in more efficient work by her employees which, of course, means higher profits. Studies made by the Illuminating Engineering Society provide recommended minimum levels of illumination for various tasks, using the footcandle as a measuring unit. A good rule of thumb, figuring 25 candles per watt per square foot to be illuminated, is to allow three watts per square foot of surface area.

Another factor in the profit and growth of your business is a favorable working atmosphere. Control of illumination, noise, and temperature, plus making sure that your employees are at ease and comfortable will guarantee their best work.

When several employees, assembling parts at a workbench in a lawnmower sub-assembly shop owned by George Hill, complained of backache, it was discovered that the wooden stools upon which they sat were too high, causing them to bend over. As soon as the antiquated stools were replaced with new adjustable ones, backaches disappeared and the workers' daily output of parts increased. This resulted in accelerated production for Mr. Hill, whose shop, today, employs an average of 20 people and allows him an annual gross profit of over $150,000.

Before going into operation in your new location, ask yourself these questions:

1. Are operating conditions as pleasant as they can be made?
2. Are fatigue elements eliminated as much as possible?
3. Are desks and machines the right size in relation to the person who will be using them?
4. Is it easy to see what must be seen?
5. Are all safety rules applied?

Building a profitable business is not only dependent on you and the work you do, but also on your ability to *hire the right employees*. To hire a person without first shopping around for the best in the field is, perhaps, the easiest way, but it can also be the costliest. Right employees will help you make money. Wrong ones can waste time and materials, even drive away customers. Bert Russell, owner of a small marble-cutting operation, feels that it's to his advantage to screen applicants and to take time to interview each individual. As a starting point, he has them fill out an application form. This provides him with a written record of work experience, education, names of former employers, and other references which he checks out and evaluates before setting up an interview.

During a first meeting Bert tries to learn as much as possible about a job applicant's background and work habits. He encourages each prospective employee to talk about himself and his work experience. If the written application and the personal interview are satisfactory, the individual is then "tested" over a 30-day probation period, after which he is hired permanently if he proves capable.

Perhaps, as in Bert's case, the kind of skill you need is hard to find You may even have to settle for "second best." But try to choose an employee who will make a good trainee, one who has aptitude and is willing to learn.

Another way for the owner of a small machine shop to make money is to get your product on qualified products lists. Major government purchasing agencies set aside contracts or portions of contracts for small business bidding, and the SBA develops sub-contract opportunities for small business by maintaining close contact with prime contractors and referring qualified small firms to them.

To take advantage of these contracts, Abe Herman, owner of a small instrument assembly plant, makes sure that his product is made right and performs adequately. To guarantee quality of the finished assembly, he installed sophisticated electronic testing equipment. Because quality is one of the chief concerns of his buyers—whether it be government, industrial user, or consumer—Mr. Herman is able to give government agencies a step-by-step account of his testing operation and is always prepared for audits of his inspection procedures. Resulting government contracts bring him an additional profit of more than $200,000 per year.

The following will help:

Evaluation Of A Contractor's Quality Program, H-50—30¢.

Quality Assurance Provisions for Government Agencies—35¢.

Both are available from Superintendent of Documents, Washington, D. C. 20402.

Eliminating accidents in your shop is, in a sense, saving money. For accidents not only can cause pain, both for you or an employee or customer who gets hurt, but they can result in financial loss as well.

There are three things to which accidents can be attributed.

1. Hazardous physical conditions, such as slippery floors.

2. Improper safety regulations

3. Human physical defects such as poor eyesight or hearing.

It is up to you as the owner of a shop to set up effective accident prevention. Establish good safety rules and see that they are enforced. Warn employees about using dangerous equipment, and when not in use, keep it screened or covered. Your goal is to help your employees understand that accident prevention rules are for their protection.

The following sources can supply you with further information on accident prevention.

From the Small Business Administration:

Small Marketers Aid No. 104—preventing Accidents in Small Stores—free

Management Aid: Annual No. 1, Chapter 19—reducing Accident Costs Through Selling Safety to Supervisors and Workers—$1.25

Books from your library:

Industrial Safety, by Roland P. Blake, Prentice-Hall, Inc.

Handbook of Accident Prevention—$2.50—National Safety Council, 415 Michigan Ave., Chicago, Ill. 60611.

If you hope to run an efficiently operated shop, it stands to reason that you must compete effectively with others in your field. Allowing your competitors to operate a production setup which turns out an item more quickly than you can and with as good, or better, quality costs you money. One way to keep the money in your own pocket is through *tool rental.*

John Garvey, who several years ago opened a small machine shop in Detroit, usually makes small parts which normally weigh no more than 5 pounds and can be handled manually. However, he wanted to take advantage of a $100,000 contract with a large automobile plant. This required loading and unloading 20-pound parts, with full containers weighing 8 tons. John's solution was to lease a fork-lift truck which cost far less than the price of labor to "hand transfer" the parts into convenient weight containers for handling.

The terms of equipment rental plans are as varied as the types of equipment available for rental and should be checked out carefully before you sign an agreement. For the most part, however, rented or leased equipment carries the same quality and service guarantee as is given in an outright sale.

In starting his business, Hugh North, owner of a small machine shop in New Jersey, needed more equipment to keep up with competition. Finding himself limited in cash resources at the time, however, he leased equipment from a company which maintained and serviced the machines for him. This move freed funds for other business needs and, indirectly, led to the acquisition of two new-parts contracts. With profit from these jobs alone, Hugh was soon able to replace the leased machines with his own, thereby building an equity upon which he could borrow.

On the other hand, Bill Conrad, owner of a machine fabricating shop, often leases machinery year round. Leasing, he claims, allows him the use of modern, profit-producing equipment without depleting funds. For example, Bill recently had the opportunity to add $300,000 to his income, building a specific, sub-contract mechanism which required the use of highly specialized, gear-cutting equipment. Since it's unlikely that in two years he will have any further need for this particular equipment, leasing eliminates the need of disposing of obsolete machinery. He also saves at tax time by charging off rental to expense, rather than capitalizing the equipment by purchasing it.

The same holds true for John Howell, whose business is the construction of trenches, ditches, and drainage outlets. Offered a contract to level a hill at a construction site, he leased, rather than bought, heavy earth-moving equipment.

Although not every type of tool or machine is available through rental, if you think that leasing equipment would be to your advantage, or benefit your business, check with the rental agencies in your area. To rent tools or lease machinery, look in the yellow pages of your phone book under Tool Renting and Leasing Services. Also check the trade journals available at local libraries.

Before you commit yourself to a business site, conduct a traffic test. Experts advise clocking a location for half-hour periods at different hours on a number of days. If you have three likely sites, for instance, you might check the traffic pattern of each for one-half hour during lunch periods and on Saturday nights.

Once you've selected your location, be assured that it and your store image will have an effect on your price policy. People expect prices to be higher, for instance, in a lavish, newly constructed mall area than they would for the same type of service or merchandise in a run-down section of town. Because a store's price line influences the way people think of its other aspects, it is important that prices be consistent with the other elements.

Your store's appearance both inside and out will affect customers' impressions about your product prices. For example, let's look at two women's apparel shops which face each other in a

Cleveland mall. The first, owned and operated by Mrs. Randolph Cunningham, features elaborate window displays and classic furnishings, denoting higher prices. Most of the customers here are older, more conservative women. Opposite, the plain window dressings and modern, inexpensive furnishings of Betty Engle's shop attract younger and less affluent women.

In all probability, your advertising more than anything else tells people about your prices. It is a reflection on whether your operation is large or small, old or new, high-price or low price. Bill Freeman, owner of "The Gourmet Shop" in a large eastern city, credits his ads for a good portion of his business. Glancing through the newspaper one can immediately identify Bill's ad. The prominently displayed logo in Old English type, and the empty white space between words and sentences, is the same as that which has appeared over the last six years in his "yellow pages" advertising. Customers get an impression of quality at a high, but fair, price.

On the other hand, Janet Findlay, who operates "Catering Services, Inc." in the same city, likes her ads to give the customer a feel of hominess and personal interest. To this end, the ads carry her message in heavy black print and include her photograph—a plump, smiling woman holding a steaming mince pie.

Other specific features of your store—products or service, employees, displays, merchandising practices, will also determine how customers feel about your operation. This image can mean the difference between repeat or lost business. When people enter a shop and find a product or service they like, they are likely to return. On the other hand, if they are displeased, they will usually communicate their displeasure to others. Sometimes a negative impression can be created by an employee. Check to see that people working for you create an impression which is consistent with your desired image.

Still, you can't be all things to everyone. Your best avenue to success is to look for ways to increase the satisfaction which your present customers find in your operation.

For the owner of a small retail store, maintaining a sufficient amount of stock on hand is imperative to the success of his business. Being out of stock, or overstocked, on an item can result in inability to serve customers properly and lead to profit loss.

How you maintain control over your stock will be largely determined by the type of merchandise you sell. Michael McCormick makes more than $30,000 each year selling handmade gift items in his little resort-town shop in New England. As a small retailer, he knows what he has on hand, what he has on order, what he has sold, and what needs to be ordered or reordered.

Because memory lapses can cause grave mistakes or omissions, Mike feels that the most effective control for keeping track of stock lies in keeping good control records. Stock can be counted on a periodic basis, or daily by counting sales. To be sure he has ample merchandise on hand at all times, Mike prefers the latter method.

If being understocked loses money for you through customer trade, being over stocked can lose it for you by tying up your working capital in slow-moving goods.

For more information on stock control ask for: *Inventory Control Small Business Bibliography* #75, free from SBA, Washington, D.C. 20416.

Avoiding accidents and damage to merchandise will save you money. Customers who slip and fall may get up and sue you for an injury, however slight. Unchecked hazards in your store may result in fire or other damage to stock and the building. Use a safety checklist to help you to reduce potential hazards and eliminate existing ones.

To help make selling easier in your store, try to display as much of your merchandise as possible in a well balanced way. Customers want to be able to see everything at a glance without having to hunt for it in drawers or on the back of shelves.

Thelma and Dick Welsh, owners of a variety store in Des Moines, feel that their well-planned layout actively promotes impulse buying and helps them maintain an annual income level of $23,000. As in many stores of this type, regular goods occupy the rear of their store, while candy, notions, toiletries and the like are placed at the entrance. Customers don't always come into the store especially to buy these particular items, but when they see them displayed, they often buy on impulse.

Another trick to easy selling is the use of paint and lighting. For getting customers to look more closely at merchandise in their pipe and tobacco store, brothers Ken and Greg Porter credit a combination of unusual lighting and wall-coloring effects, which lend a Middle Ages atmosphere to the shop. The brothers also use a novel counter arrangement in the rear of their shop to lead customers to a display of hand-carved pipes which sell for $40 to $500 each.

Many store owners today use *self-service* to reduce labor in selling goods. There are many advantages to this method. It provides open displays which enable customers to examine products at their leisure. Some people don't like the pressure of a salesperson standing by while they look at merchandise. Then, too, it eliminates the need for numerous sales personnel, thereby cutting your labor costs.

You know how it works. When the customer finds what he wants, he brings it to a service desk, conveniently set up to serve the selling floor. There an available salesperson can ring up the sale on the cash register and wrap the purchase without abandoning other customers. In this manner, since the customer waits on himself, more goods can be sold than if the salesperson had to stay with one customer during the entire buying process.

This is the type of store set-up Grant Allers used when he became a full-time breadwinner. Grant started out in a home business selling jewelry part-time, but in a few years when his hourly job in a local factory became monotonous, he quit, and opened a little shop on a business street not far from his home.

With his wife behind the cash register, and a high-school student for part-time help, he sells hand-crafted jewelry—luster rings made from shell from Mexico, lacquered brass bracelets from India, silver and turquoise bracelets fashioned by American Indians, plus numerous other handcrafted items made by local artists.

Helping to push his monthly gross income toward the $2,000 mark, Grant feels, is the self-service policy which allows his customers to browse at their leisure, trying on jewelry or sniffing a candle's aroma as they go from one display area to another. He, himself, is always in the shop to help buyers with a selection or give them a bit of history about a piece they select. This approach not only discourages theft, but adds a personal touch which brings his customers back time and time again.

GROWING WITH YOUR SERVICE

As I have previously pointed out, a successful business must lend itself to constant growth and change. We have seen how adjusting to these conditions may sometimes mean re-locating your machine shop or retail business. Now let's take a look at how the rule applies to a service operation.

Starting out with a table-desk and telephone in her kitchen, Theresa Wilder, a New Orleans housewife, was in business only two years when she found it necessary to expand her job-finding agency. Numerous phone calls and too many filing cabinets were getting in the way of preparing dinner.

Today, Mrs. Wilder has a bright, clean office in a downtown bank building. Working away from home has many disadvantages that weren't present with her in-home office. Travel time between work and home, and having little time for housewifely duties are her biggest complaints.

But there are compensations. Now she has plenty of room to spread out her work, a quiet atmosphere in which to discuss business transactions with her clients, and a nice profit picture at the end of each month.

Another instance of business growth was evidenced by Carl Painter and John Jennings. Both young men are master craftsmen in the cutting of stained glass and had worked from their respective homes for several years. However, when they met while working together on windows for a Canadian church, they formed a partnership and recently opened a shop-studio together, the Glass-Craft Art Studio. They create murals, sculptures, and paintings which they sell along with novelties, and jewelry made from cut glass.

In another new store on the opposite side of the country, Tom Bradley, a former garage mechanic has opened his expanded bicycle shop. Starting out part-time, several years ago, in the basement of his home, Tom's business grew by leaps and bounds. With the coming of the bicycle boom, he found he no longer had the space or the time to accommodate his thriving business. Moving his shop to larger quarters was imperative.

Today, Tom pays $195 per month for a shop located on a busy side street in a business section of town and averages a monthly income of $2,600. Here he stocks a minimum of 500 bicycles, including imports, which he sells at a profit of 25 percent each. Contributing to the success of his operation, he feels, is the bike repair service which he offers. When a bike is purchased, customers are assured that they can get parts and accessories whenever they need them.

TAKING A NEW LOOK AT THE LEGAL
STRUCTURE OF YOUR BUSINESS

Your best bet is to consult a lawyer on the matter of who will be capable of helping you decide on the best form for your small business. As you know, there are three principal kinds of businesses.

1. *Proprietorship,* which is what most home businesses use in starting because it is the easiest to begin and end. You do things the way you want them done. You're your own boss, subject to no restrictions, partnership agreements, or corporate charters. As sole proprietor you hold title to all enterprise assets and you own all the profits. You also must assume all losses, bear all risks, and pay all debts of the business. Should you become ill, your business could suffer, and should you die, your business could end.

2. *Partnership,* which is the simplest for two or more people to start and terminate, has the same flexibility as proprietorship. Partners are taxed separately, and all except limited partners are personally liable for debts and taxes. Should one partner die, become ill, or leave, the business must be liquidated or reorganizes.

3. *Corporation,* which operates under state laws, is the most formal structure. It has continuous and separate legal life, has its scope of activity and name restricted by a charter, has business profits taxed separately from earnings of executives and owners, and makes only the company, not owners or executives, liable for its debts and taxes.

Corporation ownership is evidenced by stock certificates. A stockholder casts one vote per share. Therefore, if one man owns a majority of stock, he can control the firm as effectively as if he were a sole proprietor.

If, in the end, you decide to incorporate your business, competent legal counsel is virtually indispensable. Your lawyer will advise you on the type and form your corporation should take, and will prepare your charter application. It will include the following:

1. The name of your company
2. A formal statement of its formation
3. The type of business
4. Location of business
5. Duration of the charter
6. Classes of stock
7. The value of shares of each class of authorized stock
8. Voting privileges of each class of stock
9 Names and addresses of incorporators
10. Names and addresses and amount of each subscriber to capital stock

11. Statement of limited liability of stockholders
12. Statement of alterations of directors' powers, if any, from the general corporation law of your state.

When the charter is received from the secretary of state, it must be recorded with the county clerk. Following that, the incorporators may hold a formal organization meeting and adopt the bylaws. Incorporation fees vary with each state. They can be as low as $10, as high as $2,000.

CONSIDERING YOU--THE NEW ENTREPRENEUR

As a self employed owner-manager you will have the satisfaction of operating a business with opportunities for using your creativity and initiative. In the face of challenges and change, you will have the pleasure of seeing your business prosper and grow under your control.

But because of the very nature of your work you must constantly motivate yourself to keep pushing forward. One of the secrets of highly successful men in any line of business is their vitality and energy. You owe it to yourself to keep in good physical and mental condition. To do this, try to keep your work in the proper perspective. Don't let it dominate your life to the exclusion of all else. A happy family life, plus an active social life, are essential to your well being. Even a hobby can serve as an escape from the pressures and frustrations of business.

You also owe it to yourself to set up a retirement plan. You can do this by using the Self-Employed Individuals Tax Retirement Act of 1962 and its amendments. This law offers income tax advantages to self-employed business people who set up retirement plans for themselves and their employees. You can take 100 percent deduction for the funds set aside for yourself, up to $2,500, which you put into an approved retirement plan. You can contribute the entire $2,500 to a plan or 10 percent of your earned income—whichever is less.

Retirement Plans For Self-employed Individuals, Document No. 5592(10-66) is available *free* from your District Director of Revenue.

INDEX